THE POLITICS OF SINCERITY

The Politics of Sincerity

PLATO, FRANK SPEECH, AND DEMOCRATIC JUDGMENT

Elizabeth Markovits

The Pennsylvania State University Press
University Park, Pennsylvania

LIBRARY OF CONGRESS
CATALOGING-IN-PUBLICATION DATA

Markovits, Elizabeth, 1975– .
The politics of sincerity : Plato, frank speech and
democratic judgment / Elizabeth Markovits.
p.   cm.
Includes bibliographical references and index.
ISBN-13: 978–0–271–03340–2   (pbk : alk. paper)
1. Communication in politics—United States.
2. Rhetoric—Political aspects—United States.
3. Honesty–Political aspects—United States.
4. United States—Politics and government—2001– .
I. Title.

JA85.2.U6M375 2008
320.97301'4—dc22
2007035892

The Pennsylvania State University Press
is a member of the Association of
American University Presses.

It is the policy of
The Pennsylvania State University Press
to use acid-free paper. This book is printed on
paper that meets the
minimum requirements of American National Standard for
Information Sciences—Permanence of Paper for Printed Library Material,
ansi z39.48–1992.

For Bennett

Let us begin by committing ourselves to the truth, to see it like it is and tell it like it is, to find the truth, to speak the truth and live the truth. That is what we will do.

—RICHARD NIXON, ACCEPTING THE REPUBLICAN NOMINATION FOR PRESIDENT, 1968

CONTENTS

ACKNOWLEDGMENTS

I suppose it's odd for a book about the problems of straight talk to have benefited from so much of it. Susan Bickford and Peter Euben proved to be terrifically dedicated "straight shooters" throughout its development, and for that I am forever grateful. I hope this book does justice to a fraction of what I have learned from Susan over the years—I can never thank her enough for her inspiration, ideas, and friendship. I also owe a great debt to Peter Euben, who moved from California to North Carolina just when I needed his insights, humor, and good company the most.

There are many others whose ideas, advice, and friendship contributed to this book. Eloise Buker, Ellen Carnaghan, Robbie Cox, Rivka Eisner, Jessica Flanigan, Jill Frank, Marilyn Friedman, Cheryl Hall, Dustin Howes, Ana Kogl, Steve Leonard, Michael Lienesch, Gerry Mara, Lara Markovits, Wynne Moskop, Carisa Showden, Erin Taylor, and several anonymous reviewers who will no doubt see their mark on the book deserve special thanks. Sandy Thatcher and the readers at Penn State University Press offered generous and helpful criticisms that have helped me reshape this project in critical ways. Phyllis Forchee, Ben Jersak, and Annelise Maloney at Saint Louis University were instrumental in preparing the final manuscript.

I am grateful to the University of North Carolina at Chapel Hill and Saint Louis University for providing me with financial and intellectual support. The Social & Political Theory Workshop at Washington University has also provided an important intellectual home here in St. Louis.

My parents, siblings, and in-laws deserve special thanks for all the good arguments about politics over the years—and for their toleration of my pointy-headedness about it all. Finally, for his patient understanding and amazing wit, I dedicate this book to Bennett Hazlip.

All errors, omissions, and oversimplifications are, of course, my responsibility.

Another version of Chapter 1 appeared in the *Journal of Political Philosophy* ("The Trouble with Being Earnest: Deliberative Democracy and the Sincerity Norm," *Journal of Political Philosophy* 14, no. 3 [September 2006]: 249–69). Thanks to Soft Skull Press for the use of David Rees's *Get Your War On* cartoon (*Get Your War On* by David Rees © 2002 by David Rees. www.softskull.com).

INTRODUCTION

During his 2000 presidential primary bid, U.S. Senator John McCain had the words "Straight Talk Express" painted on the side of a campaign bus and then rode it around the country. Of course, McCain was defeated by a "straight shooter" from Texas. However, he attracted a huge following of people who felt he was above partisan politics—a tough-talking and sincere maverick, ready to tell it like it is, no matter how unpopular that made him. The American obsession with straight talkers is as vigorous as it has ever been; McCain only crystallized something that has been a force in U.S. politics for years. We glorify the courage to speak the truth plainly, making bestsellers out of both Thomas Paine's *Common Sense* in 1776 and Bill O'Reilly's *The No Spin Zone* in 2001. A search of U.S. news sources in Lexis shows 520 hits for the term "straight talk" between January and July 2004—most hits were politics-related, but apparently we also value straight talk in gardening, home décor, and sports. Also telling is the recent interest among advertisers and marketers in "bullfighting," or the effort to purge "bull," "spin," and "pretense" from their messages to consumers in order to seem more "authentic."[1] Our collective anxiety about sweet-talking politicians, spin doctors, and outright liars leads us to seek truthful, earnest speakers we feel we can trust.

This book is a response to anyone looking for more straight talk in politics. I was attracted to this project because, like most people, I cannot stand liars—especially in politics. I began with the idea that if we could just know the truth and inspire people to tell it, perhaps we could reinvigorate the public's interest in their own political futures. As I thought about this problem, I read S. Sara Monoson's excellent work on *parrhesia* (frank speech)

1. See "Fight the Bull," http://www.fightthebull.com/index.asp/ (accessed November 11, 2005).

in ancient Athens.[2] I thought, *this is it*—we can use this ethic of *parrhesia* as our own democratic ideal! But then I began to notice that our popular culture in fact already praised something like *parrhesia:* straight talk.[3] Political theorists also have a similar ethic: sincerity. But the problem was that a lot of straight-talkers seemed deeply undemocratic: straight talk seemed to have become a trope, another tool of crafty politicians and smart advertising executives. And as I delved deeper into the historical drama of fourth- and fifth-century Athens, I noticed a similarity—they seemed to have experienced the same taming of truthfulness. So I began to ask questions: is it possible to differentiate between the bad type of straight talk and the good kind? Can we set down criteria by which to judge democratic communication? How important are one's "sincere" intentions in deliberation? What role does inequality play in these dynamics? How can we be critical of straight-talk tropes but retain some way to hold people accountable for what they say? This book is a record of my attempt to grapple with these issues. Readers will find that although much of the book focuses on ancient Athens, I have often illustrated theoretical points with contemporary political examples. Some readers will find that my political sensibilities differ from theirs. I request their indulgence for two reasons. First, it is critical for political theorists to discuss actually existing politics, with a certain degree of openness about their own political judgments. Second, this book was written between 2001 and 2006—during the height of Republican power in the United States and the entry of the United States and its allies into both the "War on Terror" and the war in Iraq. It should therefore not be surprising that many of my examples of problematic hyper-sincerity come from figures associated with the Bush administration, since it dominated the political scene in the United States during this time. I hope these references help illuminate rather than obscure what I am trying to say about democratic discourse.

Chapter 1 opens by questioning the political effects of a sincerity ideal. Because of its central importance for contemporary political theory and because of the importance of the ideal of deliberation for democratic political practices, I begin with a discussion of deliberative democracy. Through

2. S. Sara Monoson, *Plato's Democratic Entanglements: Athenian Politics and the Practice of Philosophy* (Princeton: Princeton University Press, 2000).
3. The term "straight talk" has heteronormative reverberations—reverberations that, although not the central focus of this book, are especially acute in the "hyper-sincere" rhetorical styles detailed at the end of this chapter.

an examination of Jürgen Habermas's work, I consider the function of discourse ethics in deliberative theory, paying particular attention to the assumption of sincerity and its relation to democratic accountability. As much as the Habermasian model of deliberative democracy seeks to provide a rational and institutional foundation for politics and to lessen the potential for rhetorical manipulation of the public, I argue that it instead leads to an impossible—and ultimately destructive—quest for communicative purity. I detail the various dangers this assumption holds for deliberation, from how it conceives of social knowledge and human psychology, to its privileging of consensus, to its denigration of rhetorical forms of speech. Moreover, the effects of sincerity have too often continued to silence historically marginalized voices that fall outside this ideal. I also explore how the sincerity ethic finds its ultimate expression in "hyper-sincere" rhetorical styles—ways of speaking that denigrate critics and hamstring deliberation. I then propose that we turn to classical Athenian political culture and Socrates' response to it to help us think through this dilemma of ensuring democratic accountability without enabling hyper-sincere tropes.[4]

In Chapter 2, I reconstruct the classical Athenian context and discuss its relevance to our own political life, especially the similarities between the Greek concept of *parrhesia* and the contemporary sincerity norm. Political discourse in ancient Athens evidenced a deep anxiety about the possibility of deceptive communication; *parrhesia* was a democratic norm called upon to counter the risks of deception and to ensure that leaders were accountable to the public. At the same time, we see that *parrhesia* becomes a rhetorical trope, leading to a "rhetoric of anti-rhetoric," much like our own hyper-sincere modes.

In Chapters 3 and 4, I turn to Plato's Socrates. I argue that Plato's dialogues offer a unique perspective on *parrhesia* and that reading Plato's work can help us temper our own demands for certainty while developing our capacity for political judgment. I focus here specifically on how Socrates responds to the co-optation of *parrhesia* and the rise of anti-rhetorical rhetoric in Athens. Each chapter explores an alternate view of Plato's Socrates and his relation to democratic deliberation. In Chapter 3, I discuss Socrates'

---

4. For other theorists, the obvious place to look for a discussion of sincerity is Rousseau. See, for example, Ruth Grant, *Hypocrisy and Integrity: Machiavelli, Rousseau, and the Ethics of Politics* (Chicago: University of Chicago Press, 1997). I happily leave this project to them and instead focus on the contemporary view of the importance of sincerity for politics (which would include any Rousseauian legacy) and its parallels in the ancient world.

use of irony in the *Gorgias*. Several scholars have presented Socrates as the Athenian who best fulfills the *parrhesia* ethic. However, when seen through the lens of Socratic irony, a different view of Socrates emerges. Instead of a frank speaker, we find a character playing with this ideal, drawing on Athenian oratorical traditions that seem to violate its dictates, and calling attention to *parrhesia* as a trope. While Socrates remains committed to the idea of truth in speech, his practice highlights the difficulty and vulnerability of democratic speech.[5] Chapter 4 calls into question another view of Socrates—that of the philosopher-king who condones lying to one's inferiors. This Socrates is most clearly presented in Plato's *Republic*, and the analysis here attempts to demonstrate that the story is much more complicated than often thought. Instead of being tools of an idealistic and aristocratic Platonist, Socrates' "lies" can instead be interpreted as teaching devices designed to strengthen the intellectual capabilities of the interlocutors. Both chapters complicate our understanding of Plato and Socrates and our efforts to hold the writer and character up as either heroes or antiheroes of democratic discussion. Instead, they show us how Plato's Socrates (1) disrupts conventions about the "proper" goals of deliberation; (2) reveals the crippling aggressiveness of some truth claims; (3) appreciates how verbal playfulness can grant necessary psychological distance to certain topics; (4) values the particular contributions storytelling has to make to deliberation, especially as a way to contest hegemonic political discourses; and (5) respects and helps to develop the political judgment of fellow citizens. Thus, reading the dialogues can help one appreciate the potential and difficulty of democratic deliberation; furthermore, the literary nature of Plato's work helps readers to develop the judgment necessary for the success of that democratic project. I do not mean to offer the dialogues as models of good or bad deliberation; rather, I want to provide readings that encourage an appreciation of Plato's work as instruments that help develop a critical rhetorical literacy among citizens, in addition to offering new readings of these two dialogues.

5. Irony thus described might call to mind Richard Rorty's liberal ironism, yet I purposefully refrain from making this connection as there are too many ways in which Plato's Socrates undermines such an effort by emphasizing a public, shared conception of the good (in contrast to Rorty's emphasis on the private). Moreover, the fact that we can read contingency into this setting does not mean that Plato or Socrates were themselves "liberal ironists." For more on the relationship between Rorty and Socrates' irony, see Gerald M. Mara, *Socrates' Discursive Democracy: Logos and Ergon in Platonic Political Philosophy* (Albany: SUNY Press, 1997), or John Evan Seery, *Political Returns: Irony in Politics and Theory from Plato to the Antinuclear Movement* (Boulder, Colo.: Westview Press, 1990).

Admittedly, the intertwining of Plato and Socrates complicates any effort to explain the meaning of the dialogues: is Plato's Socrates the "real" Socrates? What are the effects of Plato's literary representation of Socrates? When is Socrates speaking and when is Plato speaking through Socrates? While these are undoubtedly important questions within the literature, they do not play a central role here for several reasons. First, following Melissa Lane, I accept that "an impure (knowledge of) Socrates is what we have."[6] I am interested in Plato's Socrates, the Socrates of the dialogues. Where the "real" Socrates ends and Plato begins is not central to my work, since I am centrally focused on how the dialogues (through the character of Socrates) manipulate Athenian political and cultural resources. Furthermore, I am not convinced that we must separate out an early and late Socrates or Plato; instead, I prefer to treat the dialogues as distinct elements of an overall corpus, "each [as a] contribution to a complex, differentiated understanding of the relation of critical reason to various aspects of political life."[7] This requires me to make sense of the seeming incongruities of Plato's Socrates since I cannot ascribe them solely to changes in Plato's own (unSocratic) treatment of his teacher. As John Cooper argues:

> The classifications of "early" and "middle-period" dialogues rest squarely on the interpretative theses concerning the process of Plato's work. . . . As such, they are an unsuitable basis for bringing anyone to the reading of these works. To use them in that way is to announce in advance the results of a certain interpretation of the dialogues and to canonize that interpretation under the guise of a presumably objective order of composition—when in fact no such order *is* objectively known . . . it is better to relegate thoughts about chronology to the secondary position they deserve and to concentrate on the literary and philosophical contexts of the words, taken on their own and in relation to the others.[8]

At the same time, Plato's authorial presence remains an important element of my analysis. I am interested the literary qualities of Plato's work

6. Melissa Lane, *Plato's Progeny: How Socrates and Plato Still Captivate the Modern Mind* (London: Duckworth: 2001), 51.

7. John R. Wallach, *The Platonic Political Art: A Study of Critical Reason and Democracy* (University Park: Pennsylvania State University Press, 2001), 10.

8. John Cooper, "Introduction," in *Plato: The Complete Works*, ed. John Cooper (Indianapolis: Hackett, 1997), xiv.

and proceed from the premise that Plato consciously chose to include certain characters and events (some of which have meaning only in the context of ancient Athens) to illustrate his points. Moreover, there are times when it is important to consider how Plato grappled with the historical Socrates, especially as a response to the tumult of the years leading up to Socrates' execution. However, the dialogues are not transcripts of conversations, but one author's literary response to his environment. Thus, my goal is to interpret the dialogues discussed here, not as evidence of the difference or similarity between Plato and Socrates, but as Plato the writer's particular responses to elements of Athenian civic life, which use Socrates as a central figure.

In choosing to read the dialogues in this way, I reveal a great debt to the work of such scholars as Susan Bickford, Peter Euben, Gerald Mara, Sara Monoson, Josiah Ober, Arlene Saxonhouse, and John Wallach, among others. Whereas prior interpreters often read the dialogues as the work of an unmitigated opponent of Athenian democracy, recent works have crafted a view of Plato as a deeply embedded critic of the democracy.[9] Socrates criticizes democracy, often harshly, but that does not make the dialogues an unequivocal treatise against the institution. Instead, I share Wallach's point of view:

> Plato's criticisms are neither essentially nor particularly anti-democratic, because he regarded the political form of democracy primarily as one of many existing arrangements of political power, all of which were unjust because they wrongly ratified prevailing ethical and political "conventions" as exclusive conditions of justice . . . although the Platonic political art was certainly conducive to searing criticisms of democracy, it also reflected aspects of democratic discourse and practice.[10]

Again, I do not propose to offer a Socratic defense of democracy or to use Plato's dialogues as a model for good deliberation, but rather to demonstrate a reading of these works that encourages deeper engagement with

9. For example, Ober's reading emphasizes the aristocratic elements present in Plato's work and his effort to "liberate philosophy from engagement in the political life of the real *polis*," but it also stresses "Plato's debt to the democratic political culture of his native polis." Josiah Ober, *Political Dissent in Democratic Athens: Intellectual Critics of Popular Rule* (Princeton: Princeton University Press, 1998), 10.

10. Wallach, *Platonic Political Art*, 10, 12.

them, in addition to a greater understanding of what democratic deliberation in particular can and cannot do for our own polity. Rather than hold
Socrates up as a friend or foe of democracy, my primary goal is to examine
Plato's dialogues as a resource for thinking about our own democracy (taking care to not overstate similarities between our situations).

Given the focus on deliberation, it may seem odd that I have omitted
more than brief discussions of Aristotle's work, especially the *Nicomachean
Ethics* or the *Rhetoric*. Aristotle is the widely recognized as the ancient
who provides most direct relief from the anti-rhetorical tradition in political
theory.[11] Although this book is motivated by a concern with discourse, it is
more specifically a concern about the role of sincerity in discourse. And it
is Plato, more than Aristotle, who spends considerable time analyzing this
ethic (although rarely in a direct way); the dialogues are replete with claims
to sincerity and *parrhesia* (alongside Socrates' well-known irony). Moreover, Chapter 3 argues that while Plato's Socrates remains highly critical
of rhetorical practices in ancient Athens, the *Gorgias* also offers us a vision
of a highly rhetorical Socrates, casting doubt on straightforward readings
of his criticisms—criticisms that still dominate thinking about rhetoric
throughout both political science and popular culture. Of course, in arguing
that the dialogues can help develop judgment and in offering a set of practices to help alleviate our reliance on sincerity, I come quite close to Aristotle at times, especially to his work on *phronesis* and *ethos*; but my goal
here remains an attempt to think through a rhetorical problem—
sincerity—that occupies a central place in several of Plato's dialogues.

To return to immediate topic of this book, if sincerity poses a problem
for contemporary political practice and Plato's dialogues demonstrate the
crippling difficulties of *parrhesia*, then the listener is presented with an
enormous burden. What exactly should we be listening for in the political
realm, if not sincerity? Rather than shy away from the language of intentions and sincerity, why not look for the deeper sincerity behind complicated rhetorical modes? Plato's Socrates complicates *parrhesia*, but does
that mean we should discard frankness as an ideal? Or just that sincerity
and frankness are very complicated matters that require deeper examination of the soul of the speaker? I examine this issue directly in Chapter
5, through a discussion of Hannah Arendt and Judith Butler's work on

---

11. For more on this tradition, see Bryan Garsten, *Saving Persuasion: A Defense of Rhetoric and Judgment* (Cambridge: Harvard University Press, 2006).

performance and masks. This turn to the contemporary era is necessitated by several factors. While he turns out to treat *parrhesia* in a more complex way than previously thought, Plato's Socrates retains an emphasis on the interior of interlocutors that can prove extremely difficult for democratic political life. Moreover, my readings of the dialogues alone cannot sufficiently flesh out a vision of politics suitable for contemporary democracy. While there are important similarities between the two contexts, it would be wrong to ignore the critical differences brought about by representation and mass media. Chapter 5 argues explicitly that we should treat sincerity as irrelevant for political life and offers some alternative deliberative practices. I discuss Arendt's focus on the multiple perspectives that constitute political reality, the danger of the search for hypocrisy, the need for public masks, and the role of judgment in political practice. I make the case for a move away from the destructive politics of intimacy that cannot be addressed by theories of deliberative democracy that prize sincerity; instead, I call for an emphasis on trustworthiness as an alternative to sincerity that nonetheless can allow our commitment to democratic accountability to flourish. (While it may seem like splitting hairs, there are important differences between the two qualities.) I finish with several recommendations for reinvigorating our deliberative capacities and how we might establish this alternative vision in our own political culture.

It is important to note that de-emphasizing sincerity in politics does not leave us defenseless against falsehood in the political sphere. What is crucial is that we focus our efforts on the public person (rather than the moral interior of the person). Words and deeds are the real substance of political life and can be criticized on the basis of their correspondence to factual truth and the ethical outlook they disclose. Listeners must judge each element of a discussion anew, drawing on a rich knowledge of the context (akin to Wayne Booth's "listening rhetoric").[12] Sustained, critical listening and questioning is all-important. This does not mean that we must forgo any discussion of so-called democratic virtues. In fact, these may be central to the type of politics I am advocating. But it is critical that we refrain as much as possible in political discussion from trying to judge the interior lives of others.[13]

12. Wayne C. Booth, *The Rhetoric of Rhetoric: The Quest for Effective Communication* (Malden, Mass.: Blackwell, 2004).
13. For example, Mark Button's claims for humility as a democratic virtue seem to avoid this problem and rightfully call for attention to one's self, rather than the moral character of

Among other things, this understanding of politics calls for a serious reconsideration of current mass communication practices, a change in theoretical and empirical research models of deliberative democracy, and a renewed commitment to civic education in our public schools and universities. The current emphasis on sincerity in political life has negative consequences for how we structure and interpret political discourse. In rejecting standard interpretations of deliberative democracy and privileging practices of individual citizen judgment and the role of trustworthiness over commitments to sincerity, consensus, and "public reason," I join those trying to find a home for rhetoric in political theory, including Danielle Allen (*Talking to Strangers*) and Bryan Garsten (*Saving Persuasion*), as well as the contributors to *Talking Democracy: Historical Perspectives on Rhetoric and Democracy*. Whether we are interested in interpreting existing democracy through deliberative theory or in creating truly deliberative settings for citizens, we should neither overlook nor re-create the inequalities and anxieties that deliberative theory is meant to counteract. It is not that I want to take away our own desire for truth in politics—in fact, I am deeply committed to it. I just want us to think carefully on how we might best go about getting rid of the bull in politics and what our choices might cost us.

Before moving on, it is important to clarify my understanding of several key terms—"deliberation," "judgment," and "rhetoric." First, what do I mean by "deliberation?" Why not use "communication?" In line with its original etymology, "deliberation" here means the process of weighing various sides of an issue, giving them careful consideration; deliberation results in a judgment of some kind (but not necessarily a formal vote or consensus procedure within a particular group). Judgment, meanwhile, is the "attempt to determine, as best we may, who we are, what we want, and how we realize our ends."[14] It takes place in the absence of formal rules and methods; judgment so described is often also called *phronesis*.[15] Thus, this conception of deliberation is in contrast to more formalized treatments of deliberation that often attempt to define what counts as "reasonable" or develop specific modes of decision-making procedures in line with delibera-

---

others. See Mark Button, " 'A Monkish Kind of Virtue'? For and Against Humility," *Political Theory* 33, no. 6 (December 2005): 840–68.

14. Ronald Beiner, *Political Judgment* (London: Methuen, 1983), 145.

15. At the same time, *phronesis* is a term with many meanings for a wide variety of scholars. See Robert Hariman, "Prudence in the Twenty-First Century," in *Prudence: Classical Virtue, Postmodern Practice*, ed. Robert Hariman (University Park: Pennsylvania State University Press, 2003), 287–322.

tive theory. I will also argue here that the traditional split between reason and emotion is untenable and, along with Cheryl Hall, argue for a more complex understanding of deliberation that allows room for emotion as a constitutive element of judgment.[16] Still, "deliberation" here remains more complex than standard usages of "communication," which cover all sorts of means and ends of conveying information. At the same time, "communication," as Iris Marion Young has shown, is also an integral part of democratic practices; yet her use of the term seems to me to immediately imply that some judgment is made (that is, when "greeting" is used, judgments are formed regarding the individuals involved). So I will use "deliberation" to refer to many, but not all, communicative practices, while simultaneously arguing for a broader conception of "deliberation" than is currently the norm. I remain committed to this term because I believe, along with many others, that it offers a conception of democracy that rightly emphasizes the legitimating function of discourse.

"Rhetoric" is a term with a long and sometimes controversial history. Historically, rhetoric was considered critical to political practices and was a central part of a citizen's education; nowadays, however, it is generally ignored in political science departments and often derided in the larger political environment. In general, we have inherited two competing traditions about the place of rhetoric in politics; the perspective one takes tends to determine one's judgment of the term. Both views refer to rhetoric as speechcraft—the art of persuasion. Yet the two traditions vary greatly in their judgment of this craft. The negative view is usually attributed to Plato and is the one that worries many contemporary deliberative democrats. In this formulation, rhetoric is the province of demagogues and propagandists. Its purpose is to persuade, not inform. Its end is victory not truth. This is also the way the way "rhetoric" and "rhetorical" are often used in the media—as in "election-year rhetoric." Political scientists tend to fall into this tradition.[17]

The other tradition of rhetoric, more often associated with the Sophists, Aristotle, Cicero, Quintilian, and many others, assumes a more positive

16. See Cheryl Hall, "Recognizing the Passion in Deliberation: Toward a More Democratic Theory of Deliberative Democracy," *Hypatia: A Journal of Feminist Philosophy* 22, no. 4 (2007).

17. For an excellent discussion of the history of rhetoric within political theory, see Garsten, *Saving Persuasion*.

view of the field.[18] In their view, rhetoric is the practical complement to truth, a legitimate way of transmitting truth to others. The effectiveness, for example, of Martin Luther King Jr.'s "I Have A Dream" speech rests at least in part in his ability to frame the civil rights movement in terms of the continuing American project of liberty begun with the Declaration of Independence; his attention to audience and frames was an integral part of his ability to craft assent and community. Rather than pandering, carefully crafted rhetoric demonstrates consideration of the audience—concrete others who coexist alongside the speaker in a democracy.[19] Rhetoric is also an unavoidable aspect of all communication. According to Wayne Booth, "Rhetoric is employed at every moment when one human being intends to produce, through the use of signs or symbols, some effect on another—by words, or facial expressions, or gestures, or any symbolic skill of any kind."[20] This conception of rhetoric highlights its inescapability; all texts can be analyzed rhetorically. The rhetoric of a text also produces a specific interpretation of the world; the metaphors and terms promote particular understandings, which often have political effects.[21] It is this second, more expansive and potentially positive, understanding of rhetoric that I want to defend here, drawing out how the "Platonic" view unwisely privileges particular styles of speech in contemporary democracy, and going on in Chapters 3 and 4 to demonstrate how Plato's dialogues actually undermine the dichotomy between rhetoric and truth usually attributed to them.

18. For many of those explicitly working within rhetorical studies, some of the points made here may seem obvious; since the rise of rhetoric in ancient Athens and through to the present day, much work has been done in this field, and I do not mean to downplay its significance in any way. However, there is, both within political science and popular American culture, an aversion to rhetoric that I believe demands further attention. Moreover, rhetoricians will find here a sustained treatment of sincerity, which has heretofore received scant attention in the work on deliberative theory. They will also find an alternate view of Plato's work, long considered a foe of both rhetoric and the mass democracy that relies so heavily upon it.

19. Garsten, *Saving Persuasion*, 198.

20. Booth, *Rhetoric of Rhetoric*, xi.

21. For examples, see work by Robert Hariman (cited throughout) or George Lakoff, *Moral Politics: How Liberals and Conservatives Think* (Chicago: University of Chicago Press, 2002).

THE TROUBLE WITH BEING EARNEST

In February 2004, a crowd decked out in top hats and furs waited on a New York City sidewalk to welcome President George W. Bush's adviser Karl Rove to a fundraiser.[1] They endured the February cold, chanting slogans in support of Rove and the president. Chomping cigars and drinking champagne, they smiled and held signs for the press: Billionaires for Bush! Blood for Oil! Re-elect Karl Rove! Karl Rove is innocent! Leave no billionaire behind! When Sierra Club protesters chanted, "We want the truth and we want it now!" from the other side of the street, the Billionaires retorted, "Buy your own president!" Eventually, the police figured out what was *really* going on, perhaps realizing that actual billionaires don't often wear tiaras, and escorted the "Billionaires for Bush" behind the official protester barrier across the street.

The fur was faux, of course, and the top hats were rented. During a period when polling data reflected a polarized electorate and the United States entered two wars, political protests were not uncommon.[2] "Counterprotests" had even sprung up—prowar rallies took place across the street from antiwar protests. Invariably, both sides complained that the press

Portions of this chapter appeared in "The Trouble with Being Earnest: Deliberative Democracy and the Sincerity Norm," *Journal of Political Philosophy* 14, no. 3 (September 2006): 249–69.

1. See Michael Slackman and Colin Moynihan, "Now in Previews, Political Theater in the Street," *New York Times*, February 19, 2004.

2. See Pew Research Center for the People and the Press, "The 2004 Political Landscape: Evenly Divided and Increasingly Polarized" (released November 5, 2003), http://peoplepress.org/reports/display.php3?ReportID=196/ (accessed July 27, 2005).

ignored them, discounted their numbers, or interviewed only the most out-
rageous elements of their movement. In contrast, the Billionaires for Bush
were media darlings.[3] The street theater, coupled with the total seriousness
with which the Billionaires played their roles, was especially compelling.[4]
They often disrupted more traditional protests, confusing both sides. But
their ultimate goal wasn't confusion. Their strangeness was carefully cultivated to draw attention to their particular criticism of the president, which
was that his policies overwhelmingly favored big business and a wealthy
few at the expense of the majority of Americans. For many people, Billionaires for Bush was a thought-provoking alternative to the traditional pro-
test. But was the group, with its irony and role-playing, part of legitimate
democratic deliberation? Why couldn't they just be clear about their goals
and beliefs?

In the United States, we tend to be skeptical of such theatrics, preferring
"straight-shooters" instead. Our culture praises "truth-tellers" as vital
members of our democracy—the Spring 2002 issue of *Ms.* magazine head-
lined "The Best of 30 years of Reporting, Rebelling and Truth-telling";
conservative Atlanta talk-radio host Neal Boortz calls himself "the high
priest of the church of the painful truth"; Jim Hightower, a liberal, pub-
lishes the "Hightower Lowdown," providing "unadorned facts"; Neil
Cavuto offers his "Common Sense" on *Fox News;* and MSNBC's Chris
Matthews promises to "tell you what I really think."[5] Promoting Glenn
Beck's television show, *CNN/Headline News* bought a full-page ad in the
New York Times to point out that "this guy says it like he means it."[6] We
identify dissemblers and spin doctors with other types of government or
with our enemies in a democracy. A group like Billionaires for Bush, with
their theatrics and pretense, seems unfair. They are lying about their
motives and intentions, mucking up discourse.[7]

3. Between January 2004 and the election, 329 articles and commentaries on the group
appeared in the news, including articles in the *New York Times* and *USA Today* and on the
CBS Evening News. LexisNexis search for "Billionaires for Bush." Also see "Pressroom,"
www.BillionairesForBush.com/ (last searched and accessed July 26, 2004).

4. See the *Billionaires for Bush Do-It-Yourself Manual,* www.BillionairesForBush.com/
(accessed July 25, 2004).

5. Marlon Manuel, "Libertarian Radio Host Addresses Convention," *Atlanta Journal-
Constitution,* May 30, 2004; "Hightower Lowdown" (direct-mail newsletter), August 2004;
Chris Matthews, *Now, Let Me Tell You What I Really Think* (New York: Touchstone Books,
2001).

6. *New York Times,* December 15, 2006.

7. "Motives" and "intentions" are not always the same thing, although the terms can
often be used interchangeably. What I mean to refer to here and throughout is *internal* moti-

This chapter is an exploration of our democratic obsession with sincerity and truth-telling. I focus on two interrelated questions. First, do we lose potentially important discursive resources with an unmitigated faith in sincerity for politics? Second, might this faith hinder deliberations, leading to a less democratic public arena? Much hinges on our answers to these questions, because they deal directly with whose voices are to be considered legitimate and authoritative. I begin from a deliberative democratic standpoint: democracy is a logocentric enterprise—that is, language is at the center of democratic political projects. So it is critical that we pay attention to how we evaluate political words. Otherwise, not only can we not really understand what is going on in political discourse, but we are also more likely to make poor judgments about what sort of speech and speakers make our democracy more robust. To explore these questions, I begin with a look at the discourse ethics that underwrite much of deliberative democratic theory, then move on to critique the theory by way of an examination of the sincerity norm and its relationship to the goal of consensus in deliberation. I go on to discuss some of the dangers that the particular ethic of sincerity poses for democratic deliberation, discussing several rhetorical manifestations of a dangerous hyper-sincerity along the way.

Because it focuses on the role of language in democratic legitimation, deliberative theory is the obvious place to look to critique hyper-sincerity in public discourse. But beyond failing to consider the potential pitfalls of sincerity, deliberative theory as it currently stands gives us no satisfactory way to critique hyper-sincerity. While the particular vision of deliberative theory here is drawn from Jürgen Habermas's concept of communicative reason, a variety of philosophers and political theorists work within this literature, including scholars who remain wary (as do I) of what they see as its idealizing speech norms. The fear is that certain of the theory's claims about deliberation prejudge the arguments that might be used, excluding participants or denigrating their contributions in unfair ways. This is especially troublesome given a context of continued inequalities and both outright and subconscious discrimination. This chapter is an attempt to build upon their critique (although not necessarily in ways with which those critics would agree) through an examination of one of the norms of communicative reason—sincerity. While I am conscious of the reasons for a sincerity

---

vations (such as my commitment to an ideal), rather than external motivations (such as the possibility of a parking ticket *motivating* me to not violate the "No Parking" sign).

ethic, I question its usefulness for political deliberation. My goal here is to open debate on the potential dangers of sincerity for democratic deliberation.

The Roots of Deliberative Democracy

There has been a long-standing distinction between two basic strands of democratic political theory: liberal and republican.[8] Liberal models assume that interests exist before a political moment in a relatively coherent, ordered set. We come together to vote, which aggregates our interests, choosing the policies favored by a majority of individuals (provided they do not infringe upon various rights). Meanwhile, republican politics provides the opportunity for the elaboration of interests aimed at the common good, emphasizing the citizen's right to active participation. Here, citizens draw on a shared culture or identity to find the "common good"; this model places a high value on civility and (prior) consensus. Over the past three decades, however, a third form has emerged: the deliberative model.

Deliberative democratic theory is of concern to a wide range of political scientists and philosophers and has come to dominate much of political theory in recent years.[9] Scholars have also begun to study deliberative demococ-

8. Jürgen Habermas, "Three Normative Models of Democracy," in *Democracy and Difference: Contesting the Boundaries of the Political,* ed. Seyla Benhabib (Princeton: Princeton University Press, 1996), 21–30.

9. See Benhabib, *Democracy and Difference;* James Bohman, "Deliberative Toleration," *Political Theory* 31, no. 6 (December 2003): 757–79; Bohman, "The Coming of Age of Deliberative Democracy," *Journal of Political Philosophy* 6, no. 4 (1998): 400–425; James Bohman and William Rehg, eds., *Deliberative Democracy: Essays on Reason and Politics* (Cambridge: MIT Press, 1997); Craig Calhoun, ed., *Habermas and Public Sphere* (Cambridge: MIT Press, 1992); Simone Chambers, *Reasonable Democracy* (Ithaca: Cornell University Press, 1996); John Dryzek, *Deliberative Democracy and Beyond: Liberals, Critics, Contestations* (Oxford: Oxford University Press, 2000); Jon Elster, ed., *Deliberative Democracy* (Cambridge: Cambridge University Press, 1998); James Fishkin and Peter Laslett, eds., *Debating Deliberative Democracy* (Malden, Mass.: Blackwell Publishing, 2003); Amy Gutmann and Dennis Thompson, *Democracy and Disagreement* (Cambridge: Belknap Press of Harvard University Press, 1996); Jürgen Habermas, *On the Pragmatics of Social Interaction: Preliminary Studies in the Theory of Communicative Action* (Cambridge: MIT Press, 2001); Habermas, "Three Normative Models of Democracy," 21–30; Habermas, *Between Facts and Norms: Contributions to a Discourse Theory of Law and Democracy,* trans. William Rehg (Cambridge: MIT Press, 1996); Habermas, *Moral Consciousness and Communicative Action* (Cambridge: MIT Press, 1990); Habermas, *The Theory of Communicative Action,* vol. 1, *Reason and the Rationalization of Society,* and vol. 2, *Lifeworld and System: A Critique of Functionalist Reason* (Boston: Beacon

racy empirically, as well as offer proposals for deliberative branches of government or other reforms to increase citizens' opportunities for deliberation.[10] While many diverse views belong to this branch of democratic theory, they all share a belief in the central role of language in democracy, either as a way to interpret existing democracy or to explicate an ideal theory of democracy.[11]

In deliberative theory we have "the institutionalization of a public use of reason jointly exercised by autonomous citizens."[12] It assumes preferences are formed or reformed through deliberation, rather than aggregated in the political "marketplace" as in the liberal model. It locates the power of a political system in words and reason, rather than in the shared background of the citizenry as in republican models. State power, thus, is justified through communication.[13] This justification ideally originates in civil society (as opposed to formal institutions of government), cleansed of the corrupting influences of money and power, allowing each citizen the equality already claimed constitutionally. This model underscores the activities of speech and judgment among ordinary citizens, rather than elites, substantiating calls for greater participation in democracy. It provides an explanation of the sources of democratic legitimacy, reminding us what is at stake with the constant pressure toward greater technocratization in the economically globalizing world. Deliberative democrats challenge what they see as the increasing power of instrumental rationality, which in their view treats sentient individuals as objects to be manipulated. The theory also offers a foundation for critique, because speakers can be called to account for the validity of their statements against three universal presuppositions that theoretically underpin all communication. These are claims

Press, 1984, 1987); Stephen Macedo, ed., *Deliberative Politics: Essays on Democracy and Disagreement* (Oxford: Oxford University Press, 1999); Bernard Manin, "On Legitimacy and Public Deliberation," *Political Theory* 15, no. 3 (August 1987): 338–68; and Iris Marion Young, *Inclusion and Democracy* (Oxford: Oxford University Press, 2001).

10. See, for examples, Marco R. Steenbergen, Andre Bächtiger, Markus Spörndli, and Jürg Steiner, "Measuring Political Deliberation: A Discourse Quality Index," *Comparative European Politics* 1 (2003): 21–48, and Ethan J. Lieb, *Deliberative Democracy in America: A Proposal for a Popular Branch of Government* (University Park: Pennsylvania State University Press, 2004).

11. James Johnson, "Arguing for Deliberation," in Elster, *Deliberative Democracy*, 162.

12. Seyla Benhabib, "Introduction," in *Democracy and Difference*, 6.

13. Mark Warren, "Deliberative Democracy," in *Democratic Theory Today*, ed. April Carter and Geoffrey Stokes (Cambridge: Polity Press, 2002), 176.

to truth, claims to sincerity, and claims to normative rightness. If the arguments violate these norms, then they "will simply lack influence, especially over time, as challenges expose the arguments."[14]

At the same time, there are numerous critiques of deliberative theories, often coming from those still sympathetic to the "linguistic turn" in political theory. They range from critiques of the "pathologies" of actual deliberation, to the privileging of certain forms of communication, to the denigration of "subaltern counter-publics," to the problems with the ideal of consensus.[15] While remaining committed to the central importance of discourse in political life, I also have criticisms to make, with the hope that by unpacking the theory, I can highlight both its strengths and its shortcomings. In this section, I work through the model proposed by Jürgen Habermas, one that connects almost all of his work, but was first explicitly discussed in his Gauss Lectures in 1971 (published in *On the Pragmatics of Social Interaction*), and refined in *The Theory of Communicative Action* and *Between Facts and Norms*. Habermas's work provides the foundation for many other deliberative theorists; it is, then, a good starting point for my own critique. I am aware that there are a variety of theories of deliberative democracy, some of which more clearly exhibit the problems that I identify here and some of which go to great lengths to avoid them. I stick with Habermas's formulation because it contains the authorizing concepts and categories for much of deliberative theory.

In *Between Facts and Norms*, Habermas aimed to demonstrate the link between the formal institutions of the democratic state and informal processes of opinion and will formation in civil society. According to his theory, constitutional democracies are legitimated by the "consensus theory of truth"; that is, by the potential assent of all other rational persons who

14. Ibid., 183.
15. Susan Stokes, "Pathologies of Deliberation," in Elster, *Deliberative Democracy*, 123–39; Adam Przeworski, "Deliberation and Ideological Domination," in Elster, *Deliberative Democracy*, 140–60; Iris Marion Young, "Communication and the Other: Beyond Deliberative Democracy," in Benhabib, *Democracy and Difference*, 120–35; Young, *Inclusion and Democracy*; Nancy Fraser, "Rethinking the Public Sphere: A Contribution to the Critique of Actually Existing Democracy," in Calhoun, *Habermas and the Public Sphere*, 109–42; Gerald F. Gaus, "Reason, Justifications, and Consensus: Why Democracy Can't Have It All," in Bohman and Rehg, *Deliberative Democracy*, 205–42; Bonnie Honig, "Difference, Dilemmas, and the Politics of Home," in Benhabib, *Democracy and Difference*, 257–77; Ernesto Laclau and Chantel Mouffe, *Hegemony and Socialist Strategy: Towards a Radical Democratic Politics* (New York: Verso, 2001); and Chantal Mouffe, "Democratic Citizenship and the Political Community," in *Dimensions of Radical Democracy*, ed. Chantal Mouffe (New York: Verso, 1992), 225–39.

could enter the discussion. Democracy is legitimate because it strives not for majority rule, but for openness and rationality. Theoretically, democracies achieve consensus through an intersubjective discussion of experience that allows people to "harmonize" worldviews and actions. The agreement is reached neither through force nor strategic bargaining, but through the communicative power arising from the rationality of deliberation. While it remains a central point of debate among deliberative democrats, many theories maintain that this action is undertaken with an eye on consensus.[16] If the goal of discussion is not consensus, then the endeavor is not "communicative," but "strategic," meaning that participants are not treating one another as equals, but as objects to be defeated or won over. Only communicative action can provide a true basis for democracy because only this type of motivation is grounded in mutual respect and accountability.

The opinion formed in deliberation has force by virtue of its "publicity," or moral traction.[17] That is, after a group of equal and autonomous individuals debate an issue in an arena in which information flows freely, reason will carry the best option forward; it will have communicative power to the extent that it secures publicity (by virtue of its reasonableness). While this ideal may be extraordinarily difficult to achieve, public decisions are judged as legitimate according to the extent to which they conform to this model of rational deliberation. Even when communicative acts fail to achieve this ideal, it remains in play; according to Habermas, one always implicitly assumes that the communicative endeavor in which one is about to take part will be pure and undistorted.

For many deliberative democrats, pure communicative action takes place

16. For example, Warren ("Deliberative Democracy") does not think consensus is part of the theory, while Steenbergen et al. ("Measuring Political Deliberation") think it is. Also see Joshua Cohen, "Procedure and Substance in Deliberative Democracy," in Bohman and Rehg, *Deliberative Democracy*, 407–37, for views on "limited consensus." See Seyla Benhabib, *Situating the Self: Gender, Community, and Postmodernism in Contemporary Ethics* (New York: Routledge, 1992); Johnson, "Arguing for Deliberation"; and Danielle Allen, *Talking to Strangers: Anxieties of Citizenship since Brown v. Board of Education* (Chicago: University of Chicago Press, 2004), for more on the general debate. My view is that making consensus any sort of ideal (even one we acknowledge to be practically unobtainable) gives some people ammunition to use against others, e.g., arguing that their intentions in joining the deliberation are problematic. There remains a significant difference between tolerating certain types of speech and appreciating them. In any case, I hope this criticism will be seen as one more voice in the argument against making consensus (rather than the more limited "understanding") a goal of democratic deliberation.

17. Jürgen Habermas, *The Structural Transformation of the Public Sphere* (Cambridge: MIT Press, 1989).

against a backdrop of universal validity claims, or discourse ethics, that allow communication to run smoothly. They are claims to truth, normative rightness, and sincerity. That is, "agreement in the communicative practice of everyday life rests simultaneously on intersubjectively shared propositional knowledge, on normative accord, and on mutual trust."[18] Different types of statements thematize only one of the validity claims at a time. For example, an expressive statement like "I feel satisfied" only explicitly raises the claim to truthfulness, while a claim like "that car is blue" only explicitly raises the claim to truth. However, "it is a rule of communicative action that when a hearer assents to a thematized validity claim, he acknowledges the other two implicitly raised validity claims as well."[19] So the sincerity claim is always in play, regardless of whether one asserts it explicitly or not, or whether one is talking about her own feelings or transmitting a fact to another person.

Habermas considers sincerity to be one of the three criteria of rationality, and other prominent theorists have also endorsed this ethic.[20] In addition to deliberative democracy's explicit focus on sincerity, John Kang has argued that both libertarian and communitarian thought also rely on sincerity assumptions.[21] Scholars working in communication studies and journalists have also noted the importance of sincerity in contemporary politics.[22] Finally, I believe that our current civic ideology leads most people (at least in the contemporary United States) to assume sincerity is impor-

18. Habermas, *Moral Consciousness and Communicative Action*, 136.

19. Habermas, *Theory of Communicative Action*, vol. 2, 121.

20. In addition to Habermas (*Between Facts and Norms*, 318–19), a number of other theorists explicitly discuss the ethic of sincerity. See, for example, Robert E. Goodin, "Sequencing Deliberative Moments," *Acta Politica* 40, no. 2 (July 2005): 182–96; Paul Grice, *Studies in the Way of Words* (Cambridge: Harvard University Press, 1989), 27; Gerry Mackie, "All Men Are Liars: Is Democracy Meaningless?" in Elster, *Deliberative Democracy*, 89–92; Steenbergen et al., "Measuring Political Deliberation," 26; and Warren, "Deliberative Democracy," 183. For another discussion of Habermas's use of sincerity, see Davide Panagia, "The Force of Political Argument," *Political Theory* 32, no. 6 (December 2004): 825–48. Panagia's contrast of William Hazlitt's *The Plain Speaker* and Habermasian argument is an alternative take on my argument, but one that I will not explore here.

21. John M. Kang, "The Irrelevance of Sincerity: Deliberative Democracy in the Supreme Court," *Saint Louis University Law Journal* 48, no. 305 (April 2004): 307. Also, see Kang for the arguments of other theorists on behalf of sincerity, including John Rawls, Cass Sunstein, Joshua Cohen, John Dunn, Frank Michelman, Amy Gutmann, and Dennis Thompson.

22. See John B. Thompson, "The New Visibility," *Theory, Culture and Society* 22, no. 6 (2005): 31–51, and Paddy Scannell, *Radio, Television and Modern Life: A Phenomenological Approach* (Malden, Mass.: Blackwell Publishers, 1996), chap. 3. See also David Runciman, *The Politics of Good Intentions: History, Fear, and Hypocrisy in the New World Order* (Princeton: Princeton University Press, 2006).

tant for political discussions. We expect people not to lie about their intentions and beliefs—to be sincere, rather than strategic—when telling us what they think. The value of sincerity is easy to see; we don't want liars and obfuscators to have a platform in our deliberations. The deception that might flow from a speech situation unbounded by norms of sincerity would seem to threaten the very possibility of a logocentric polity. Theorists often use "sincerity" interchangeably with "truthfulness" and "authenticity," which also calls to mind the idea that a speaker is not hiding anything pertinent to the discussion.[23] She is not only not deceitful, but also offers a complete account of the relevant information. She is what she claims she is, without complicating hidden designs on the discussion and without making false statements she knows to be false. Sincerity means intentionally telling people what one thinks, not holding back pertinent details, and not lying; there is a consistency between what one says and what one believes.[24]

Sincerity is also linked to the ideal of rationally motivated consensus. The agreement to which the speaker is oriented will result from the rationality of the statements made, not from some pathos intentionally and strategically elicited by a gifted speaker. If one believes unforced, rationally motivated consensus is possible, then there is no reason to strategically position arguments (thus disconnecting actual beliefs from statements) because with enough discussion, the group will recognize the truth of the argument or else convince one otherwise. Since one is not trying to "win," there is no good reason to misrepresent one's beliefs or to pander to the audience's prejudices. And so sincerity often involves a claim to not use rhetoric—to not try to strategically choose words in order to persuade, but

23. I am aware of Lionel Trilling's argument in *Sincerity and Authenticity* (Cambridge: Harvard University Press, 1972), in which he posits that sincerity, a concept that refers to one's relation to the public (that is, one avows only one's true feelings to others), was replaced with authenticity, which implied transcendence of the social. Nevertheless, I collapse the two terms here, as the meanings are not always kept separate within the literature I discuss, because they are for Trilling "cognate ideals," and because both of Trilling's terms refer to a purity of the self.

24. Amanda Anderson argues that Habermas's use of sincerity does not refer to the individual: "In this recasting of sincerity as a communicative presupposition, Habermas moves away from the idea of sincerity as anything approaching a substantive virtue, or even an attribute of persons." *The Way We Argue Now: A Study in the Cultures of Theory* (Princeton: Princeton University Press, 2006), 168. For many deliberative democrats, the focus is, in fact, on institutions, not individual virtue. Yet there is some slippage (as "proceduralism can seem to make appeal to ethos or virtue," 173), and both academic (especially empirical studies and applications of deliberation) and popular discourse has tended to collapse these communicative presuppositions into individually identifiable traits. See also Anderson, *The Way We Argue Now,* chap. 7.

rather to rely on the rational power of one's facts, one's sincerity, and the normative appropriateness of what one says. One is sincere—that is, one's intentions are sincere, and so one has pledged to not misrepresent oneself in order to achieve a goal.

The norms themselves "converge in a single claim to rationality . . . [which] is necessarily built into the way in which the species of talking animals reproduces itself."[25] This claim grounds Habermas's model in a distinctly human capacity for reason through speech, providing an alternative to social steering through money or power (economic or bureaucratic imperatives). It is universal, both in the sense that each person has this capacity (according to "ethnopsychiatry")[26] and in the sense that it follows from the imperative of mutual recognition and reciprocity. These dynamics are embedded in the thought processes of every human being; "truth" consists of what every "rational" being would concede to in a discussion.[27] The endeavor also requires the attribution of communicative freedom to the other persons in the dialogue and openness to the points of fellow discussants. Through communicatively expressed reason, subjects act democratically to move toward a consensus regarding their shared situation and what to do about it.

Discourse ethics, or validity claims, form the background consensus for discussion. That is, we assume everyone in a discussion is operating according to these rules that purport to ground speech in truth. If they are violated—thus disrupting the achievement of a rational consensus—these norms can be used as a foundation for critique. These claims can be questioned and defended, identifying points of agreement and disagreement, making explicit what was implicit in the original communicative act. To redeem claims to truth or normative rightness, the actor must provide reasons to interlocutors. To redeem one's sincerity, reasons are insufficient; this claim can only be redeemed through consistent behavior or third par-

---

25. Habermas. *On the Pragmatics of Social Interaction*, 85.
26. Ibid., 132.
27. This assertion (that rationality in speech is hard-wired in the human mind) seems to me a tremendous and interesting claim, which I unfortunately have neither the time nor expertise to explore here. Suffice it to say, the "innateness" of language and language usage is not universally accepted by linguists. For accessible arguments for and against the "innatist" view, see Steven Pinker, *The Language Instinct* (New York: Morrow, 1994); Terrence W. Deacon, *The Symbolic Species: The Co-evolution of Language and the Brain* (New York: W. W. Norton, 1997); or Geoffrey Sampson, *Educating Eve* (New York: W. W. Norton, 1997). I thank to John H. McWhorter, *The Power of Babel* (New York: Times Books, 2001), 8–9, for this information.

ties.[28] Sincerity thus requires a community and is related to one's reputation. According to Habermas, discourse ethics provide the basic logic behind human communication in the social sphere (or "lifeworld") and thus always have a "steering effect" on deliberations, even when left unfulfilled.[29]

To explain how liberal democracies can and should work, these dynamics are then abstracted to a grand scale.[30] This is made possible by mass communication, which allows discussion to take place in spite of physical absence. As the "conversation" expands, anonymity grows and contexts become more generalized, leading to a more abstract discussion—but one that remains firmly within the realm of "ordinary language" (accessible to nonspecialists) and grounded in discourse ethics. Different associative groups, meeting at various intervals and for various durations, exist within civil society to generate and sustain these deliberations. So deliberations are not limited to such formally "political" venues as legislatures, town meetings, or presidential speeches. Instead, this arena is decentered. According to Iris Marion Young, "Society is bigger than politics and outruns political institutions . . . the processes of communication that give normative and rational meaning to democracy occur as flows and exchanges among various social sectors."[31] Likewise, W. Lance Bennett and Robert Entman argue that "the public sphere is comprised of *any and all locations, physical or virtual, where ideas and feelings relevant to politics are transmitted or exchanged openly.*"[32] A narrower definition, while more focused and easier to work with, would ignore the massive variety of locations in which people communicate ideas that bear on their and others' political perspectives and actions. This enlarged and decentered view of the public sphere helps us recognize the diverse spaces in which democracy takes place. Discourse begins in this periphery and thus depends on the opportunities available and capacities exercised there.[33] The process sorts these influences, and pub-

---

28. Habermas, *Theory of Communicative Action*, vol. 1, 41, and Habermas, *On the Pragmatics of Social Interaction*, 91.

29. Habermas, *Between Facts and Norms*, 340.

30. Scholars have noted the potential problems with this abstraction. See Benjamin Lee, "Textuality, Mediation, and Public Discourse," in Calhoun, *Habermas and the Public Sphere*, 402–18.

31. Young, *Inclusion and Democracy*, 46.

32. W. Lance Bennett and Robert M. Entman, "Mediated Politics: An Introduction," in *Mediated Politics: Communication in the Future of Democracy*, ed. Bennett and Entman (Cambridge: Cambridge University Press, 2001), 3; emphasis in original.

33. Habermas, *Between Facts and Norms*, chap. 8.

lic opinion becomes focused (in contrast to the liberal notion of aggregated opinion). It is focused to the extent that the debate has been rational and exhaustive, meeting all objections, transforming itself as better reasons come into view, and defending itself from further challenges. This opinion then meets with the core—the institutionalized political system—and legally binding decisions are made.

As I discussed earlier, discourse ethics can be used to call discussants to explain themselves further. This notion of accountability is central to deliberative theory. While the terms may differ—"reciprocity," "account-ability," "deliberative uptake," or "reflexive challenge"—the crucial and shared assumption is that participants in a deliberation have a mutual respect that renders them willing to justify their claims to one another.[34] Deliberative democracy rests on this recognition of a responsibility to give reasons and explain oneself to other members of the polity. It also requires listening to the reasons and objections of others; accountability is an inter-active and potentially transformative activity, not just a resignation to pres-enting a reason for an action or belief and moving on.[35]

This democratic belief in mutual accountability rests upon and requires universal moral respect or equality. All those affected by political decisions should be included in the process and given equal political rights to commu-nicate their ideas. One could imagine (and indeed history has seen) an oli-garchic accountability—a sort of lords of the round table, which excludes large portions of the population, but in which members of a certain ruling class are deemed equal to one another and therefore worthy of holding one another accountable. Or "accountability" could exist where all the members of the polity are theoretically included, but many remain outside the delib-erative process because they have been coerced into silence through threats of physical violence (the Mississippi Sovereignty Commission, active in intimidation efforts from 1956 through 1973, comes to mind). Thus, to be a deliberative *democracy*, all members of the polity must *actually* have "the same symmetrical rights to various speech acts, to initiate new topics, to ask for reflection about the presuppositions of the conversations, and so

34. See Gutmann and Thompson, *Democracy and Difference*; Young, *Inclusion and Democracy*; Bohman, "Deliberative Toleration"; and Seyla Benhabib, "Toward a Deliberative Model of Democratic Legitimacy," in *Democracy and Difference*, 67–94.

35. I use "accountability" because it applies well to the expectations of both government officials and citizens. Furthermore, "accountability" is etymologically related to an act of speech, highlighting the communicative aspects of this relationship. See Chapter 2 for further discussion of the meaning of accountability.

on."[36] Democratic accountability provides this foundation for democracy; tyrants and dictators are not accountable, but democrats respond to the claims made upon one another. From Herodotus's distinction between democratic Athens and monarchic Persia (*Histories* 3.80) to the current calls for more participation and accountability in global governance, the concept stands at the heart of the democratic sensibility.

For many deliberative democrats, the quality of accountability in a democracy rests upon universal discourse ethics. When one disagrees with a speaker, it is because one finds her to have the facts wrong, or to be saying something we find ethically problematic, or to be disingenuous. These three communicative norms provide a rational foundation from which fellow citizens can critique speakers and call them to account for what they say. In conjunction with formal mechanisms of accountability, such as sunshine and libel laws, reelection procedures, and so on, discourse ethics provide the basis for accountability. It is the way to ensure that when someone makes statements and is questioned by others, that person is not providing false information with impunity. Sincerity in particular is meant to counter the potential for manipulative speech or outright trickery in a deliberative democracy. In a polity based on the power of words, the legitimacy of the process rests on the quality of information and ideas; dissemblers pose a particularly insidious problem for democracies. A democratic speaker is assumed to reveal her views transparently, shunning obfuscations, double-talk, and cheap emotional (and strategic) appeals. When a speaker makes a claim, her sincerity is taken to indicate her commitment to mutual accountability and democracy.

The Problem with Straight Talk

While I share the impulse to locate a rational foundation for political life and am drawn to sincerity as a guarantor of communicative validity, there are several reasons to pull back from embracing the ethic for politics. Before moving on to my examination of the sincerity norm, I want to first discuss the ideal of consensus in these theories.[37] The goal of consensus shapes the

36. Benhabib, "Toward a Deliberative Model," 78.
37. For a useful and extended discussion of the role of consensus (and its relation to "understanding") in deliberative democracy, as well as its historical antecedents and its contribution to the "bad habits" of our current democratic practices, see Allen, *Talking to Strangers*, chap. 5.

sincerity norm because it has to do with one's intentions in deliberation. Meanwhile, consensus privileges certain styles of political speech. For example, language that may be considered combative and uncooperative is devalued. Such language reflects a problem with the speaker's intentions— they are not oriented toward unforced consensus.[38] By recognizing one deliberative result as legitimate, deliberative democrats run the risk of ignoring certain styles of speech and denigrating important outcomes other than consensus. They can neglect the idea that deliberation can be a forum for thinking through a problem together or can lead to an understanding of "where another person is coming from," without necessarily reaching the same conclusion about what action to take. As I noted before, the ideal of consensus is certainly not something on which deliberative democrats agree; what I want to provide here is another argument in support of removing consensus as an ideal of democratic communication, highlighting the relationship between consensus and sincerity.

Expansive mutual accountability is the central component of democratic politics. However, deliberative theories can be too quick to leap from this foundation to an ideal of communication based on validity claims leading to rational consensus. Accountability entails giving an account when called to do so. In the democratic political arena, it may mean that a person works through a problem with other people, possibly changing one's own beliefs through discussion (the deliberative ideal), but also perhaps maintaining one's prior preferences or remaining stumped by the impossibility of any decision. If one deeply holds certain beliefs, a radical openness to ideas that contradict those beliefs seems unlikely and undesirable.[39] While we would hope that Ku Klux Klan members could be convinced of their error, we are unlikely to permit ourselves to be converted to it. Would it be irrational or antidemocratic for contemporary U.S. citizens to refuse to seriously entertain arguments supporting slavery?[40] Furthermore, it is not clear why reci-

---

38. At the same time, forms of hyper-sincerity often limit the possibilities of reaching understanding, since they claim a monopoly on truth and reject the usefulness of debate. Yet the way in which they do this still rests on an understanding of speech and politics that remains committed, at least ideally, to consensus. That is, if only that stubborn other person would listen to my sincere (and therefore true) statements, we could come to a consensus.

39. See Gaus, "Reason, Justifications, and Consensus."

40. This does not mean that those espousing undemocratic views do not deserve justification of policies affecting them. "Even if certain citizens do not themselves engage in tolerant perspectives taking, these facts in no way undermine their reflexive challenge." Bohman, "Deliberative Toleration," 768.

procity cannot entail forms of negotiation in which one gives up something in order to keep the shared world from coming undone.

At its heart, political discussion is how participants work through communal problems together. This discussion may lead to consensus, but can also lead to other specific sorts of mutual understanding in which we acknowledge our differences and move forward with the realization that we may never agree to the same means and ends (yet also without killing one another). Privileging consensus above all other goals may have the perverse result of conceptualizing politics as a zero-sum game in the eyes of participants, leading to more dogmatism and violence in political life. According to Bryan Garsten, "The call for unanimity . . . implicit in the creation of an authoritative public source of judgment chafes and constrains; it is from that implied unanimity that dissenters feel alienated; and it is against the asserted sovereignty of that unanimity that they rebel."[41] There is often residual disagreement; and while decisions must be made, they often entail a loss that must be acknowledged.[42] This can be achieved with bargaining or negotiation, which can play an important role in reducing the possibility of violence through a substantive acknowledgment of the conflict. Habermas's conception also poorly describes "strategic consensus"; that is, consensus not motivated by reasons, yet one that is not *forced* through threats or rewards. It is a communicative moment in which one participant agrees with another, not because she is necessarily convinced (she may not even really care about this issue), but because she wants to keep the discussion moving, or deepen the trust between participants. Finally, as Susan Bickford argues: "Denigrating strategic action only obscures the difficult complexity of actual political interaction, in which strategic and communicative interaction are intertwined, and I am not convinced that this intertwining should be regarded with regret. Trying to purify this mix of motives leaves us unable to appreciate the complexity of human interaction, and reinforces a romantic ideal both of politics and who we are as citizens."[43] To make consensus the proper result of political discussion can lead to a dangerous idealization, opening the possibility that some participants will criticize others for being uncooperative simply for disagreeing, or that others will refrain from voicing important reservations because of the pressure to con-

---

41. Garsten, *Saving Persuasion*, 185.

42. For more on sacrifice and loss in political life, see Allen, *Talking to Strangers*.

43. Susan Bickford, *The Dissonance of Democracy: Listening, Conflict, and Citizenship* (Ithaca: Cornell University Press, 1996), 18.

form. We have to maintain both the possibility of a transformation of beliefs through discussion *and* the understanding that consensus may not (and should not necessarily) occur. This is admittedly a more tragic view of the political realm, but it is one that recognizes the persistent messiness of political life.

But why does deliberative democratic theory often have so much trouble imagining outcomes different from consensus in ways that do not configure them as somehow deviant? This has much to do with the theory's conceptualization of rational speech. In this view, reason provides a foundation for political life, an impartial and objective way to adjudicate conflict. But giving reasons does not necessarily mean that participants will or should arrive at the same place, or that even when they do agree, that such agreement rests on the same reasons. In some cases, their reasons may simply be incommensurable. For example, the foundational qualities of the claims underwriting both sides of the abortion debate leave the two sides without a basis for agreement. A charge of "murder" does not leave much room for a claim of "reproductive rights." A mutual understanding of the impossibility of full reconciliation can be an important part of living together. Furthermore, the jarring quality of some speech not oriented toward consensus can serve an important role in helping us understand how far apart our perspectives may be. One website, www.bigbadchinesemama.com, a parody of mail-order bride websites that feature stereotyped Asian women, is specifically tagged to lure those looking for pornography websites through Internet search engines.[44] In this way, the author lures in men looking for a "demure lotus blossom," and then invites them in for some verbal abuse: "After all, us 'Orientals' are known for our hospitality and genteel demeanor. We aim to please . . ." The combativeness of the website is the crux of the message and perhaps the best way to express the offense caused by the stereotypes critiqued by the author.[45]

In other cases, a speaker may remain open to consensus but make demands of her audience that may be seen as burdensome or uncooperative. For example, Gloria Anzaldúa's essay "En rapport, In Opposition: Cobrando cuentas a las nuestra" argues for a *rapprochment* among feminists of

---

44. http://www.bigbadchinesemama.com/ (accessed July 28, 2004).
45. If deliberation is a process of judgment based on the imperative of mutual accountability, then it is not clear that this is "deliberation" when taken as an individual instance. But that doesn't also mean that it doesn't provide a necessary background for individual deliberation to take place or is not a part of a larger-scale notion of public sphere deliberation.

color.[46] Pieces of the work are in Spanish, with no translation offered. Such a move may be seen as rather uncooperative—this is not language that is easily understood by all readers. The reader must undertake a translation effort or else know that she is only partially getting it. Anzaldúa refuses to bridge the distance herself, requiring the reader to meet her along the way. This technique helps the reader understand the predicament of someone like Anzaldúa, coming out of a colonial experience and wary of continued cooperation with those who automatically expect her cooperation. Anzaldúa speaks in two languages because that is how she exists in the world; persuading people to recognize her (and others) as she is *is* the goal. Her use of Spanish clues the reader into the fact that without an appreciation of this part of the writer's identity, the reader does not really understand what is going on. While it is tempting to argue that the author really just wants to be understood in the end, to argue that consensus is her aim is to flatten her work and to remove the anger and criticism that animate it. Claims of complete understanding can serve to co-opt another person's standpoint, which that person has individually cultivated and experienced, perhaps in explicit opposition to the person now claiming to "get it." As Elizabeth Kiss warns, "An abstract preference for connection over separation ignores the reality that, for the less powerful members of any society, connection often means invasion and intrusion rather than intimacy."[47]

With this criticism in mind, I am ready to move to the sincerity norm itself. Ideally, the norm could serve to hold members of a community accountable to one another, creating the very possibility of binding decision-making. Václav Havel's "The Power of the Powerless" and George Orwell's "On Politics and the English Language," as well as his novel *1984*, implore us to recognize the importance of truth and to reject verbal obfuscations in political life. But truth and sincerity do not necessarily guarantee each other, and an unexamined idealization of sincerity may have perverse effects in a system based on deliberation.

Many deliberative democrats have recently come to acknowledge the ways a "gentlemen's club" of deliberation might be privileged by some

46. See Gloria Anzaldúa, "En rapport, In Opposition: Cobrando cuentras a las nuestra," in *Making Face, Making Soul, Haciendo Caras: Creative and Critical Perspectives by Feminists of Color*, ed. Gloria Anzaldúa (San Francisco: Aunt Lute Books, 1990), 142–48.

47. Elizabeth Kiss, "Alchemy or Fool's Gold? Assessing Feminist Doubts About Rights," in *Reconstructing Political Theory: Feminist Perspectives*, ed. Uma Narayan and Mary Lyndon Shanley (University Park: Pennsylvania State University Press, 1997), 6–7.

conceptions of the theory: "We cannot *define* deliberation—as do some deliberative democrats—in terms of individuals' prior commitment to reasonableness, nor to their intentions to seek consensus, not even to their respect of opponents. Barring the epistemological and political problems of identifying such commitments, it would in effect depoliticize deliberation, limiting it to the easy kinds of politics that can take place once these commitments are secured."[48] But deliberative theory has yet to fully explore the extent of the "reasonableness" assumptions. Even for those who do not assume an ideal speech situation marked by civility and ending with consensus, sincerity still plays an important role in democratic communication.[49] Yet a focus on the ethic of sincerity can lead to the sort of pathologies of deliberation that these theorists hope to avoid. An unquestioned belief in the value of sincerity for political deliberation too easily collapses the relation between claims to truthfulness and truth claims and contributes to an undemocratic epistemology; oversimplifies human psychology, ignoring the possibility of multiple and complexly related intentions; denigrates "rhetorical" forms of speech; and privileges a seemingly nonrhetorical mode of communication: hyper-sincerity.

Telling It Like It Is

There is a metadiscursive claim to "truth-telling" at work in the sincerity norm. The claim that one's statements conform to objective reality is posed by deliberative democrats as a separate validity claim (the truth claim) from the claim that one is telling the truth as one sees it (the truthfulness claim), but these two often converge.[50] While the distinction between sincerity and truth claims is important for analytic philosophy, the two are fairly indistinguishable in practice, as Habermas himself indicates.[51] If one is being sincere, then it is impossible to make a statement that one believes to be false. A truthful person cannot "really" state something that she does not believe to be true (although it is possible to "really" believe something that is not true). Sincere Speaker X may in fact be wrong, but cannot believe

48. Warren, Deliberative Democracy," 182.
49. Ibid., 183.
50. A similar claim can also be made in regard to normative rightness. As Plato long ago pointed out in the *Crito*, just because almost everyone in a society agrees on something, it is not necessarily normatively right. So consensus can become a substitute for moral appropriateness. My thanks to Gerry Mara for pointing this out.
51. Habermas, *Theory of Communicative Action*, vol. 2, 121.

this to be the case while making that statement. Thus, an explicit claim to sincerity carries with it an implicit (metadiscursive) claim to know.

This norm actually entails two components: acting with sincerity regarding your own intentions and not casting doubt on the sincerity of others.[52] Of course, one should question validity claims that appear to be violated, but trust remains an important component of smoothly functioning communicative action. The participant calling the claim into question must initiate the disruption. Especially in instances in which the speaker's rhetorical style apparently conforms to "rational" argumentation, critics may be deemed uncooperative and distrustful and unable to participate in a conversation. "Rational" qualities often include a demonstration of high literacy or expertise, the use of abstract language (as opposed to storytelling or joking), and the use of zero-degree tropes. By "zero-degree" I mean a style that explicitly claims to lack any rhetorical flourishes, in which words and reasoning stand alone.

Furthermore, Habermas acknowledges that the criticism cannot be made and debated in certain cases, because of threats to the speaker's own ego and identity, leading to the appearance of consensus in spite of the fact that the speaker has violated a norm.[53] To question someone's sincerity and to allow your own sincerity to be questioned requires a tremendous psychological capacity and goes against many of the norms of "polite society." In the end, those questioning a speaker's sincerity may be branded "uncooperative," while those who violate the norm may never have to redeem their claim. Whether criticism increases or decreases often depends on the particular speaker's reputation and rhetorical style. Moreover, many of those who might otherwise question a speaker avoid doing so because of a dislike of conflict and a wish to avoid appearing hostile.[54] This norm has especially affected women's involvement in political discussions.[55]

If all communicative action implicitly rests upon mutual trust, then the very claim to sincerity imposes a call for the listener to also accept the truth claim in a statement unless she knows it to be false and explicitly questions

52. Habermas, *On the Pragmatics of Social Interaction*, 64, 90.
53. Ibid., 155–70. Families with asymmetrical power relations provide an example of such distorted communication.
54. Jane S. Mansbridge, *Beyond Adversary Democracy* (New York: Basic Books, 1980), 34, 273–74.
55. Pamela Johnston Conover, Donald D. Searing, and Ivor M. Crewe, "The Deliberative Potential of Political Discussion," *British Journal of Political Science* 32, no. 1 (2002): 21–62, especially 54–55.

it in discussion. Given the enormous complexity of the issues that arise for deliberation, as well as the notoriously low levels of voter knowledge, there are many instances in which one has to use the information provided by others. Citizen Y is unlikely to have firsthand information on every issue debated; she feels she must depend on "expert" opinion, whether from academic journals, newspapers, or talk radio. The "truth" (facts and their extralinguistic meaning) to which one has access often depends on the supposed truthfulness of the speaker; the sincerity claim often underwrites the truth claims that can lead one person to listen to Rush Limbaugh for political insight and another to the BBC. At the same time, and as Machiavelli demonstrates in *The Prince*, plainly styled language has long been the hallmark of speakers professing their sincerity; whether that speaker actually speaks the truth is another matter.

Because of this practical collapse of truth and truthfulness, the sincerity norm can also contribute to a naturalization of the world. When we claim to describe the world as it really is and ourselves as we really feel, we often implicitly make a claim that discourse should correspond to a world from which words somehow stand apart. The world exists naturally, there to be described, and my description, because it is merely words, does not shape it. Joan Scott's discussion of "experience" makes a similar argument: "What could be truer, after all, than a subject's own account of what she has lived through? It is precisely this kind of appeal to experience as uncontestable evidence . . . that weakens the critical thrust of histories of difference."[56] When transparency is assumed, we are less likely to probe the construction of the individual. It also creates an uncontestable claim—if one is truthful about one's experience, for example, how could competing or contradictory claims be legitimate? Who is going to disrespect the speaker enough to claim that she doesn't *really* know how she feels about her own life, especially given what we know about people's dislike of conflict and confrontation? The anecdotes that make up one's experience are not a transcription of actual events, however; and even if they were, they are shaped by myriad social factors, many of which could have been otherwise. Moreover, memory is a malleable storehouse of knowledge; studies of eyewitness testimony have demonstrated its unreliability.[57] The easy acceptance of claims based on one's own lived experience can blind us to the possibility

56. Joan Scott, "Experience," in *Feminists Theorize the Political*, ed. Judith Butler and Joan W. Scott (New York: Routledge, 1992), 25.

57. Elizabeth Loftus, *Eyewitness Testimony* (Cambridge: Harvard University Press, 1996).

that not only are those experiences not *necessary* events in our lives, but also that our interpretations of experience create memories and stories that could be quite different from actual events.

Because the sincere speaker shuns artifice, she is able to see the world clearly, while those who admit a place for rhetoric are prisoners of verbal illusions. This is like the complaint made of advocates of "political correctness." According to critics, they have constructed an artificial world through speech and are not willing to say what is really there, instead making tortured rhetorical stretches to avoid offense. In contrast, the sincere speaker can see the world for what it really is. She is not trapped by discursive illusions and psychological confusion, but instead has a clear view of the *real world*. If the speaker can see the world clearly, why not trust her? And since the speaker is brave enough to refuse the demands of decorum, willing to tell it like it really is, she has proven her commitment to truth. Furthermore, this implies that there is *a* world to be seen clearly and, recalling Machiavelli's comparison of himself to a landscape painter, *a* privileged vantage point from which to gain an understanding of *the* truth.[58] The idea that reality depends on one's perspective (and that these varying perspectives are legitimate) has no place. Since one should trust one's fellow citizen, and since some speakers are especially trustworthy and can understand the world for what it is, rather than what they want it to be, why all the need for public discussion?

The Certain Self

In his discussion of the realist rhetorical style (to which I will return later), Robert Hariman argues that in this style of professedly sincere speech, "self-assertion is the essential speech act . . . once discourse . . . has been discarded as a means for completing a political scenario, and incapacitated as a source of political motives, the individual becomes the principle of cohesion by default."[59] The individual's authenticity is the measure of validity, and the sincere speaker is one with an authentic, unitary self. She disdains ritual language, role-playing, fancy constructions, in favor of

58. Niccolò Machiavelli, *Selected Political Writings*, ed. and trans. David Wootton (Indianapolis: Hackett, 1994), 6. Machiavelli does acknowledge various perspectives, but places himself as the one person who can understand all of them, thus seeing the real truth behind the situation.

59. Robert Hariman, *Political Style: The Artistry of Power* (Chicago: University of Chicago Press, 1995), 42.

straight talk. This person is dispassionate—the assertive self is in control. The irrational emotions do not obscure clear thinking. This tendency helps reinforce a false understanding of our relationship with language as something standing apart from reality, a tool to be used only in a descriptive (as opposed to productive) manner. It also helps privilege a stereotypically masculine style of talk—self-confidence, certainty, and a seemingly dispassionate tone demonstrate the speaker's commitment to the discussion. Moreover, because the sincere speaker is unitary, there is no split self, no self-consciousness that would allow the speaker to manipulate her own words for greatest effect.[60] Expressions of belief are authentic in that the speaker truly holds them without reservation. Yet this ignores the fact that whenever we speak, we choose words—there are no necessary and natural political statements.

This emphasis on an individual's assertions oversimplifies human psychology. It assumes that the speaking individual can see her own intentions clearly and that those intentions are both stable and unitary (or at least not conflicting). It also assumes that the individual has ready access to language that expresses her feelings clearly and that those words correspond to a stable intention in the individual. But we make statements contingently, stilling for a moment the constant flux and uncertainty of ourselves to say something. There are always gaps between what we are able to express and what is going on in a particular situation. Appreciating this complexity does not mean silencing ourselves or never making any positive statements; however, it does require that we know what it is that we are actually doing.[61]

60. For Trilling, authenticity is the quality that implies this unitary self; sincerity was replaced with authenticity precisely because of the rejection of the split self allowed by a sincere relation of the self to the social world. Yet the point here stands because the sincere person, as opposed to the insincere person, has an exact correspondence between actual self and representation of self, thus denying any mediating influences between the self and the world (whereas, for Trilling, the authentic person refuses the demands of representation and display to others altogether). In these terms, both sincerity and authenticity pose problems for contemporary democratic politics.

61. Micah Schwartzman's work on judicial sincerity addresses this problem by arguing for a more minimal conception of sincerity, which only demands a consistency between belief and statement, leaving aside the demand for thorough introspection and acknowledging the problem a demand for "single-mindedness" poses. Schwartzman is right in arguing that while psychological complexity throws more demanding notions of sincerity into question, we can still identify egregious cases of insincerity; yet, as Chapter 5 will make clear, I still believe it is extremely difficult and, more important, politically dangerous, to use an individual's *intentions* as a foundation for political judgments.

The sincerity norm can take for granted that a person would have only one motive when engaging in discussion and privileges the idea that a person will only communicate one thing by what she says. However, there are many situations in which we say something and may mean several things; this saturation of meaning is not a pathology of speech, but a rich resource. Instead of a straightforward, single intention that can be expressed simply, intentions may be multilayered. In unintentional irony, a person is not even consciously aware of all the possible extralinguistic meaning in her statement (i.e., a prescription drug addict condemning alcohol abuse). By thinking about her multiple intentions in making such statements (i.e., concern about drug abuse in society and unresolved anxiety about her own life), she can come to a better understanding of her social world. Other times, the multiplicity of intentions may be known to the speaker—a political cartoon exists both to entertain and criticize. But the joking and hyperbole on which such cartoons rely muddy the idea of a single, transparent intention. Storytellers and songwriters also come to mind—can we know their "true" intentions? In other situations, a person may actually want or feel something for two reasons, one that the listener may find attractive and another that she may find unacceptable (i.e., a person supports an environmental regulation because it is normatively right, but also because the person's family member stands to profit from its enforcement). Full disclosure becomes much more complicated and threatening; we have trouble imagining how the second motivation could *really* coexist with the first.

A person may have multiple intentions when engaged in a communicative act; full disclosure may be impossible, too lengthy, or may obstruct the point of the discussion. Multiple intentions are not necessarily devious—they are often just a fact of human psychological complexity. As I will discuss in Chapter 3, hidden or unclear intentions may compel the listener to a deeper engagement with the matter at hand, forcing an intellectual engagement that strengthens the group endeavor (and it may just as well fail). Further, how one's intentions are perceived has its own impact. We cannot fully determine how other people will perceive what we do or say. In light of this, we must make our understanding of deliberation more complex—otherwise, critics can too easily discredit certain speakers as insincere, uncooperative, or devious. For example, if one uses irony or joking in a communicative endeavor, one may be thought of as obscure or as lacking seriousness. This can occur in two ways. First, the very use of irony or joking may erroneously signal to the listener that the speaker does not take the matter seriously. Second, practices like irony, parody, and sarcasm are often misunderstood, leading to confusion.[62] But irony also relies on this duality—a straightforward joke is unlikely to be a funny or intellectually stimulating one. What is crucial here is that the intentions of the speaker are not entirely transparent; what looks like insincerity may actually be a useful mode of communication. This is also not to say that irony is necessarily a "better" form of speech than straight talk; things called "ironic" may also be flip, antipolitical, or self-defeating. Instead, I want to highlight the difficulties of thinking of political deliberation in terms of intentions.

One could argue that irony is parasitic on sincerity—that is, irony is only irony because we usually assume that people are being sincere. But irony can be more complicated than that. In the type of irony I have in mind, we may never really know what the ironic speaker means. As Chapter 3 will make clear, it is not a simple matter of taking the meaning to be the opposite of what is expressed; the ironist may mean exactly what she is saying, the opposite of that, or some combination of the two. Instead of feeding off sincerity, the most interesting irony calls into question the usefulness of the distinction between sincerity and insincerity. Given its instability, it seems logical that there might be instances in which irony or joking are unacceptable, as when one appears in a court of law. If our attention to sincerity might be relaxed a bit, when is it appropriate to do so? However, to decide beforehand under what circumstances or how irony should be deployed would be to fall again into what we want to avoid— prejudging the reasonableness of arguments. We cannot know beforehand what particular configuration of circumstances and personalities might call for irony. The force of irony—what makes it unique and powerful—is its strangeness and its spontaneity.

Admitting Rhetoric

A variety of modes of speech are omitted from strict conceptions of deliberative democracy. Young has pointed out the absence of greeting, rhetoric, and storytelling in deliberative democratic theory.[63] John Dryzek likewise argues:

---

62. For a good example, see the letters posted to the website authors at http://www.blackpeopleloveus.com/ (accessed July 28, 2004).

63. Young, "Communication and the Other" and *Inclusion and Democracy*.

Some deliberative democrats, especially those who traffic in "public reason," want to impose narrow limits on what constitutes authentic deliberation, restricting it to arguments in particular kinds of terms. . . . A more tolerant position, which I favour, would allow argument, rhetoric, humour, emotion, testimony or storytelling, and gossip. The only condition for authentic *deliberation* is then the requirement that communication induce reflection upon preferences in non-coercive fashion. This requirement in turn rules out domination via the exercise of power, manipulation, indoctrination, propaganda, deception, expressions of mere self-interest, threats (of the sort that characterize bargaining), and attempts to impose ideological conformity.[64]

We still need to better understand why there is such opposition to admitting rhetoric and exactly what the stakes are. I believe that the disagreement surrounding the place of rhetoric in deliberation stems from the notion that the use of rhetoric brings into question one's sincerity (and one's commitment to consensus). A common way to impugn an opponent is to claim that the person is using "rhetoric." The speaker is pandering, playing with words in order to win. For critics, rhetoric is insincere—it is language specifically chosen in order to persuade. Rhetoric involves an acknowledgment that words are chosen and tied to a particular situation and audience. And if one's words differ depending on who is listening, then language is strategic, which calls into question the deliberative motives. For many people, rhetoric is akin to the "manipulation" and "propaganda" criticized here by Dryzek.[65]

Meanwhile, other deliberative democrats argue that they either do not banish rhetoric from deliberation or that rhetoric has no place in certain areas of it. For example, Benhabib argues both of these points:

Each of these modes may have their place within the *informally structured process of everyday communication among individuals who share a cultural and historical life world.* However, it is nei-

64. Dryzek, *Deliberative Democracy and Beyond*, 1–2. Benedetto Fontana, Cary Nederman, and Gary Remer, the editors of *Talking Democracy: Historical Perspectives on Rhetoric and Democracy* (University Park: Pennsylvania State University Press, 2004), also note the rejection of rhetoric in deliberative theory.

65. See, for example, Chambers, *Reasonable Democracy*, and Thomas Spragens, *Reason and Democracy* (Durham: Duke University Press, 1990).

ther necessary for the democratic theory to try to formalize and institutionalize these aspects of communicative everyday competence, nor is it plausible—and this is the more important objection—to build an opposition between them and critical argumentation. Greeting, storytelling, and rhetoric, although they may be aspects of informal communication in our everyday life, cannot become the public language of institutions and legislatures in a democracy for the following reason: to attain legitimacy, democratic institutions require the articulation of the bases of their actions and policies in discursive language that appeals to commonly shared and accepted public reasons. In constitutional democracies such public reasons take the form of general statements consonant with the rule of law. The rule of law has a certain rhetorical structure of its own: it is general, applies to all members of a specified reference group on the basis of legitimate reasons.[66]

Yet it is not clear that Benhabib has *not* built an opposition between the other modes and argument, as she seems to disallow greeting and storytelling. This passage also seems to limit deliberative democracy to the formal spheres of government, which is certainly not the sole originating location of understanding in a democracy. Benhabib's deliberative democracy here consists of statements formally promulgated by such institutions, but elsewhere she favors a decentered model.[67] She bars some types of rhetoric from the "public language of institutions," which remains only a small component of the cacophony of deliberative democracy. The language used in this arena must be pure and abstract, cleansed of the corrupting and particularizing influences of rhetoric (although Benhabib acknowledges that this is its own rhetorical style). But one of deliberative theory's most appealing aspects is that it helps explain opinion formation throughout society, not just in the formal "core." The average citizen is more likely to encounter associational life and mass media on a regular basis than the formal institutions and statements of government. Moreover, something like greeting surely has something to do with the cooperation and conflicts that exist in legislatures prior to promulgations of law (as Vice President Cheney and Senator Patrick Leahy would surely attest after their June 2004

66. Benhabib, "Toward a Deliberative Model," 82–83.
67. Ibid., 73–74.

exchange on the Senate floor, in which the vice president told the senator to "go fuck yourself"). The titles of bills, the preambles and "Findings" sections of legislation, and Supreme Court opinions, for example, often contain narrative and imagery—sometimes helpful, sometimes troubling— that many would characterize as rhetorical.[68] Finally, it is not clear that the ideal of language purged of such elements would necessarily be more "commonly accepted" and legitimate.

While often perceived by critics to be a distinct element of speech, rhetoric is a quality of all (human) language use, one that is thoroughly intertwined with any utterance. Since the "linguistic turn," we know that all communication bears a relationship to the social context in which it is uttered. In contrast to the claims of hyper-sincerity, "all language is already artificial, all speaking is unplain by design."[69] There is no speech that is completely natural, unchosen, and necessary. Each statement has rhetorical elements by virtue of the fact that it appears in our world and has an effect based on its particular expression and context. *Pace* Young, scholars of rhetoric tell us that rhetoric is not a separate class of communication from storytelling and greeting, but rather a master category by which all statements can be dissected and understood. Sometimes rhetoric is used more self-consciously than at other times (the point of classical rhetorical study), but it is always a part of communication: "Rhetoric is employed at every moment when one human being intends to produce, through the use of signs or symbols, some effect on another."[70] Just as storytelling and humor have rhetorics, so do mathematics and social scientific analysis.[71] So we do ourselves a disservice to believe that rhetoric could be separated from communication, idealizing a false possibility that empowers hyper-sincere speakers (this does not mean that all hyper-sincere speakers are intentionally using such a style; nevertheless, their style has particular political effects). Rhetoric depends on context, which always exists, and to acknowledge rhetoric is to recognize that statements and speakers are always situ-

68. See, for example, see the Findings sections of the Patriot Act (HR 3162), or Texas v. Johnson, 491 U.S. 397 (1989), in which Chief Justice Rehnquist's dissenting opinion abounds with narrative and rhetorical language.
69. John Haiman, *Talk Is Cheap: Sarcasm, Alienation, and the Evolution of Language* (Oxford: Oxford University Press, 1998), 110.
70. Booth, *Rhetoric of Rhetoric*, xi.
71. See D. N. McCloskey and Robert Solow, eds., *The Consequences of Economic Rhetoric* (Cambridge: Cambridge University Press, 1988) and *The Vices of Economists, The Virtues of the Bourgeoisie* (Amsterdam: Amsterdam University Press, 1996), for more on the rhetoric of seemingly abstract and scientific statements.

ated. In different contexts, the same statements can mean very different things; meanwhile, "all successful communication within any given domain will depend on tacit shared assumptions about standards and methods."[72] As Young argues: "Rhetoric announces the situatedness of communication."[73] This fact is an unavoidable feature of communication. One speaks quite differently at an academic conference than one would in rural Louisiana. To speak in the same way at both locations simply would not make sense. Both the occasion and the audience are different, and the wrong voice would unduly limit the prospects of being heard. But, as Garsten points out, rhetoric requires the exercise of *judgment*, and the contemporary landscape is marked by a deep aversion to risk and uncertainty; deliberative theory deals with this aversion by asking people to accept one authoritative public point of view that obviates the need for the risky work of persuasion and individual judgment.[74]

For many deliberative democrats, there is a sharp line between sincere (and therefore true) speech, which leads to a democratically legitimate end, and other forms and aspects of speech. If these norms are intentionally violated, action moves to a strategic level in which behavior is influenced not by the power of words, but by the imperative of "maximizing gains and minimizing losses in the context of competition."[75] Yet this binary is too harshly drawn and impossible to preserve; many things may be going on in a speech situation. No form can *a priori* be judged to ensure truth and democratic legitimacy; it must be judged in light of the complex relations between speakers, language, and political reality. This is especially true in light of the fact that in a mass democracy, most people will come to political discussion through media, rather than in the "safe havens of deliberation" that attempt to overcome the asymmetries of mass media. Although proposals for deliberative forums are on the rise and some forums hold great promise, the fact remains that most people will most often experience formal democratic debate from their couch. This is a monologue, not a discussion, and rhetoric will play an even greater role here than in face-to-face communication. This creates certain challenges for deliberative theory as scholars try to spell out exactly how mass communication can form part of a healthy deliberative democracy. As Simone Chambers points out:

72. Booth, *Rhetoric of Rhetoric*, 18.
73. Young, "Communication and the Other," 130.
74. Garsten, *Saving Persuasion*, 10, 189–91.
75. Habermas, *On the Pragmatics of Social Interaction*, 13.

"If theories of deliberative democracy assume that all such [asymmetrical and mediated] public exchanges are 'bad,' they limit themselves and risk becoming overly utopian and irrelevant to the real workings of large modern democracies . . . we must look to the possibility of a deliberative orator."[76]

The goal thus becomes to try to tease out what qualities make for a good deliberative orator. Chambers, following Aristotle, counsels an attention to *ethos*, or the character of the speaker: "What guarantee do we have that such appeals are not used to manipulate hearers in illegitimate ways? One answer is to turn to *ethos*. We should only be listening to those with virtuous characters."[77] For many interpreters, Aristotelian *ethos* involves one's public reputation and long-standing moral qualities, developed through years of practicing *phronesis*. I do not think it is a stretch to argue that most people would include the quality of sincerity in a description of a "virtuous character." Given my wariness of sincerity, it should come as no surprise that I have reservations about this particular gloss on *ethos*. However, given the fact of asymmetrical and mediated democracy, *ethos* seems critical. The question is, what sort of *ethos*? An *ethos* of sincerity? Or is there another possibility?

Hyper-Sincerity

Two master tropes of hyper-sincerity dominate our public life: the cult of plain speech and the realist rhetorical style. These zero-degree tropes take the tendencies I have discussed to their most extreme. They make truth claims through a unitary and simple self, able to objectively see the world for what it is; they prove their sincerity through their expressed opposition to rhetoric and artifice and their use of plainly styled speech. This abuse of sincerity seems to be encouraged by particular social and cultural conditions—times of particular stress, such as we see in Athens during the Peloponnesian War or in the United States after the events of 9/11/2001. While deliberative democratic theory certainly does not *cause* these problems, it perhaps leads us down a path where we cannot anticipate or critique such problems.

John Haiman identifies a "cult of plain speech" in the contemporary

---

76. Simone Chambers, "Behind Closed Doors: Publicity, Secrecy, and the Quality of Deliberation," *Journal of Political Philosophy* 12, no. 4 (December 2004): 400–401.

77. Ibid., 403.

United States that prizes seemingly plain, blunt language, short words, and simple grammar that cut out the ornament and (appear to) get right to the meaning.[78] Haiman connects this phenomenon to the historical rejection of rhetoric in the West, as well as to a hypermasculine and anti-intellectual American culture:

> Real men will tolerate the jibberjabber of fluent wordsmiths— lawyers, pundits, spin doctors, poets, speech writers, admen, schoolmarms, journalists, politicians, therapists, highbrow academic nerds (in a word *wimps*)—only with contemptuous reluctance and always view them, if they view them at all, with the thinly veiled disdain which the salt of the earth reserve for "the croissant crowd": gigolos, maitre d's, feminist performance artists, and Woody Allen. In the company of such men, it is a badge of virility to flout the rules of grammar of the only language you know; grammaticality (to say nothing of multilingualism) is for sissies.[79]

People who speak "plainly" are seen as more natural and real, and therefore trustworthy. They can hold others to account because they are not confused by the temptations of fancy words. Rhetoric is denigrated to the point that a rustic, folksy style is affected.[80] Yet this plainspokenness is something that is cultivated, practiced, like any other speech. We learn, whether consciously or not, to dress our speech plainly to take advantage of the credit that this style can procure for a speaker. Of course, and as Haiman points out, this style is most suited to the American tough guy, one who, through speech if nothing else, is (like) a "common" person. Whether it comes from George W. Bush or a farmer, this style takes on the credibility of the farmer—plain, unaffected, and perhaps most important in politics, *real*. Voices that do not fit this model are suspect, often shut out of the conversation.

The realist rhetorical style identified by Robert Hariman takes this hyper-sincerity one step further. Like the cult of plain speech, it proposes

78. Haiman, *Talk Is Cheap*, 102–6.
79. Ibid., 107.
80. See, for example, Geoffrey Nunberg's analysis of George W. Bush's pronunciation of "nuclear" as "nucular." Nunberg argues that this particular pronunciation is a "folk etymology," an affected and intentional rhetorical choice. *Going Nucular: Language, Politics, and Culture in Confrontational Times* (New York: PublicAffairs, 2004).

to rid the world of the artifice of rhetoric, making a metadiscursive statement that authenticates the speaker and undermines potential critics. But
the realist style also makes certain assumptions about the social world as a
place dominated by self-interested actors, natural laws, and necessary
choices imposed by the situation. Hariman's description of Machiavelli's
The Prince is instructive: "This style begins by marking all other discourses
with the sign of the text: It devalues other political actors because they are
too discursive, too caught up in their textual designs to engage in rational
calculation."[81] It aligns itself with the "real, natural" world by claiming
objectivity and transparency. It "affects a lack of affectation" and thereby
acts as a zero-degree trope; it does not admit a power to move you through
its artistry with words, but claims to do so through its clear depiction of
reality. A "realist" text, then, purports to be a description of reality and
therefore immune from charges of bias. It relies on a separation of discourse
and reality, arguing that a speaker's statements are just reflections of the
"real world," not contributions to that reality. The author's truthfulness
serves an antidemocratic purpose, closing the open discursive space required
for democracy. There is no need for individual citizen judgment or true
deliberation, since the speaker already has access to the truth and can be
trusted.

Hariman identifies the realist style with Machiavelli, but notes that it is
used by a variety of speakers, and "operates as a powerful mode of compre-
hension and action in the modern world."[82] James Arnt Aune argues that
it is "the default rhetoric for defenders of the free market. The realist economic style works by radically separating power and textuality, constructing the political realm as a state of nature, and by depicting its opponents
as prisoners of verbal illusions."[83] In other work, I have documented the
use of this rhetorical style by the World Bank to defend economic globaliza-
tion.[84] If the world is defined by natural laws and can be objectively
described, then it is the realist voice that can be trusted to provide this
description. The realist speaker can see the truth, has no other designs on
the situation other than helping you out, and will not use fancy language

81. Hariman, *Political Style*, 17.
82. Ibid., 13.
83. James Arnt Aune, *Selling the Free Market: The Rhetoric of Economic Correctness*
(New York: Guilford Press, 2001), 40.
84. Elizabeth Markovits, "Economizing Debate: Rhetoric, Citizenship, and the World
Bank," *Poroi: An Interdisciplinary Journal of Rhetorical Analysis and Invention* 3, no. 1 (June
2004), http://inpress.lib.uiowa.edu/poroi/poroi/index.html/ (accessed October 30, 2006).

to confuse and convince you (like other people do). Rather than respect fellow citizens, the realist plays the part of big brother, patronizing their intelligence while lauding it (in their ability and bravery in recognizing a frank person like the realist).

Machiavelli provides us with an interesting twist—reason to doubt the sincerity of realist rhetoricians. Machiavelli himself claims to be artless and to have rejected the conventions of his time when writing *The Prince*. Unlike others, he will tell Lorenzo di Medici how things really are:

> I have not ornamented this book with rhetorical turns of phrase, or stuffed into with pretentious and magnificent words, or made use of allurements and embellishments that are irrelevant to my purpose, as many authors do. For my intention has been that my book should be without pretensions, and should rely entirely on the variety of the examples and the importance of the subject to win approval. I hope it will not be thought presumptuous for someone of humble and lowly status to dare to discuss the behavior of rulers and to make recommendations regarding policy.[85]

Of course, his use of metaphor as well as his later claims about the need for the appearance of artlessness while deceiving calls these opening lines into question. Machiavelli explicitly calls on the prince to cultivate the appearance of nonchalance and to conceal his motives in order to appear natural.[86] Machiavelli offers numerous examples of successful leaders who gave the appearance of power and control in order to gain it and who acted graciously while plotting against their enemies. Here we see how the *appearance* of sincerity is what *really* matters. While the successful political actor cultivates this appearance, she is also always ready to deceive: "It is essential to know how to conceal how crafty one is, to know how to be a clever counterfeit and hypocrite."[87] But as the Dedication claims, Machiavelli is an exception to these rules of artifice; he alone tells the unadorned truth in a world full of liars.[88]

---

85. Machiavelli, *Selected Political Writings*, 5–6.

86. Hariman, *Political Style*, 32. See also Victoria Kahn, "Virtù and the Example of Agathocles in Machiavelli's Prince," *Representations*, no. 13 (Winter 1986): 68–83, and Eugene Garver, "After *Virtù*: Rhetoric, Prudence, and Moral Pluralism in Machiavelli," in Hariman, *Prudence*, 67–97.

87. Machiavelli, *Selected Political Writings*, 54.

88. I am concerned here only with the rhetorical effects of Machiavelli's prose. For more on Machiavelli's possible intentions, see Mary G. Dietz, "Trapping the Prince: Machiavelli and the Politics of Deception," *American Political Science Review* 80, no. 3 (1986): 777–99, and

The Difficulties of Democratic Accountability

If accountability coupled with widespread equality is the cornerstone of democracy, then language plays a central role in our politics because it allows the communication that creates accountability. And if language is the means by which we hold one another accountable, then it seems critical to maintain a sense of ethics in speech, a way to criticize one another that is mutually acceptable. Yet speech remains an imperfect and frustrating medium. While emanating from our collective concern with truthfulness in politics, the realist rhetorical style and the cult of plain speech serve to hinder democratic deliberations. In particular, the realist style is an aggressive and intimidating way to shut out other voices. If the goal of the sincerity norm is to honor the imperative of universal moral respect by enabling democratic accountability, the manifestations of hyper-sincerity discussed here should give us pause. Perhaps most frustrating is that all sorts of invocations of sincerity, not simply hyper-sincerity, may also pose problems for democratic communication. Those claiming sincerity often implicitly claim the unquestionability of their perspective and the certainty of their views, in addition to making a metadiscursive comment that tries to separate rhetoric from discourse.

For these reasons, it is also important to shift attention from the speaker's intentions to our own capacities as listeners and readers. One can implore and critique a speaker on behalf of "validity claims," but ultimately it is only through one's own intellectual efforts that one can judge what the speaker may be saying. While trust can be important in deliberation, thoughtful skepticism may be of greater consequence. Constant and potentially exhausting engagement is the price we pay for the opportunities of democratic deliberation. By acknowledging the lack of foundations, we can better appreciate the requirements of citizenship and appreciate exactly what is *democratic* in our democratic deliberations. We can also begin to build the judgment required of citizens in a deliberative democracy.

Recall the Billionaires for Bush from the start of this chapter. They are insincere, often uncooperative, performers. Even when asked directly about their intentions, the member guide encourages them to "get comfortable to responding 'like a Billionaire' and staying on message in many of the

the subsequent debate, John Langton and Mary Dietz, "Machiavelli's Paradox: Trapping or Teaching the Prince," ibid. 81, no. 4 (December 1987): 1277–88.

possible situations that could arise."[89] Contrasting them with the object of
their protests, George W. Bush—a plainspoken straight-shooter, infamous
for his lack of grammaticality—it is not clear that the Billionaires for Bush
are operating in a way that lessens the potential for democratic deliberation.
Instead, their insincerity helps draw attention to what they see as an
undemocratic situation. The performance gets the Billionaires for Bush
onto the nightly news and in the morning papers, opening a debate about
whether the group is just obnoxious or really onto something (and what
that something might be). Habermasian discourse ethics might cause us to
overlook such messages and groups; given the discussion here, it seems
unhelpful to draw conclusions about the group or others like it before really
looking what they are doing. So what alternatives do we have? How else
can we limit rhetorical manipulation? In the next chapter, I argue that by
revisiting the ancient Greek concept of *parrhesia* (frank speech) and Socrates' response to it, we can gain insights into the role of straight talk in
democratic politics and begin to formulate other ways to ensure the legitimacy of democratic discourse.

89. See the *Billionaires for Bush Do-It-Yourself Manual*, www.BillionairesForBush.com/
(accessed July 25, 2004).

MIDWIVING SOCRATES

In Book 1 of the *Republic*, Thrasymachus, a foreigner in Athens, finds himself in the house of Cephalus, engaged in a heated debate about justice with
Socrates—whom he likens to a snotty child in need of a wet nurse (344a).[1]
Thrasymachus is an aggressive but reluctant interlocutor, who joins in only
after he becomes exasperated with Socrates' arguments; when he enters the
debate, he "roars" in, like "a wild beast" (336b). After asserting that people
reject injustice only because of their own fears of suffering it, Thrasymachus tries to leave. But the Athenians will not let him: "Those present . . .
made him stay to give an account of what he had said" (344d–e). They
refuse to allow Thrasymachus his assertions without putting his arguments
up for scrutiny. But Thrasymachus is not a good deliberative partner; he
refuses the demands of accountability. Why is that?

It is interesting that Thrasymachus is not Athenian. Socrates' constant
questioning and nitpicking exasperates him, as it did Socrates' fellow
Athenians. But Socrates is not the only one pressing Thrasymachus to justify his statements here; the others—all raised in democratic Athens, with
its norms of accountability—are too. Thrasymachus is isolated and frus-
trated. "How am I to persuade you, if you aren't persuaded by what I said
just now? What more can I do? Am I to take my argument and pour it into
your very soul?" (345b–c). The idea that the discussion might lead to a
new judgment on an issue is literally foreign to him. Because he does not

---

1. All citations taken from John Cooper's edition of *Plato: The Complete Works*.

understand the importance of explaining oneself to others, he is incapable of continuing the deliberation. Over the course of Book 1, matters improve little for Thrasymachus; he turns insulting, sweats profusely, blushes in front of Socrates—the "wild beast" returns.

Isocrates, a contemporary of Socrates, wrote in the *Antidosis* (15.254): "Because there has been implanted in us the power to persuade each other and to make clear to each other whatever we desire, not only have we escaped the life of wild beasts, but we have come together and founded cities and made laws and invented arts." As Isocrates makes clear, the Athenian relationship with language was a matter of civic pride. A person like Thrasymachus, at first unappreciative of the power of language and debate, remains like a wild beast throughout Book 1; he sullenly concedes Socrates' argument only because he is unable to fully participate in the kind of debate that defined democratic Athens.

Democratic Accountability in Socrates' Time

If Thrasymachus *had* been raised in Athens during the fifth and fourth centuries, he would have found himself presented with the opportunity to join in the collective decision-making processes of the polis sometime after he celebrated his eighteenth birthday.[2] While many of the other perquisites of citizenship were only available once a citizen reached thirty years of age (jury duty, selection to the body that controlled Assembly agendas [the Boule or Council of Five Hundred], and election as *strategoi* [military leader]), the young Thrasymachus could have attended the Assembly meetings where the *demos* discussed and voted on policies about forty times each year. Participation in the Assembly formed the core of Athenian citizenship; it was here that the *demos*'s claim to power, the essence of *demokratia*, was centered. While other institutional components of Athenian democracy were undoubtedly important, it is the Assembly that best captures the idea of democracy. Here, decisions about the future of Athens were made by a simple majority of the citizens present after discussion by any citizen who wanted to speak. Deliberations opened with the ritual

2. In practice, a citizen would begin participation in the assembly around the age of twenty. R. K. Sinclair, *Democracy and Participation in Athens* (Cambridge: Cambridge University Press, 1991), 31.

question: "Who of the Athenians has advice to give?"[3] An Athenian Thra-symachus could then have proffered advice on the Council's recommenda-tions or offer entirely new proposals—provided his proposals did not contravene existing law and that he addressed the same issue only once. He could have been shouted down if he had failed to keep the interest or sup-port of the audience, or he might have received a gold crown if the advice had been considered especially good. Through public speech, citizens exer-cised judgment through deliberation, considering and voting on most mat-ters of state, from war plans to public honors.

In this way, the Athenian democratic state was logocentric; the power of speech was praised by Pericles, lampooned by Aristophanes, and studied by Thucydides (as part of what Ober calls the "speech/fact/power triad").[4] The Athenians considered persuasion a divine force (the goddess Peitho) and, as Isocrates points out, the very thing that allowed humans to reach beyond their own animality. Outside the Assembly, words bound citizens in other complex ways. The Athenian citizen was likely to serve on a jury, where cases were brought, argued, and judged by ordinary citizens, not govern-ment officials. Ritual oath-taking was required for public officials. The city also demanded oaths of witnesses in jury trials, anyone participating in the examination of new citizens or officials (*dokimasia*), in the scrutiny of citi-zen rolls (*diapsephisis*), and in the examinations of officials after they left office (*euthunai*).[5] And although Assembly attendees did not take an oath, each session opened with a curse on anyone who would deceive the *demos*. While rooted in the previous monarchic and oligarchic regimes, speech as a means to persuade (rather than to command) was the legitimating power in the democracy.[6] In this chapter, I will examine the practices that enabled and reinforced this logocentricity, which in turn gave rise to Socratic ques-tioning and Plato's dialogues; much as Socrates describes himself as an intellectual midwife in the *Theaetetus* (148e–151d), the Athenian culture of accountability helped nurture and bring forth the particular discursive practices described in Plato's dialogues.

3. Josiah Ober, *The Athenian Revolution: Essays on Ancient Greek Democracy and Political Theory* (Princeton: Princeton University Press, 1996), 23.

4. Ibid., 20.

5. See Susan Guettel Cole, "Oath Ritual and the Male Community at Athens," in *Demokratia: A Conversation on Democracies Ancient and Modern*, ed. Josiah Ober and Charles Hedrick (Princeton: Princeton University Press, 1996), 227–48.

6. Language taken from Jean-Pierre Vernant, *The Origins of Greek Thought* (Ithaca: Cornell University Press, 1982), 49.

Two intertwined concepts are central to the practices of logocentric democracy in Athens during the fifth and fourth centuries—accountability and citizen dignity. Peter Euben describes accountability as follows:

> In many respects the Greek idea of accountability has the same range, breadth, and ambiguity as our own. To render an account is to provide a story or description of events or situations as well as to explain oneself (often to a superior). To give an account is to give reasons (i.e., on this account I am going). Things (or someone) of no account lack importance, worth, value, and consequence. To call to account is to hold someone responsible or blame them: to take account of is to consider, include, recognize; something unaccountable is unforeseen, incalculable, or mysterious.[7]

Most basically, accountability means a responsibility to explain oneself to others. In contemporary political life, accountability is a buzzword—"We need more accountability." But why? What is so important about it? Accountability serves two crucial roles in a democracy. First, it acknowledges the social embeddedness of individual citizens. If I hold all the power necessary to act in all the ways that I would like and that affect me, there would be no need for others to be held accountable. (Indeed, I have probably become a tyrant and thus not accountable to others.) Moreover, mechanisms of accountability are critical to the exercise of public power because those with that power may be tempted to use it to advance their private interests at the expense of shared interests (again highlighting our embeddedness). So accountability recognizes that our political lives are structured around one another, and that we do not individually hold enough power to achieve all that we would like. Second, and perhaps more important, accountability is a necessary condition for democratic arrangements—I could certainly recognize my dependence on others without having any way to influence them, or I could try to use physical strength to get others to do my bidding. In contrast, mechanisms of accountability allow mutual influence and cooperation; they are part of a moral strategy to deal fairly with our own interdependence.[8] When directed toward leadership, they provide those citizens currently without power a means by which to hold

---

7. J. Peter Euben, *Corrupting Youth: Political Education, Democratic Culture, and Political Theory* (Princeton: Princeton University Press, 1997), 97.
8. Thanks to Susan Bickford for this particular gloss on the point.

the powerful answerable for government policies and failures. It is a basic feature of both representative and large-scale direct democracies. When one calls for accountability, it is at once an acknowledgment that that particular citizen matters, and a summons to that citizen to use his rights and powers in a socially accepted manner. Without accountability, power faces no limits, because those with power can decide how to use it with no regard for the will of others. The result would be a state in which Thrasymachus's view of justice as the will of stronger prevails.

Of course, accountability had specific institutional forms in Athens. But such details do not obscure the central point—to be held accountable is to be forced (although one may volunteer the account before compulsion is necessary) to justify oneself, to offer reasons why one does something, whether in the present or the past. A general notion of accountability in politics means that this explanation is a routine part of government, not just something that applies in an irregular or voluntary way.

The Development of Democratic Accountability in Ancient Athens

Accountability was an indispensable component of Athenian democratic political culture. In the mind of the Athenians, "to have officials held accountable was the key to responsible government: unaccountability meant lawlessness."[9] Herodotus identifies it as the central difference between monarchy and democracy (*Histories* 3.80), and it is a theme in drama, political theory, and oratory through to the fourth century. Classical literature often juxtaposed the benefits of Athenian accountability of officials (and the concomitant societal openness) with contrasting qualities in its enemies: Persia, ruled by unaccountable monarchs, and Sparta, home of the deceitful warriors.[10] The accountability of officials was one way Athens defined its own civic identity; it was special and different because it placed limits on authority. Jean-Pierre Vernant traces the changes within Athenian society itself, as it moved from guidance by sacred pronouncements imposed by an unquestioned monarch to a democracy in which "creations of the mind and the operations of the state [were to] be equally

9. Jennifer Tolbert Roberts, *Accountability in Athenian Government* (Madison: University of Wisconsin Press, 1982), 6.

10. For more on the Athenian characterization of Spartans as deceitful, see Jon Hesk, *Deception and Democracy in Classical Athens* (Cambridge: Cambridge University Press, 2001).

subject to a 'rendering of account.' "[11] This particular arrangement of power came about with the gradual evolution from kingship to oligarchy to democracy in Attica, as different leaders attempted to maintain social cohesion through democratic reform. However, it is worth noting that "accountability" was not a democratic innovation. Instead, its roots lie in the norms of reciprocity of the archaic oligarchies.

In the Homeric world, reciprocity—the "principle and practices of voluntary requital"—joined leaders and followers in a symbiotic relationship; it was marked by an ethical code that limited the bounds of acceptable behaviors.[12] Like accountability, it bound people to one another, calling on them to acknowledge their social embeddedness (although unlike accountability, it did not necessarily entail giving an account). But this system had no practical mechanisms of external enforcement—no laws, institutional mechanisms, or this-worldly higher authorities to which one could appeal. Instead, it rested on an ethical code and religious oaths. Its violability would help give rise to a new form of authority—*turranos*. As Arlene Saxonhouse reminds us, tyranny involves a freedom from *metra*, the limits that form the ordered world.[13] Tyrants are not bound by the conventions of society, and become the measure of all things. With them, reciprocity fades; this is the point of the story of Gyges' ring in Herodotus. He is free to do whatever he pleases, because his actions remain unseen, and norms of reciprocity (let alone accountability) cannot be invoked against the unknown.

Formal (although not democratic) accountability actually comes into play in Athens in the aristocratic regimes before Solon's reforms. During that period, Athenians developed procedures for supervising officials (the nine archons were already in place), including the roots of classical era *euthunai* (post-tenure review), *dokimasia* (pre-office scrutiny), and *eisangelia* (impeachment).[14] Unlike the later forms of these procedures, these functions were performed by the Areopagus, an elite body composed of all former archons. They were considered worthy to judge those citizens holding

11. Vernant, *Origins of Greek Thought*, 52.

12. Richard Seaford, "Introduction," in *Reciprocity in Ancient Greece*, ed. Christopher Gill, Norman Postlewaite, and Richard Seaford (Oxford: Oxford University Press, 1998), 1.

13. See Arlene Saxonhouse, "The Tyranny of Reason in the World of the Polis," *American Political Science Review* 82, no. 4 (December 1988): 1261–75.

14. Martin Ostwald, *From Popular Sovereignty to the Sovereignty of Law: Law, Society, and Politics in Fifth-Century Athens* (Berkeley and Los Angeles: University of California Press, 1986), 7–9. See also Sinclair, *Democracy and Participation in Athens*, 18–19.

office, not because of their experience, but because they too were from the upper classes, and were thus their equals.[15]

Democratic accountability takes root some time before the 430s. The Assembly already existed, although its duties seem to have been largely limited to ceremoniously approving or vetoing measures presented by the aristocratic Areopagus. Over the course of several archonships, beginning with Solon and firmly in place after the reforms of Ephialtes, and the emergence of what Ober calls "citizen dignity," the power to hold one's leaders and fellow citizens accountable for their actions spread beyond the oligarchy to the Assembly of the *demos*, all free- and native-born males. While the exact dates of specific reforms (as well as the reasons for them) remain a subject of debate among classicists, by the middle of the fifth century the reforms were in place.

This spread of accountability to include all citizens would not have been possible without citizen dignity, the idea that all the members of the *demos* were free, equal, and secure in their status as citizens.[16] Critical to citizen dignity was the abolition of debt slavery. Political equality was secured once it was no longer possible for a citizen to lose his citizenship or fall under the power of another citizen because of economic reverses. The dignity of the citizen was hard-won over time, and *enacted* through legal and political practice rather than given by some higher power or natural law. Citizens were free and equal because of the law and because of their exercise of political power.

Perhaps even more important for democratic accountability, now any citizen could take legal action against any other citizen, including indicting individuals for crimes against the polis (a process termed *eisangelia*).[17] Vernant attributes this to Solon's newly developed "principle that the wrong done to a particular individual is actually an attack on all," which "gave each person the right to intervene formally on behalf of anyone who had suffered an injury."[18] Furthermore, the existing mechanisms of account-

15. According to Kurt A. Raaflaub, "equality . . . became a pillar of oligarchic ideology." "Democracy, Oligarchy, and the Concept of the 'Free Citizen' in Late Fifth-Century Athens," *Political Theory* 11, no. 4 (November 1983): 527.

16. Ober, *Athenian Revolution*, 101.

17. *Eisangelia* is often referred to as "impeachment," a convention I will follow, although I want to point out that it is slightly misleading as both a general, who was formally elected, and an orator, who only manages to not be shouted down by the Assembly members and serves in no official capacity, could face *eisangelia*.

18. Vernant, *Origins of Greek Thought*, 79.

ability were transferred from the oligarchic institutions of the past to more democratic bodies, and new procedures for holding both citizens and officials to account were introduced. An *eisangelia* was now initiated in the new Boule (Council of the Five Hundred) or the Assembly, rather than the Areopagus. With the exception of the *strategoi*, magistrates were limited to one-year terms, and were selected by lot. Juries now performed the *dokimasia* in most cases. Incoming archons and Boule members were subject to scrutiny by the Boule; and by the fourth century, laws limiting Boule membership to the top three census classes were ignored, leading to a representative body (in contrast to the Areopagus). The *euthunai* was also democratized; citizens selected by lot conducted the audits, and a procedure by which any citizen could lodge a complaint against a magistrate was introduced. Solon also introduced *ephesis,* a procedure for appealing an archon's decision to a body of citizens (the *heliaia*); archons thus became answerable for their decisions to a democratic body.[19] Not only were officials accountable, they were now accountable to any free citizen of Athens, not just those they considered their social equals.

Furthermore, this spirit of accountability was not limited to officials. Several ancient figures complain about or satirize the supposed *un*accountability of the *demos* in Athens (Aristophanes, Diodotus in Thucydides). However, there is evidence of a culture of accountability that extended throughout the citizenry.[20] First and foremost, it is rooted in the development of a spirit of civic-mindedness among the Athenian citizen body. Ober refers to Solon's reforms as making "Athenians potentially responsible for one another's welfare."[21] The prohibition of debt slavery, the ability of all citizens to bring one another to trial, a public interest in formerly private matters (religious celebration, marriage, care of orphans, the establishment of the *agora,* and standardized measurements),[22] and the *ephesis* procedure all point to a new emphasis on civic unity and a belief in the political and intellectual capabilities of regular citizens. With the Peisistratids' public works programs and Cleisthenes' reform of the *demes* (*deme*s were the groups into which the citizens were divided; Cleisthenes reorganized the *deme*s along geographical rather than kinship lines), the new civic spirit

19. Ostwald, *From Popular Sovereignty,* 12.
20. Euben, *Corrupting Youth,* chap. 4.
21. Ober, *Athenian Revolution,* 38.
22. Philip Brook Manville, *The Origins of Citizenship in Ancient Athens* (Princeton: Princeton University Press, 1990), chap. 6.

was even more firmly instilled in the public mind; Athenians now belonged to one of ten tribes, based not on kinship and loyalty networks, but on local political units. With the development of a democratic political culture, all citizens were invested with an interest in the stability of the state and a means to affect that stability. And beyond a shared civic spirit, the Athenians also developed a system of mutual accountability that even more firmly tied the citizen to the polis.

Institutional Mechanisms of Accountability

Mutual accountability began early in the citizen's life. Again, imagine that Thrasymachus is a native-born Athenian male. Regardless of social class, after his eighteenth birthday he would find himself subject to his first scrutiny as a citizen—the *dokimasia*. Here, fellow citizens in his *deme* would question him—was he eighteen years old? Was he freeborn of two Athenian parents?[23] As already mentioned, the examinee would take an oath promising to vote honestly, thus potentially presenting himself for inspection by his fellows (a challenge to a claim of citizenship would be resolved by a jury and perhaps the Council of the Five Hundred). Of course, the culture of accountability had its drawbacks, undoubtedly leading some to avoid political involvement and permitting mechanisms of accountability to be used as tools of revenge and intimidation. For example, in the wake of the Peisistratid tyranny, the Athenian upper classes subjected the public to a *diapsephismo*, an opening of the citizenship rolls for a general scrutiny, leading to a "reign of terror" in which citizens were forced to prove their citizenship to the vengeful upper classes.[24] Philip Brook Manville argues that it was in this context of suspicion and retribution that Cleisthenes' proposals were developed (and for this reason were so popular with the public).

Scrutiny of one's life did not necessarily end with acceptance by the *deme*. A citizen would be subject to a further *dokimasia* upon selection for office (generally by lot; *strategoi*—military leaders—were elected). While this examination was limited to those serving in an official capacity, it is important to remember that an Athenian citizen (especially in the fourth century) would most likely serve in such a capacity at some point in his

23. Ibid., 18.
24. Manville, *Origins of Citizenship in Ancient Athens*, 174.

life.[25] This scrutiny involved more questions than the *dokimasia* preceding acceptance by the *deme*. Here a citizen was asked not only about his lineage, but also whether he had treated his parents respectfully, paid his taxes, and fulfilled his military duties and religious obligations. If the candidate was up for the office of *strategos*, he was also asked if he had legitimate Athenian children and whether or not he owned property. The audience was then asked if anyone had complaints about the candidate. If rejected, a situation that does not seem to have happened with much frequency, the candidate was simply ineligible for office.[26] Once installed, several procedures existed for checking up on those holding office, including *apophasis* (report of investigation), *probole* (complaint to the Assembly), and *endeixis* (laying of information, much like presenting information to a judge in order to get a warrant).[27] *Eisangelia*, or impeachment, might be considered the culmination of such checks. It was usually reserved for high crimes, such as treason or acceptance of bribes, and appears to have been used most frequently against the *strategoi*.[28]

These mechanisms, like all legal actions in Athens, required that a citizen take the initiative in scrutinizing the officeholder or *rhetor* (speaker) under suspicion. Although Jennifer Tolbert Roberts has found numerous instances of politically motivated actions, the reliance on citizens (rather than public investigators and prosecutors) for a great many of the institutions of accountability fostered a useful hypervigilance among the Athenian citizenry. Although *apragmosyne* (minding one's own business) was considered a Greek virtue, it existed alongside the Periclean and Corinthian descriptions of Athenians as restless and self-reliant found in Thucydides.

25. Euben, *Corrupting Youth*, 95; Manville, *Origins of Citizenship in Ancient Athens*, 19; Sinclair, *Democracy and Participation in Athens*, 69. Meanwhile, although Athens is famous for its selection of magistrates by lot, others note that "lots were drawn not among all citizens thirty and over, but only among those who had offered themselves as candidates." Bernard Manin, *The Principles of Representative Government* (Cambridge: Cambridge University Press, 1997), 13. Hansen divides Athenian political activity into two categories—active and passive. While no citizen was forced to be an active participant—that is, put forward proposals and arguments in the Assembly—"passive" citizenship required "enough common sense to choose wisely between the proposals on offer" through listening and voting. Mogens Herman Hansen, *The Athenian Democracy in the Age of Demosthenes: Structures, Principles, and Ideology* (Norman: University of Oklahoma Press, 1999).

26. It does appear that the *dokimasia* was used "after these upheavals [oligarchies of 411 and 404] . . . to eliminate those with oligarchic sympathies even after amnesty explicitly forbade such political retribution." Euben, *Corrupting Youth*, 96.

27. Sinclair, *Democracy and Participation in Athens*, 159.

28. Apparently, more Athenian generals faced execution as a result of *eisangelia* than died on the battlefield. Hansen, in Roberts, *Accountability in Athenian Government*, 19–20.

At the same time, *apragmosyne* seems to be a particularly archaic virtue—akin to the *sophrosyne* (moderation) and *aidos* (modesty) that Athenians of a more oligarchic bent often contrasted to the perceived license and excesses of democracy. For committed democrats, however, watchfulness was key.

In case of lapses in public vigilance, the system also contained a number of repetitive, automatic mechanisms of accountability. In the fourth and possibly fifth centuries, officials were required to submit a report to the Assembly during each *prytany* (the unit of the ten-month Athenian calendar); the Assembly then opened the floor to complaints and took a vote of confidence on each official.[29] If any official failed to receive this affirmation, he was thereby removed from office and awaited a formal trial. The *euthunai* was another automatic procedure, occurring when any person serving a public function vacated office (since *strategoi* could be reelected, they could serve for many years before being subjected to the *euthunai*). While the first part of the procedure consisted of a financial audit (with fines prescribed for any malfeasance) conducted by a jury and officials selected by lot, the second part was open to the general public. It took place in the *agora* and allowed any citizen with a complaint to make against an official to do so to the *euthunos* of the particular magistrate's tribe.[30] Until this process was complete, the rights of the officeholder were curtailed—he was unable to travel, transfer property, or make an offering to a god.[31] Even after the oligarchies of 411 and 404, those who participated in the regimes were granted amnesty only after they had passed the *euthunai* themselves.

Critics would complain that this system ensured that officials were accountable, yet the citizenry remained free to fail, free to make bad decisions, free to ruin Athens for everyone else. Yet there were other mechanisms that applied to the public at large. I have already noted the initial *dokimasia* faced by each new citizen. As a new citizen's first experience as a citizen, this scrutiny would have initiated citizens into this culture of accountability. Later, if our imaginary Athenian Thrasymachus decided to take a more active role in the political sphere, yet did not want to take an official position or had already served his two possible nonconsecutive terms in the Council, he might become a rhetor, offering his advice to the

29. Roberts, *Accountability in Athenian Government*, 15.
30. As Euben notes, it is significant that Socrates' characteristic questioning of his fellow citizens tended to happen in and around this same place. See Euben, *Corrupting Youth*, 105.
31. Roberts, *Accountability in Athenian Government*, 18.

Assembly and perhaps making proposals. And "although the 'accustomed speakers' were no doubt frequently heard in the Assembly, there is considerable evidence for more casual and occasional participation by a much wider group of speakers."[32] As either a sporadic or frequent speaker, Thrasymachus might be shouted down by others at the Assembly, ridiculed by comedians, and subjected to the gossip that attended most public figures. Formally, a rhetor would be open to *eisangelia* if he was thought to have given bad advice to the *demos* or accepted a bribe. There was also a *dokimasia rhetoron* for speakers; mistreatment of parents, prostitution, failure of military duties, and squandering of one's inheritance could rescind one's right to speak before the Assembly.[33] He would also remain vulnerable to a *graphe paranomon* (an indictment for making an illegal proposal) for a year after making the particular proposal to the Assembly. The *graphe paranomon* could be lodged against those suggesting a law either because the form in which it was made was illegal or because the substance of the law conflicted with an existing law.[34]

As with all other legal actions, individual citizens (not a public prosecutor) would bring charges against other citizens when necessary. Again, citizen vigilance was key. In Athens, this right came with risk—if the charges were deemed frivolous and the prosecution unsuccessful, there were high penalties to be paid, at least from the late fifth century onward. All citizens had the right to make proposals and speak in front of the Assembly, and they were all held responsible for those activities. The consequences for wrongdoing could be quite severe. Roberts finds no record of anyone put to death for an illegal proposal, although it may have been called for by the citizen-prosecutor, while prosecution for *eisangelia* could and did bring a death sentence.[35] Most often, charges entailed hefty fines, ideally so large that the citizen charged could not pay, causing his fine to be doubled and resulting in the loss of his civic rights.[36] And if Thrasymachus found himself convicted of a *graphe paranomon* three times, he lost his right to make any future proposals, a hallmark of Athenian citizenship. After one year, an illegal proposal that had become law could still be struck down, but the rhetor was no longer held liable.

32. Ober, *Athenian Revolution*, 25.
33. Josiah Ober, *Mass and Elite in Democratic Athens: Rhetoric, Ideology, and the Power of the People* (Princeton: Princeton University Press, 1989), 109–10.
34. Roberts, *Accountability in Athenian Government*, 153.
35. Ibid.
36. Sinclair, *Democracy and Participation in Athens*, 154.

Other mechanisms of accountability deserve mention here. The first, ostracism, applied to all citizens, not just officeholders, and is an infamous sign of the darker side of Athenian accountability. Instituted at the end of the sixth century, the law allowed the citizenry to banish a powerful individual for ten years.[37] Once a year, the Assembly voted on whether to hold an ostracism vote that year; if yes, the vote was held a bit later and citizens (at least six thousand of them) wrote the name of the person they wished to see exiled on a potsherd. The citizen receiving the most votes was ostracized. There was no debate about the matter in the Assembly meetings and no formal opportunity for those likely to appear on a potsherd to defend themselves. However, the period between the first and second votes was probably a time of informal campaigning. Through exile, it was hoped that the power of any single individual could be controlled by the *demos;* if someone gained too much influence, he would perhaps find his name on a great many potsherds.

While not often considered as part of accountability procedures, the *antidosis* was another way in which citizens could, in theory, be forced to explain themselves to one another. If a citizen was nominated to pay for a liturgy (to produce a play at a theater festival) and believed that a different citizen was better suited because he was wealthier, he could propose an exchange of property to test the claim if the rival declined to take on the cost. There is no record of any actual exchange taking place, but Ober notes that the institution encouraged the wealthy to spy out one another's assets, and ensure that no one shirked their public duties.[38] Thus we see a specific procedure by which one wealthy citizen could hold another to account, to force another to explain his finances to the public (or else quietly take on the liturgy himself). Again, complaints were left up to the citizens and helped to strengthen the general culture of accountability in Athenian society.

And what of the Athenian juries (*dikasteria*), lampooned for their unaccountability by Aristophanes in the *Wasps?* Jury verdicts could not be appealed, and jury members were not subjected to the *euthunai* at the end of their term (although they did take an oath at the start of their service). While no formal means existed to ensure the accountability of jurors, Adriann Lanni has demonstrated that, contrary to Aristophanes' complaint,

37. Records show only ten ostracisms and none by the end of the fifth century.
38. Ober, *Athenian Revolution,* 28.

Athenian juries were subject to a certain form of supervision—the *corona*.[39] The *corona* consisted of the bystanders at the open-air lawcourts, likely coming for a day's entertainment, but at the same time fulfilling an important role. Lanni argues that their presence inhibited those in court from making false assertions and "insured that the jurors could not make collective judgments without the immediate knowledge of a section of the community."[40] While the system here is admittedly informal, it helps dispel the idea that jurors were free to be absurd; coupled with the phenomenon of gossip, jurors knew that their decision would be public and that they were not anonymous.

Accountability for *Idiotai*

So far, I have detailed ways in which specific citizens—the wealthy, those who took part in any of the public offices, and rhetors—were held accountable to the *demos*. But what of the *idiotai*, those citizens who were able to avoid active civic involvement? I have discussed the *dokimasia* that each citizen underwent, but there remained other, less formal mechanisms by which the seemingly apolitical citizen was tied to his fellows. First, there was the practice of ritualized oaths and sacrifice. Oath-taking marked many relations and episodes of the citizen's life. Susan Guettel Cole explains how this practice tied males to the larger political community: "The language of oaths and the actions of oath sacrifice functioned as a part of the network of public rituals that symbolized obligation to the collective power of the whole group."[41] While the *idiotai* were exempt from many of the specific oaths taken in a public context, oath ritual was rooted in the archaic period and characterized aspects of private relationships between men, inculcating a sense of responsibility to one another, bound by verbal agreement.

In addition, gossip functioned as a form of social control in Athens, as well as a means of information-sharing.[42] Although it is often considered a private matter, gossip depends on community and is intimately tied to one's reputation in the community. Having a particular reputation could affect one's private relationships, making it more or less difficult to get certain

---

39. See Adriann M. Lanni, "Spectator Sport or Serious Politics? οἱ περιεστηκότες and the Athenian lawcourts," *Journal of Hellenic Studies* 117 (1997): 183–89.

40. Ibid., 189.

41. Cole, "Oath Ritual," 228.

42. Virginia Hunter, *Policing Athens: Social Control in the Attic Lawsuits, 420–320 B.C.* (Princeton: Princeton University Press, 1994), chap. 4.

things done. Moreover, if an Athenian later found himself in court (which was not necessarily something one could choose to avoid), his reputation would likely serve as evidence (and be described anew for any who hadn't already heard the gossip). Gossip served to form a backdrop and resource in judicial proceedings, including *dokimasia,* in which one's family relations, sexual behavior, abuse of alcohol (or abstention from), and financial situation were fair game. In Athenian society, gossip served as a reminder of the interdependence of members of the community.

Finally, and relatedly, the institution of comedy provided another forum in which to review private citizens. Of course, the average private individual would not likely be named directly on stage—this was reserved for public figures and seems to be limited to Old Comedy. But they might find themselves lampooned as part of a generic type (the money-obsessed Strepsiades in *The Clouds*), or because of a particular decision made by the *demos* (the continuation of the war with Sparta in *The Acharnians*). Although highly informal, comedy served as a way to review the *demos* as a whole. As with oath-taking and gossip, comedy certainly affected those who did participate in greater ways. However, I mean to demonstrate that, contrary to some critics, the average Athenian (even those who chose a relatively apolitical life) remained tied to this overall culture of accountability.

Democratic Ideology in Socrates' Time

Isegoria

Each citizen may have had the right to bring charges against another citizen for dereliction of one's public duties, and the *demos* as a whole engaged in scrutinies and accountings, but what was to prevent someone like Thrasymachus from lying during his *dokimasia?* From going back on his oath to a fellow citizen? From leaving out essential details when discussing his handling of public funds? Or from intimidating, even implicitly, those who would lodge complaints against him? In this *logocentric* polity, the system of accountability depended on a civic ideology celebrating free, honest, and transparent speech. *Isegoria* (equal right to speak) was an obvious component of this. At the same time, it was likely an aristocratic holdover, something members of the upper classes expected of one another in the archaic councils and not something they expected the *hoi polloi* to make use of to any great extent.[43] However, over time democrats began to demand or use this right to address the Assembly, and the celebration of free speech became a critical complement to the institutions of accountability, as well as part of Athenian civic identity.

As equality of speech spread to the masses, we also see the rise of teachers of the art of persuasion; a young man like Thrasymachus (who himself taught the subject) would find that he could compete with those who had been blessed by upper-class birth by engaging the services of a teacher of rhetoric. These teachers, the "Sophists," gave rise to a new class of political leaders; their "typical clients were young men who wanted to think smart, talk smart, and win success in the democracy."[44] The word *rhetorike* first appears in Plato, but was likely current at the time.[45] For many, it was a thing to scorn, a way of describing *peitho* (persuasion) divorced from truth and destructive of the foundations of Athenian democracy.[46]

However, it would be too easy to ascribe the denigration of rhetoric simply to the rise of Sophism, for as Jon Hesk has shown, the "emergence of these ideas about rhetoric and deceit can be located in political, legal, and cultural discourses which defined Athenian democracy itself."[47] Hesk draws on Pericles' funeral oration to demonstrate how democratic Athens contrasted its supposedly innate values of openness and honesty with those of the "other," the "tricky" Spartan.[48] While tyrants and Spartans deceived, Athenian citizens were truthful and frank. Likewise, in *Against Leptines*, Demosthenes connects truthfulness to Athenian self-identity, arguing that

43. See Raaflaub, "Democracy, Oligarchy"; also see Arnoldo Momigliano, "Freedom of Speech in Antiquity," in *Dictionary of the History of Ideas: Studies of Selected Pivotal Ideas, Volume II*, ed. Philip Weiner (New York: Scribner's, 1973), 252–63, and J. D. Lewis, "*Isegoria* at Athens: When Did It Begin?" *Historia* 20 (1971): 129–41.

44. Robert W. Wallace, "The Sophists in Athens," in *Democracy, Empire, and the Arts in Fifth-Century Athens*, ed. Deborah Boedeker and Kurt A. Raaflaub (Cambridge: Harvard University Press, 1998), 204.

45. George A. Kennedy, "Historical Survey of Rhetoric," in *Handbook of Classical Rhetoric in the Hellenistic Period, 330 B.C.–A.D. 400*, ed. Stanley E. Porter (New York: E. J. Brill, 1997), 3. See also Stephen Halliwell, "Philosophy and Rhetoric," in *Persuasion: Greek Rhetoric in Action*, ed. Ian Worthington (New York: Routledge, 1994), 222–43. Frederick Ahl argues that the tradition of "figured speech" stretches back much further into Greek tragedy. Ahl, "The Art of Safe Criticism," *American Journal of Philology* 105, no. 2 (Summer 1984): 174–208.

46. At the same time, the development of rhetoric and the rise of sophism, while often viewed as destructive of democracy, were impossible without the democracy. See Wallace, "Sophists in Athens," 205–6.

47. Hesk, *Deception and Democracy in Classical Athens*, 4.

48. Ibid., 26; Thucydides, *Peloponnesian War* 2.39.1.

Leptines' supposed dishonesty marks him as un-Athenian.[49] The civic ideology regarding speech was thus part of Athenian self-definition.

Anxieties about the possibility of deception can also be seen in archaic and classical literature, beginning with Homeric poetry. Euripides' *Ion* and *Andromache*, Aeschylus's *Agamemnon*, and Sophocles' Theban cycle all deal with the problem of truth and fears of deceit (especially by females, who never were incorporated into the Athenian citizenry). The concern extended to the comedic stage, as seen in Aristophanes' *The Clouds*, in which he ridicules a Socratic "Thinkery" and accuses the philosopher of sophistry. Furthermore, Greek historical literature is replete with stories in which the tyrants of previous eras used deceit to achieve their ends. Herodotus opens his *Histories* with the story of Gyges' betrayal of King Candaules of Lydia and his own rise to power. His stories of Peisistratus's first tyranny and of Deioces' ascension as monarch of the Medes also make clear that archaic rulers were neither accountable to their people nor bound by truth in their quest for power. Pride in having developed some means to overcome the deceptions of unjust rulers helped mark the Athenian democracy as special and different, although it by no means alleviated anxiety about the ever present possibility of deceit.

Finally, the concern was also manifest in the development of philosophy around this time. The sophistic challenges in the fifth century shifted the focus from traditional moral authority to the realm of appearances (*doxa*) and a focus on the impossibility of absolute knowledge. In contrast to both traditional authorities and the innovations of sophism, early philosophers worked to define their own notion of "truth," which came to refer to an objective reality and unchanging abstract principles. According to philosophy's critique, the problem with the mythic tradition lies in its irrational foundation, while the Sophists were unable to articulate any version of "truth" outside the speaker's desire or convention. These intellectual developments were possible only in the context of democracy (with its celebration of free speech and the accompanying encouragement of intellectual speculation).[50] The innovations also had ramifications for the democracy. And as the traditional foundations of Athenian life were disrupted, the anxiety about deceptive speech only increased.

All these factors contributed to widespread complaints about the use of

49. Hesk, *Deception and Democracy in Classical Athens*, 164.
50. Wallace, "Sophists in Athens," 205.

rhetoric in the Assembly. By the fourth century, critics complained that the celebrated Athenian *isegoria* had given rise to the use of oratory as a tool of those bidding for personal power.[51] The trope of deceptive rhetoric was picked up by myriad Assembly speakers; "the orators . . . gloss deceit as 'katapolitical' (against the polis) by associating its perpetrators with sophistry or sycophancy."[52] Ordinary Athenians viewed exceptionally skillful orators with suspicion (while at the same time greatly enjoying their performances).[53] If a speaker was able to successfully pander to the audience, so the argument goes, then he could manipulate the Assembly into courses of action contrary to the best interests of the *demos*, actions that instead only contributed to the profit or power of that speaker. While *isegoria* allowed each citizen the possibility of addressing the Assembly, it did not guarantee that one would receive a hearing; skillful oratory was required if one wanted to not only project one's voice through the noisy crowd, but also remain on the *bema* (speaker's platform) long enough to finish one's point. Given this situation, concern about the hazards of clever speech was persistent. Democracy in Athens was dependent upon spoken language as the medium by which political ideas circulated in society and binding decisions were made, creating a situation in which the vagaries of language were linked to the success of the democracy.

As democracy expanded, Athenian political culture drew on existing terms, like *isegoria*, to describe the new rights afforded to all citizens (in what Ober calls the "transvaluation of existing terms").[54] But given this configuration of anxieties and psychopolitical needs, *isegoria* was not enough to sustain democratic accountability—the archaic concept could not deal effectively with the Athenian obsession with deception and aristocratic attacks by those suspicious of the power of the common citizen, especially given the rise of rhetoric during this period.[55] Over time, the Athenians developed a set of formal, legal mechanisms in an attempt to ensure the truthfulness of speakers. For example, male prostitutes were not allowed to

---

51. Monoson, *Plato's Democratic Entanglements*, 59.
52. Hesk, *Deception and Democracy in Classical Athens*, 165.
53. Ober, *Mass and Elite in Democratic Athens*, chap. 4.
54. Ibid., 339.
55. The Athenians curbed some freedoms of speech in response to these anxieties. The city developed a number of libel laws by at least the fourth century, declaring certain things, such as "this man beats his father," unsayable, or *aporreta*. Max Radin, "Freedom of Speech in Ancient Athens," *American Journal of Philology* 48, no. 3 (1927): 215–30. Also, Diopeithes' decree in 432 made it illegal to deny the gods or to teach new meteorological doctrine. Momigliano, "Freedom of Speech in Antiquity, 258.

speak before the Assembly (by way of the *dokimasia rhetoron*, mentioned earlier) because it was thought that anyone who had sold his body would be more likely to betray the polis for his own gain. In addition, there are five extant references from the fourth century to laws against deceiving the public.[56] A rhetor could face serious charges for accepting a bribe, a reflection of the value attached to public speech and its transparency (although, as Barry Strauss notes, the prohibition against bribery existed alongside the archaic appreciation of reciprocal gift-giving).[57] The formal systems of accountability helped to counteract some of the less desirable consequences of skillful oratory. At the same time, however, these measures would not suffice. *Isegoria* was too narrow—not only in that it was an oligarchic hangover, but also because it bestowed a right without fully invoking a great enough sense of responsibility. The civic ideology supporting the institutions of accountability in Athens required a new vocabulary that both articulated the Athenian faith in speech and established a concept to which good citizens could aspire.

Parrhesia

It is into this landscape that the notion of *parrhesia* appears around the second half of the fifth century.[58] If the concern was that citizens in a polity founded on speech would not be able to differentiate between "true" and "untrue" speeches, and would be vulnerable to persuasion through gratifying rhetoric rather than ethical rightness or sound logic, then it comes as no surprise that the cherished *isegoria* of Athenian citizens would be replaced by a term that emphasized not just the right to speak, but also a duty to speak the truth. According to Ober, the term also implied an appreciation for "individual freedom of thought," for it would not be possible to speak frankly if one had not thought through and informally discussed various ideas.[59] *Parrhesia* celebrated the intellectual strength of the Athenian, as well as his commitment to truth and honesty in political life.

What was *parrhesia*? For Athenian democrats, it described the speech of a person who spoke without reservation, ornament, or regard for personal

---

56. Hesk, *Deception and Democracy in Classical Athens*, 52.

57. Barry S. Strauss, "The Cultural Significance of Bribery and Embezzlement in Athenian Politics: The Evidence of the Period of 403–383 B.C." *Ancient World* 11, nos. 3 and 4 (August 1985): 67–74.

58. Ober, *Mass and Elite in Democratic Athens*, 296.

59. Ibid.

safety. To have the quality of *parrhesia*, a speech must criticize someone who has the power to somehow injure the speaker (e.g., the *demos*). *Parrhesia* was considered a central element of Athenian democracy and an ideal of debate in the Assembly.[60] The concept underwrote accountability in speech as a limit to the possibilities of deceptive oratory that threatened the public good and preoccupied Athenian thought. *Parrhesia* could be used by speakers to call others to account; it also legitimated the culture of accountability as a norm against which one's words could be scrutinized. It "became the frontline of defense against flattery, bullying, corruption, deception, or incompetence on the part of the speakers."[61] It posited a particular view of the ideal speaker: "*Parrhesia* is a kind of verbal activity where the speaker has a specific relation to truth through frankness, a certain relationship to his own life through danger, a certain type of relation to himself or other people through criticism . . . and a specific relation to moral law through freedom and duty."[62]

Parrhesia became a core element of the Athenian democratic identity. It marked a break with the past and celebrated Athens's democratic revolution; according to Saxonhouse, "It affirmed the rejection of an awestruck reverence for the hierarchical ordering of a society and the ancient traditions that supported it."[63] From extant sources, the word first appears in Euripides' plays, *Hippolytus* (performed in 428) and *Ion* (uncertain date).[64] *Ion*, which according to Michel Foucault centers on the issue of *parrhesia*,[65] dramatizes the autochthonic founding of Athens, and implies that the Athenian people took the role of *parrhesiastes* (frank speaker) from the gods when the immortals were no longer able to speak the truth themselves (in this case, the oracle at Delphi fails when Apollo cannot admit his seduction of Creusa, mother of Ion).[66] The word also appears in other Euripidean works to denote free speech in private matters (*Electra, Orestes, Bacchae,*

60. Monoson, *Plato's Democratic Entanglements*, 54.
61. Jeffrey Henderson, "Attic Old Comedy, Frank Speech, and Democracy," in Boedeker and Raaflaub, *Democracy, Empire, and the Arts*, 257.
62. Michel Foucault, *Fearless Speech* (Los Angeles: Semiotext(e), 2001), 19.
63. Arlene Saxonhouse, *Free Speech and Democracy in Ancient Athens* (Cambridge: Cambridge University Press, 2006), 208. Saxonhouse's analysis of *parrhesia* and shame offers much to complement and challenge the analysis here.
64. Momigliano, "Freedom of Speech in Antiquity, 259.
65. Foucault, *Fearless Speech*, 27, 36–38.
66. According to Foucault, this term (*parrhesiastes*) did not come into use until the Greco-Roman period (ibid., 11). While it may be historically inaccurate then to call a fifth- or fourth-century Athenian a "*parrhesiastes*," I will nonetheless employ it as useful shorthand.

and *Phoenician Women*).[67] It appears at least once in Aristophanes (*Thesmophoriazusae*).[68]

Parrhesia also became an important theme in Greek oratory by the fourth century. Demosthenes would invoke the ideal when criticizing commonly held views.[69] At other times, democrats used it to criticize the *demos* itself—as in, *parrhesia* does not exist in this city because the citizens prefer flatterers to the truth.[70] Orators preferred it to *isegoria*, using the latter term only very occasionally (five or six times total for Demosthenes, Isocrates, and Aeschines, compared to *parrhesia's* appearance fifty-six times in the same works).[71] *Parrhesia* was held as an ideal component of a good polity, whether it was used as a celebration or criticism of the public.

To be sure, for some, *parrhesia* indicated a chatterer, one who holds nothing back and lacks critical judgment.[72] These criticisms were always offered in the context of a larger criticism of democracy as a form of government and refer to *parrhesia* as a sort of self-indulgence; oligarchs saw it as evidence of the absurdity of democracy, specifically as the lack of two virtues, *apragmosyne* (minding one's own business) and *aidos* (modesty). Isocrates used the norm as an ideal by which to critique Athenian democracy; but in *Areopagiticus*, he argues that *true* democracy is inconsistent with *parrhesia*, which is part of the lawlessness and lack of self-restraint in the present Athenian democracy.[73] More dramatic criticisms come from the Old Oligarch, who was entirely disdainful of democracy (in contrast to Isocrates, who may be thought of as a loyal critic). For him, *parrhesia* appears in its most negative sense—as mindless chatter, free speech to the point of gibberish. This occurs because the *demos*, even the least educated and "vulgar" persons, are allowed to speak their minds.[74] A source like the Old Oligarch plainly preferred *isegoria*. According to Arnoldo Momigliano, "*Isegoria* implied equality of speech, but did not necessarily imply the right to say everything. On the other hand, *parrhesia* looks like a word invented

67. Momigliano, "Freedom of Speech in Antiquity," 259.

68. Ibid.

69. Monoson, *Plato's Democratic Entanglements*, 60.

70. See Ober, *Mass and Elite in Democratic Athens*, 321.

71. Momigliano, "Freedom of Speech in Antiquity, 260.

72. Foucault, *Fearless Speech*, 11.

73. Ibid., 83; at the same time, Philip Harding ("Comedy and Rhetoric," in Worthington, *Persuasion*, 196–221) argues that Isocrates drew on comedic invective to paint a satirical picture of Athenian democracy in the speech and that his characterization of democracy is that of a loyal and humorous critic.

74. Foucault, *Fearless Speech*, 78–79.

by a vigorous man for whom democratic life meant freedom from traditional inhibitions of speech.''[75] For oligarchs, that shamelessness was what
was wrong with democracy, while democrats viewed the removal of archaic
restrictions on free citizens as the strength of Athens (especially when coupled with *parrhesia's* emphasis on truthful speech). Unlike *isegoria, parrhesia* would promote political equality in the face of deep class divisions by
making it a moral duty of all citizens to speak out when democracy needed
advice.

Parrhesia served as a foundation of the democracy, empowering Athenian institutions of accountability. Citizens not only had a right to speak
publicly, but they also had a duty to the polis to speak when circumstances
called them to do so—and to speak truthfully. In this way, citizens could be
made accountable to one another, and power regularly faced the limits
imposed by active questioning. That *parrhesia* was a powerful norm is clear
from the fact that it became a trope for orators—it was so much a part of
the Athenian identity that speakers would invoke its meaning to signify
their commitment to the public good.

Contemporary Sincerity Claims and Ancient *Parrhesia*

Like Jürgen Habermas's requirement of sincerity in deliberation, *parrhesia*
was meant to shore up the deliberative foundations of Greek democracy,
connecting speech and rationality, allowing *logos* to prevail. Yet the concept
differs from our contemporary view in several ways. *Parrhesia* was practiced in a highly charged political context. An Assembly speaker risked
fines, ostracism, and execution, so a good measure of courage was required
to offer one's advice to the democracy. In fact, speakers often cited the fact
that they were speaking at all as evidence that they spoke with *parrhesia*—
why else would one take the risk? Closely connected to this point is the fact
that to speak with *parrhesia* meant one was speaking critically; democracy
could not flourish without citizens willing to go against the common opinion and offer a better one. This sense of risk is often missing from theories
of deliberative democracy. While we do not have a comparable system holding citizens accountable for their words, risks and impediments persist—
especially when one makes statements at odds with prevailing views.

75. Momigliano, "Freedom of Speech in Antiquity," 260.

Engagement in the public political sphere often requires courage.[76] The expression of unpopular or radically innovative points may require a speaker able to withstand a great deal of questioning and, on occasion, physical intimidation and contemporary forms of ostracism. Theories of deliberative democracy would benefit from greater attention to the highly charged nature of some political contexts, as well as to the courage needed for political deliberation.[77] For the most part, Habermas's ideal deliberations are stripped of the threat of power and intimidation, and speakers are categorically equal, yet greater attention to issues of risk and courage would expand the explanatory capacities of deliberative theory, providing more insight into how and when issues are brought to the table and by whom.

Normative theories of deliberative democracy would also benefit from a stronger appreciation of the sense of "duty" that was crucial to the Greek concept. For Athenian democracy to flourish, it required citizens who felt a moral obligation to speak their minds fully and to criticize when necessary. To critically examine an issue with the public good in mind and to do so while open to all possibilities (even unpleasant ones) was the duty of the Athenian citizen. If a citizen felt the debate lacked an important perspective, he was morally required to express it. Habermas seems to assume this will happen because rationality exists; there is no explicit entreaty that citizens push the public deliberation further, nor a sense that they have a moral duty to criticize when necessary. The consensus theory of truth assumes that erroneous facts and ethical beliefs will simply lack influence. Yet we often already draw on the idea of a duty to speak the truth (e.g., those who criticize "political correctness"). These speakers believe that they are brave enough to go against the pressures of our time and that this bravery is evidence of their trustworthiness.[78] Explicitly incorporating a more

76. See Holloway Sparks, "Dissident Citizenship: Democratic Theory, Political Courage, and Activist Women," *Hypatia* 12, no. 4 (Fall 1997): 74–111. In this particular article, Sparks discusses courage in the context of dissident political *action*, contrasting it with the attention that has been paid to speech in deliberative democratic theory. I make no strong distinction here between political speech and political action, but only want to draw attention to the idea of courage in political engagement.

77. Habermas does claim that some discursive interactions will fall short of their goals because to question (and demand redemption for) some validity claims would be too great a threat to the speaker's identity. *On the Pragmatics of Social Interaction*, 156. This is an important point—one that gets lost in most of the discussions.

78. At the same time, I find that many critics of political correctness (and multiculturalism) are not really "going against" the mainstream; in fact, they are criticizing new innovations in social thought and are actually quite conservative in their outlook. Thus, it has become a trope, rather than real evidence of bravery. This, however, is the similar to the points I will make regarding *parrhesia*.

demanding view of citizenship would be an important normative addition to deliberative theory.

Even given these differences, both the sincerity ideal and *parrhesia* share several characteristics, making an examination of the Greek treatment of the concept especially useful for contemporary debates. First, neither exists for its own sake. Both the claim to sincerity and *parrhesia* are viewed as essential components of *democratic* deliberations, ensuring the accountability of speakers. Both aid in discovering an insight into a particular situation in order to make the correct choice regarding action.

Second, both make a claim to transparency. Ideally, the intentions of the speaker are public and fully disclosed in both cases. According to Habermas, the claim "signifies that I sincerely mean the intentions that I express exactly as I express them."[79] When I say "I am going to vote for Lara," this norm implies that I am truly going to vote for Lara (for any number of reasons) and when I say "I am going to vote for Clare because she has the best plan for schools in our town," it implies that I am truly voting for Clare on the merits of her education plans, and not *really* or *primarily* for something else. I may vote for a person because of a variety of other reasons as well, but a pattern of voting for, say, my old business associates when I have told the interlocutor that my primary interest lies in education reform, would draw suspicion. When a partner in a supposedly monogamous relationship tells the other that she loves that person, it is assumed by the listener that the speaker has not omitted any pertinent facts, such as the fact that she also loves two others. The extent of disclosure varies according to particular contexts, but all details that could be considered relevant by the *listener* should be acknowledged by the speaker; otherwise, the mutual trust that the sincerity claim serves will break down.

Parrhesia, similarly, refers to speech that gives a "complete and exact account of what [one] has in mind."[80] No relevant details are omitted, and the intentions of the speaker are clear. Furthermore, no superfluous, emotionally manipulative tropes are used to convince the audience; Foucault explicitly contrasts *parrhesia* with rhetoric.[81] Monoson points to *parrhesia* as an oratorical strategy deployed specifically to counter the fears of rhetoric in Athens; by invoking *parrhesia*, a speaker "economically affirmed two points absolutely necessary to defend against Athenians' suspiciousness

79. Habermas, *On the Pragmatics of Social Interaction*, 91.
80. Foucault, *Fearless Speech*, 12.
81. Ibid., 20–21.

about expert oratory: the personal virtue and integrity of the speaker, and the priority of the public interest over personal pleasures."[82] As Chapter 1 demonstrated, theories of deliberative democracy often share this suspicion of rhetoric.

Third, both concepts (*parrhesia* and the sincerity norm) make a truth claim. If the speaker is thought of as particularly truthful, his statements are likely to be accepted as true without validation; this is at the heart of the "trust us, we're experts" phenomenon. As for *parrhesia*, Monoson claims that it "is equated with 'telling the truth as one sees it' . . . [it] did not . . . entail any assertion of a view's alignment with an absolute, transcendent standard . . . [or] the certain flawlessness of the *logos* itself."[83] In her view, *parrhesia* is only a comment on the integrity of the speaker and his relation to his expressed *logos*—namely, that he sincerely believes it to be correct. It is unclear, however, how such a claim does not assert its own correctness. Is there a case in which an orator spoke of deeply believing in what they conceded to be a possibly erroneous view? I agree, then, with Foucault: "The *parrhesiastes* says what is true because he knows that it is true; and he knows that it is true because it is really true."[84] Foucault found no case of a Greek who spoke (or claimed to speak) with *parrhesia* who expressed any doubt about the correctness of his view.

According to Ober, "For most Athenians, the shocking 'postmodern' conclusion that all knowledge is political . . . was simply a truism; neither the possibility nor the normative desirability of apolitical forms of knowledge about society or its members ever entered the ordinary Athenian's head."[85] Thus, the ancients had a "democratic" conception of knowledge. Yet the conception of knowledge accompanying invocations of *parrhesia* turns on the context. If I state (with *parrhesia*) that I really *feel* apprehensive about the Sicilian expedition, then there is yet room for the social construction of knowledge and political action. But if I state that embarking on the Sicilian expedition will bring disaster, I also implicitly make a claim to know firmly something that others do not. And an orator more often spoke in support of or opposition to a particular plan of action, not of his own feelings about that plan. Frankness in this context implies superiority over other viewpoints; the speaker can see the truth and is unencumbered

82. Monoson, *Plato's Democratic Entanglements*, 60.
83. Ibid., 53.
84. Foucault, *Fearless Speech*, 14.
85. Ober, *Athenian Revolution*, 149.

by personal needs, whether psychological or material. And if *parrhesia* is deployed as part of a critical stance, then by implication it comes from outside the "collective practices of public communication," and instead from the intellectual efforts of a particular individual rhetor.[86] It is with the rise of *parrhesia* that we see the development of the critical, independent consciousness that is traditionally attributed to Socrates. This necessarily implies at least some other epistemology than that of "democratic knowledge," at least in contexts where speakers invoked *parrhesia* (or related tropes, as we will see with Cleon).

Shifting to the contemporary world, the sincerity claim functions quite similarly. As was made clear in Chapter 1, asserting that one is speaking truthfully can amount to a claim that one has access to the single truth about a situation. At the same time, if one speaks from a truly "modern" standpoint, the basis for one's truthfulness would seem to be quite different from an Athenian's. As discussed by Foucault, ancient "truth" was ensured by a moral quality possessed by the speaker, allowing that person to perceive and judge correctly (in contrast to the modern notion of "truth," stemming from an initial condition of doubt and redeemed by the presentation of evidence). Yet in the contemporary political context, the claim to truth is in fact more like this ancient concept than the modern "scientific method." It is often supported by a moral claim—to sincerity. When a person looks for political information, they choose a source because they believe that source to be trustworthy. For example, a person may read the *St. Louis Post-Dispatch* rather than the *Chicago Tribune* because she believes the *Post-Dispatch* reporters are held to a higher standard of journalism and because she lacks the time and expertise to do her own research. In other cases, a person may trust one friend's opinion more than another's; the person trusts her friend Dianya for voting cues because she knows Dianya shares her values. People often take voting cues from the media, politicians, pundits, and family members, not because they necessarily investigate and compare information, but because they trust those sources and are too busy to do the digging themselves. We also often align ourselves with those who have a similar moral outlook; during an election, a person may rely on the voting guides put out by any number of civic organizations, but she is unlikely to use guides published by organizations

86. Ibid., 150.

with diametrically opposing views. In contrast to Foucault's claim about the fundamental difference between ancient and modern truth claims, practical political decisions are in fact often made on the basis of judgments about a speaker's moral quality, rather than through appeal to scientific standards of evidence.

Finally, both *parrhesia* and the sincerity norm call for judging the spoken claim against the speaker's previous behavior. Habermas's claim to sincerity can only be redeemed through consistent behavior or through interrogation by third parties. One's statements and actions must cohere; missteps cast doubt on the sincerity of one's intentions. Likewise, *parrhesia* was redeemed by the behavior of the speaker. According to Monoson, "Orators . . . cited their deeds to bolster the claim to personal integrity."[87] Furthermore, because of *parrhesia*'s association with risk, a speaker often proved something about his character simply by the act of speaking in the Assembly.[88] One's actions had to correspond with one's words in order for a speaker to be considered a *parrhesiastes.* In an interpretation upon which Monoson builds, Foucault finds Socrates to be the ideal frank speaker, one whose *logos* is in harmony with his *bios.*[89]

While *parrhesia* and Habermasian sincerity share certain elements, and while contemporary deliberative theory would benefit from more attention to risk and courage, I want to underscore that current conceptions of both terms (sincerity and *parrhesia*) are problematic for democratic politics. The two claims develop into similar metarhetorics, ones that deny their rhetoricity even as they profit from it. They neglect the problems discussed in the previous chapter, such as the discounting of important forms of communication and the privileging of other problematic ones (i.e., hyper-sincere styles). The rightful concern with differentiating between truth and falsity has led to a focus on the personal sincerity of speakers, attention that perversely hinders our deliberative potentials. Despite our differences, we share this predicament with the ancient Greek democrats.

87. Monoson, *Plato's Democratic Entanglements,* 160.
88. Ibid., 60, 160.
89. Foucault, *Fearless Speech,* 91–107. The sense of accountability is much stronger in Socratic *parrhesia* (as opposed to "democratic" or traditional *parrhesia*). In the Assembly, a speaker was rarely called to give an account of his *entire* life. He merely cited past or present deeds. According to Foucault, Socrates would transform the idea of *parrhesia* from a public to a personal ethic.

Perversions of *Parrhesia*

To use *parrhesia* in Athens was to engage in speech devoid of rhetorical ornament, and the ethic appealed strongly enough to Athenians to become a trope of Assembly debate by the fourth century, after having first appeared in the late fifth. However, the transformation of *parrhesia* into a trope is distinctly at odds with its original meaning. As a rhetorical strategy, *parrhesia* could by manipulated by speakers to conceal their true intentions, whatever those may be; coupled with the claim to transparency inherent in it, *parrhesia* perhaps could serve as an effective mask for deception. In democratic Athens, we thus see the rise of a "rhetoric of anti-rhetoric," amazingly similar to the hyper-sincere styles of the current era.[90] The typical argument would go something like this: unlike my opponent, I will not flatter you, for it is against our best interest; I will use *parrhesia*, although you probably will not like it. While not explicitly invoked or identified as a rhetorical device there, this trope is perhaps most familiar in Thucydides' portrayal of the Mytilenean Debate.[91] That Cleon (or Thucydides' portrayal of Cleon) drew on this value to support his argument is not irrefutable, considering that he does not explicitly claim *parrhesia* for himself. Yet his speech conforms neatly to descriptions of *parrhesia*, and Thucydides would have been familiar with this ideal.[92]

Following an uprising against the Athenian imperial power by the Mytilenean people, the Athenian Assembly decided in 427 B.C.E. to kill all the adult males and enslave the women and children of the island. Thucydides reports that the Athenian citizens quickly reconsidered the decision, finding it too cruel, and convened another meeting to discuss the matter; this sec-

---

90. Term taken from Hesk, *Deception and Democracy in Classical Athens,* chap. 4. Ober uses the term "anti-public speech meta-rhetoric." Ober, *Political Dissent in Democratic Athens,* 98.

91. See also Saxonhouse's discussion of the debate in *Free Speech and Democracy,* chap. 7.

92. According to Arnoldo Momigliano, "Freedom of Speech in Antiquity," 259–60: "Thucydides, of course, knew both words [*isegoria* and *parrhesia*] and, of course, used neither. Not simply because he was never satisfied with simple formulas. Discussion he appreciated above all things, but he recognized that freedom of speech is inseparable from good faith, both in the speaker and in the listener, and must be used to foster reason against unreason. The debate between Cleon and Diodotus is not only the most profound discussion about imperialism ever held in the ancient world before Saint Augustine; it is also the most searching analysis of the conditions in which discussion is useful in a democracy. If you attack, not the objective validity, but the good faith of your opponent, you introduce an element which will poison democratic proceedings. Even more than Pericles' Funeral Speech, Diodotus' speech represents Thucydides' contribution to the theory of freedom of speech."

ond discussion is known as the Mytilenean Debate and consists of speeches by Cleon and Diodotus. Cleon speaks in a language that appeals to self-interest and justice, while his opponent Diodotus argues for the more lenient policy based on claims of expediency. Cleon begins his speech by exhorting the Athenians to trust their own laws, not men and their changing minds. He appeals to their democratic leanings—"Ordinary men usually manage public affairs better than their more gifted fellows. The latter are always wanting to appear wiser than the laws" (3.37).[93] Anyone who disagrees with his view must "have such confidence in his rhetoric . . . or be bribed to try to delude us with elaborate sophisms" (3.38). Although he does not explicitly invoke *parrhesia*, Cleon sets up a dichotomy between rhetoric and his own intentions that continues throughout the speech:

> You ask, if I may so say, for something different from the conditions under which we live, and yet comprehend inadequately those very conditions; *you are very slaves to the pleasure of the ear, and more like the audience of a rhetorician than the council of a city. In order to keep you from this, I proceed* to show that no one state has ever injured you as much as Mytilene . . . *the truth is that* great good fortune coming suddenly and unexpectedly tends to make people insolent. . . . No hope, therefore, that rhetoric may instill or money purchase, of the mercy due to human infirmity must be held out to the Mytileneans . . . *the orators who charm us with sentiment may find other less important arenas for their talents* . . . I say that if you follow my advice you will do what is just towards the Mytileneans, and at the same time expedient. (3.38–40, emphasis added)

Cleon claims to be the one who can see the true path, the one concerned with justice, while the other speakers simply want either to win with a pleasurable speech or are actually traitorous. According to his own words, he is only speaking to save Athens from itself (not for his own gain) and has disdained the rhetorical ornaments favored by others (and by the audience, implying that he is putting himself at risk by speaking out). He paints himself as an ideal *parrhesiastes*.

93. All quotations taken from Thucydides, *The Peloponnesian War* (New York: The Modern Library, 1982).

However, like Machiavelli and contemporary hyper-sincere speakers, Cleon is using speech to denigrate speech, arguing that the constant speech-making of which Athenians are so fond will destroy them. Like Pericles, he is willing to criticize the *demos*, yet it is clear from the speech that, unlike Pericles, he does not value the role of democratic deliberations. He calls for haste and revenge, rather than the timely deliberation that Pericles praised. Although he makes an explicit appeal to the "common" man, he belies this faith with his own disparaging remarks about deliberation and plays on their fear of deceptive rhetoric.

Furthermore, in his introduction to the speech, Thucydides calls Cleon "the most violent man at Athens, and at that time by far the most powerful with the commons" (3.36). This comment provides two important insights. First, Cleon's desire for haste and insistence upon the execution of the Mytileneans may have had more to do with his predisposition toward violence than with the justness of that decision. Second, while Cleon criticizes those who would tell the *demos* what they want to hear, and pander to their whims, Thucydides here implies that this is perhaps the type of politician Cleon is.

Moreover, Cleon's sort of pandering undermines the very ability of the *demos* to deliberate. He appears to celebrate the native intelligence of the Athenian public, but praises those who accept advice uncritically: *don't think too much, trust me, I know what's good for Athens.* He states: "Those who mistrust their own cleverness are content to be . . . less able to pick holes in the speech of a good speaker . . . these we ought to imitate" (3.37). He makes use of the democratic ideals of free and critical speech, but he invokes upper-class ideals of moderation and restraint at the same time—a man with *sophrosyne* is better equipped to make political decisions than the pesky intellectual. Cleon's anti-intellectualism is ironic given that the rise of sophism and the weakening of archaic values are what allowed him to become a rhetor in the first place, but makes more sense if one considers it in terms of the truth claim inherent in *parrhesia:* if a speaker has a clear view of the situation at hand and can shepherd the *demos* into the correct decision, what need is there for intellectualizing? Indeed, what good could come from undermining such clarity?

As Cleon's opponent Diodotus notes, "The most difficult opponents are those who also accuse one of putting on a rhetorical show for a bribe" (3.42). How can one deal with Cleon's antirhetorical rhetoric? Diodotus's response bodes ill for *parrhesia* and democracy:

It has become the rule also to treat good advice honestly given as being no less under suspicion than bad, so that a man who has something rather good to say must tell lies in order to be believed, just as a man who gives terrible advice must win over the people by deception. Because of these suspicions, ours is the only city that no one can possibly benefit openly, without deception, such if anything does good openly to the city, his reward will be the suspicion that he has something secretly to gain from this. (3.43)

Once the debate moves to questions of the speaker's authenticity, the cycle of accusation and counter-accusation becomes endless. As Arnoldo Momigliano points out, "If you attack, not the objective validity, but the good faith of your opponent, you introduce an element which will poison democratic proceedings."[94] Whether or not Diodotus *had* to hide his own intentions (and argue on the basis of expediency rather than justice)[95] seems to me less important than whether the right decision was made. But Cleon's invocation of his own trustworthiness and the criticism of language helps to create an obsession with intentions that stifles debate.

Subversions of *Parrhesia*

Parrhesia retains a certain allure for democrats, especially in the current political climate in which deception and fears of deception seem to play a prominent role. But Plato's Socrates may be warning us that *parrhesia* actually undermines more productive efforts to counter the dangers of deceptive rhetoric.

According to Foucault, the Platonic Socrates does not use the word *parrhesia* often;[96] it appears fifteen times in the entire corpus. At the same time, Foucault cites Socrates as developing a kind of *parrhesia* that stressed the relationship between one's *bios* and *logos*. He discusses one particular dialogue, *Laches*, at length, as *parrhesia* is a central frame and is explicitly mentioned three times in the short work. In it, two men from eminent families, Lysimachus and Melesias, discuss the type of education best for

94. Momigliano, "Freedom of Speech in Antiquity," 260.

95. See, for example, Leo Strauss, *The City and Man* (Chicago: University of Chicago Press, 1964), 234.

96. Foucault, *Fearless Speech*, 91.

their sons; while these two have no great achievements of which to speak, they admit this openly and are therefore speaking with *parrhesia*.[97] Over the course of their discussion, they are joined by Laches and Nicias and agree that Socrates (presented here as a young man, not yet well known) would be the best teacher because, as Laches says, "I have had experience of his deeds, and there I found him a person privileged to speak fair words and to indulge in every kind of frankness."[98] The Socratic education is concerned with care for the soul; the dialogue form, which requires that his partner be actively engaged and repeatedly tested, is the ideal educational tool. According to Foucault, it is because of the harmony present in his own life that Socrates is able to serve this function.[99] He is a *basanos*, or touchstone; he can cross-examine others and call them to account for their own lives because he lives up to his "fair words." In this way, he is the true *parrhesiastes*.

This form of *parrhesia* differs from its earlier incarnation. Both deal with truth, are critical, and require courage. But Socratic *parrhesia* differs in that it brings attention to the *bios* of the one tested.[100] It implies a personal relationship between the speaker and listener, which Foucault contrasts to the public one between speaker and Assembly; the sense of personal integrity is much stronger and it will be tested. It is opposed to sophism and self-ignorance, rather than to flattery of the demos. It takes place as a *"parrhesiastic* game" between two people.[101] The goal is to educate and test rather than to persuade. Socrates not only truly believes what he says, but also lives according to those words. According to Foucault, Socrates exhibits a Dorian harmony (which Plato finds to be the "courageous" harmony) between his *logoi* and *erga* (practices).

While I share Foucault's interest in this development, and believe that attention to *bios* or *ergon* was a critical addition to the idea of *parrhesia*, I do not think Socrates just "appropriated" this ethic for philosophy. This "testing" of speakers was already a component of the Athenian culture of accountability, at least to a greater degree than Foucault acknowledges; we

97. Ibid., 92.
98. 188e–189a; alternate translation cited and discussed in Foucault, *Fearless Speech*, 99.
99. Aristide Tessitore, in contrast, points out that "this surface impression of harmony is, however, qualified by a subtle comic irony." Tessitore, "Courage and Comedy in Plato's *Laches*," *Journal of Politics* 56, no. 1 (February 1994): 122.
100. Foucault, *Fearless Speech*, 96, 101.
101. Ibid., 95, passim.

can see Socrates drawing on this tradition to develop his own practices.[102] For more on the relationship between Socratic and political *parrhesia*, we can turn to Monoson's work. She argues that Plato recognized democracy's claim to *parrhesia* and believed a true commitment to democratic *parrhesia* required a move to philosophy: "But Plato does not simply appropriate the ideal for philosophy, empty of its contemporary political associations, and give it an entirely new meaning. Rather, Plato subtly manipulates its patriotic, political associations to illuminate the relation of this democratic practice to philosophy, as well as to engage his readers in thinking about how far a devotion to this democratic ideal will lead one, gently, to interest in philosophy."[103]

In the *Gorgias*, Monoson sees *parrhesia* as an attitude required in order to engage in a search for the truth; hence, Socrates lauds Callicles for his frankness.[104] *Parrhesia* requires personal courage and exposes one's deeply held beliefs to examination; this is part of politics for Socrates and central to his critique of Athenian democracy. When he criticizes *parrhesia* in the *Republic*, Monoson reads him as trying to point out that *parrhesia* will become chatter (in which all views are held to be equal) and destructive without the active intervention of philosophy to critically identify truly good ideas and policies. Likewise, I believe Plato's Socrates drew on the democratic political culture of Athens, remained deeply embedded in it, and struggled to make sense of its tensions and problems.[105] Socrates acknowledges the oligarchic criticism of *parrhesia*, aware that it could give rise to demagogues like Cleon. At the same time, he wants to retain and renew a deep commitment to living within the truth, aware that without it we are left only with either unthinking allegiances or none at all, worshipping spiteful gods, cowering before the Tyrants, fetching Leon from Salamis regardless of the loss to the integrity of Athens.[106]

102. See Euben, *Corrupting Youth*, chap. 4. See also Wallach, *Platonic Political Art*.

103. Monoson, *Plato's Democratic Entanglements*, 161.

104. Ibid., 162–63. See also Wallach, *Platonic Political Art*, 117, for more on Socrates' commitment to free speech.

105. "The critical discourses of Athenian democracy can then be read not as a storehouse of antidemocratic views but as a set of rich resources for resisting hegemony and renewing democracy." John Wallach, J. Peter Euben, and Josiah Ober, "Introduction," in *Athenian Political Thought and the Reconstruction of American Democracy*, ed. Wallach, Euben, and Ober (Ithaca: Cornell University Press, 1996), 22. For more work using this same approach, see Wallach, *Platonic Political Art*, especially chap. 1.

106. During the rule of the Thirty Tyrants in 404, Socrates and four other Athenians were called before the Tyrants and ordered to arrest Leon; while Socrates refused, the others com-

However, I part ways with Monoson here. I maintain that instead of either appropriating or subtly transforming *parrhesia*, Socrates subverts the conventional understandings of it. By doing so, he demonstrates the difficulty of securing a stable ethical foundation for deliberation. We often read Plato's incorporation of discursive modes other than philosophy (i.e., myth or tragedy) as his way of establishing the legitimacy of philosophy over these more traditional genres.[107] In contrast, I will argue in the next two chapters that Socrates uses various discursive modes (namely, irony and myth) as foils against which the dangers of the purity sought by Athenian *parrhesia* can be more clearly seen. Plato's dialogues offer us a glimpse of a particular response to a particular sort of democratic political problem. Instead of transparent discussion backed up by consistent action, Plato's Socrates forces us to deal with the larger ambiguities of communicative interaction; he is ironic in both his words and his actions, he deploys myth, and he aims for *aporia* (admission of doubt) rather than consensus. The dialogues help us to appreciate the diversity of perspectives that make up the social world, a basic understanding that is essential to the democratic project. By studying the various ways Socrates makes points, the way he questions one's ability to know something for certain and the value of frankness—not to mention his basic strangeness[108]—Plato dramatizes on several levels the importance of multiplicity for democracy. In contrast, *parrhesia's* truth claim can often eliminate competing viewpoints, obliterating those who disagree. Of course, *parrhesia* calls for individual critical thought, which more obviously places value on the individual's perspective. Because of this situation, *parrhesia* is a concept laden with tension—deeply appealing but problematic nonetheless. The following chapters will explore these tensions through an examination of, first, the ironies of the *Gorgias* and, second, the mythmaking of the *Republic*.

---

plied with the order, capturing Leon and bringing him back to Athens. The Tyrants then executed Leon and confiscated his vast estate. See *Apology* 32c–d.

107. See Andrea Wilson Nightingale, *Genres in Dialogue: Plato and the Construct of Philosophy* (Cambridge: Cambridge University Press, 1995).

108. For more on Socrates' strangeness, see Alexander Nehamas, *The Art of Living: Socratic Reflections from Plato to Foucault* (Berkeley and Los Angeles: University of California Press, 1998) and *Virtues of Authenticity: Essays on Plato and Socrates* (Princeton: Princeton University Press, 1999).

SOCRATIC IRONY AND THE ART OF POLITICS

On October 9, 2001, in the wake of September 11, writer David Rees posted the first installment of *Get Your War On* on the Internet:

From *Get Your War On* by David Rees © 2002 by David Rees. Used by permission of Soft Skull Press. http://www.softskull.com/.

The comic strip portrays a group of sarcastic office workers left to deal with the aftermath of 9/11 and the "War on Terror." The comic slowly attracted readers via email spread friend to friend, which later prompted the publication of a collection, a national book tour, and syndication in *Rolling Stone* magazine. According to Rees:

> When other people started getting into it they would write me and say, "You know this is how my friends and I have been talking—we didn't think that anyone else was having these conversations." The strength of the strip wasn't that it promoted a radical new point of view or anything. It was just that it was one of the

first things out of the gate to actually express what thousands of people were thinking and saying. It just wasn't finding a reflection in the media.[1]

Why was this perspective missing from the public sphere? Immediately after September 11, various writers proclaimed an "end of irony," arguing that our pre-9/11 era of ironic detachment had served us poorly. "No longer will we fail to take things seriously," proclaimed Roger Rosenblatt in *Time*.[2] According to this argument, U.S. culture had been mired in an irony and cynicism that made it impossible to distinguish good from evil. September 11 reoriented dangerously jaded Americans, shaking them out of their post-1960s ironic haze.

At the same time, the post-9/11 "death of irony" was not entirely new. The attempt to make the world safe from the dangers of irony had swelled two years before, with Jedediah Purdy's book *For Common Things: Irony, Trust, and Commitment in America Today.* The book provided a warning against the distrust and cynicism that Purdy believes springs from a culture that idolizes Seinfeldian detachment:

> The point of irony is a quiet refusal to believe in the depth of relationships, the sincerity of motivation, or the truth of speech— especially earnest speech. In place of the romantic idea that each of us harbors a true self struggling for expression, the ironist offers the suspicion that we are just quantum selves—all spin, all the way down.[3]

In Purdy's eyes, the ironist's position is false because of its claim to be both part of the world and not part of it: "The ironist goes to the party and, while refusing to be quite of it, gets off the best line of the evening."[4] It is this divided self that strikes opponents as a disingenuous defense mechanism. Purdy argues that this mood was the result of the corruption and broken promises of recent American history, while others see it as the

1. Tim Dickinson, "Have Clip Art, Will Dissent," *Mother Jones*, April 3, 2003, http://www.motherjones.com/news/qa/2003/04/we_340_01.html/ (accessed March 8, 2004).
2. Roger Rosenblatt, "The Age of Irony Comes to an End," *Time*, September 24, 2001.
3. Jedediah Purdy, *For Common Things: Irony, Trust, and Commitment in America Today* (New York: Knopf, 1999), 10.
4. Ibid.

nightmarish hangover of the too-radical 1960s. Purdy presented the indictment, and 9/11 delivered a final blow.

But not everyone bought it. *Get Your War On* was soon joined by a new
issue of the satirical weekly *The Onion*, which included such headlines as
"God Angrily Clarifies 'Don't Kill' Rule," "Hijackers Surprised to Find
Selves in Hell," "Not Knowing What Else to Do, Woman Bakes American
Flag Cake." For many Americans, the reaction to 9/11 included both horror
and anger at the attacks, as well as a deep dissatisfaction with the United
States' role in the existence of the Taliban and its response to the attacks.
For them, irony could provide an important alternative to the earnest
solemnity and bandwagon politics that seemed pervasive in the mainstream
media immediately following 9/11.[5] It's not that these ironic responses did
not recognize right and wrong as critics like Rosenblatt claimed—there is a
clear sense of violation and anger in much of this work. But there is also
a deeper acknowledgment of the complexity and difficulty of politics. For
example, *The Onion* headlines acknowledge the more general sense of
unease throughout the country ("Not Knowing What Else to Do") and
then mock the superficiality and inadequacy of the response ("Bakes American Flag Cake"). For those who found themselves emailing Rees's work or
Onion articles to one another, such headlines are trenchant and funny
without losing seriousness. They invite self-examination by mocking our
pretensions. Ironically, these ways appeal because they seem more
"authentic," that is, they better reflect the multiplicity inherent in ourselves and in our democracy.[6]

5. Over time, the ironic response also turned out to be quite popular. According to a
2004 Pew Research Center report, 21 percent of people aged eighteen to twenty-nine claimed
to get their news from *The Daily Show* and *Saturday Night Live* (compared to 23 percent
who rely on the network's nightly programs and 37 percent who rely on cable news channels).
The Pew Research Center for the People and the Press, "Cable and Internet Loom Large
in Fragmented Political News Universe," January, 11 2004, http://peoplepress.org/reports/
display.php3?ReportID = 200/ (accessed December 14, 2006). This stands in stark contrast to
the results from 2000, in which only 9 percent reported getting political information from
comedy shows. While studies have shown both positive and negative effects of this trend, a
study from the National Annenberg Election Survey indicates that *The Daily Show* viewers
"are more likely to know the issue positions and backgrounds of presidential candidates than
people who do not watch late-night comedy." Annenberg National Election Survey, "Daily
Show Viewers Knowledgeable about Presidential Campaign, National Annenberg Election
Survey Shows," September 21, 2004, http://www.annenbergpublicpolicycenter.org/naes/
2004_03_late-night-knowled ge-2_9–21_pr.pdf/ (accessed December 14, 2006).
6. Meanwhile, the success of such books as Harry Frankfurt's *On Bullshit* (Princeton:
Princeton University Press, 2005) and *On Truth* (New York: Knopf, 2006) also demonstrates
people's continuing anxiety about the possibility of deception and rhetorical manipulation.

Critics often complain that ironists are unaccountable: by at least partially disavowing what they say, ironists distance themselves from their words. For hyper-sincere speakers, with a certain view of the truth and of the self, irony is an affront; it signals a lack of seriousness, a willingness to play games with the truth in order to assert the ironist's superiority over others. However, it is not irony but the development of sincerity into a trope—along the lines of hyper-sincerity a la Bill O'Reilly or Cleon—that causes citizens to doubt the possibility of truthfulness and leads to suspicion and pessimism. Rather than being the root of cynicism, perhaps irony can be a way to mitigate it, making democratic accountability a real possibility.

This chapter argues that irony can be a vital component of a democratic civic education and deliberations, in part because of the revitalizing challenges it can pose to democratic discourse. To that end, it examines Plato's case against rhetoric in democratic Athens through an examination of irony in the *Gorgias*. Given the long-established dichotomy between rhetoric and *parrhesia*, a Platonic dialogue that explicitly discusses both concepts—in fact, one that is often considered to have established this dichotomy—is an important resource for thinking about this question. At the same time, the dialogue is especially compelling because it also contains some of Socrates' most notorious and perplexing ironies alongside the calls for *parrhesia* and sincerity. Why does Plato emphasize the importance of truth and *parrhesia* for politics in a dialogue laden with Socratic irony and one in which commentators seem especially dubious of the sincerity of the interlocutors' replies to Socrates?[7] Attention to the dialogues' drama and historical context suggests that the *Gorgias* is actually quite similar in substance to the *Phaedrus*, despite the fact that it also contains Socrates' most aggressive attacks on the practices of rhetoric. Since this project is explicitly concerned with the relevance of sincerity, rhetoric, and irony to politics, the *Gorgias*, with its explicit discussion of the role of leadership in a democracy, is yet again a useful resource.

The analysis proceeds in two stages; first, I examine Socrates' apparent mockery of his interlocutors and try to make sense of this particularly odd practice. I then go on to explore the meaning of two specific ironies of the *Gorgias*—Socrates' indictment of rhetoric and his claim to be the one true *politikos* in Athens. I connect the deployment and substance of these ironies

---

7. See, for example, Charles H. Kahn, "Drama and Dialectic in Plato's *Gorgias*," *Oxford Studies in Ancient Philosophy* 1 (1983): 75–121.

to a democratic, rhetorically conscious politics, while bearing in mind that the Socratic philosophy presented by Plato also poses serious challenges to democratic politics. The chapter ends with a brief discussion of the roles of power and consensus in democratic discourse.

Scholars take radically different positions on the *Gorgias*. Some, like Gregory Vlastos, see the Socrates of this dialogue as a teacher who tries to instill moral autonomy in his students, while others argue that he is in fact a "deliberative authoritarian."[8] Some, like Euben, see the *Gorgias* and its Socrates as "polyphonous" and democratically reflexive, while others, like Benjamin Barber, argue that this Socrates is a boor who "manipulates and dominates to his own advantage," thus engaging in the *eristic* rather than deliberation.[9] Some view Socrates' performance in the *Gorgias* as a source of democratic practices (i.e., "respectful shame" in Christina Tarnopolsky's work or Socrates' use of *parrhesia* in Monoson's work), while others view Socrates' practices in the dialogue as deeply problematic and often unfair to the interlocutors.[10] To complicate matters even further, even among Socrates' "supporters," we hear of his "frigidity"[11] and the dangers of his irony.[12] While the present study obviously owes a great deal to Vlastos and Euben, as well as to Monoson and Foucault, I also want to take seriously these conflicting views of Socrates and this particular dialogue, using Plato's presentation of Socrates as a way to think about democratic deliberation and its difficulty, as well as the potential value of irony for political life. What can we learn from this diversity among interpreters? Why did Plato leave so many questions, while also seeming to emphasize authority, truth, and hierarchy?

One of very few things we do know is that Plato probably meant to portray Socrates in a generally positive light. So even when we are con-

---

8. Antony Hatzistavrou, "Socrates' Deliberative Authoritarianism," *Oxford Studies in Ancient Philosophy* 29 (Winter 2005): 75–113.

9. Benjamin R. Barber, "Misreading Democracy: Peter Euben and the *Gorgias*," in Ober and Hedrick, *Demokratia*, 363. See the same volume for the full debate between Euben and Barber.

10. See Christina Tarnopolsky, "Prudes, Perverts, and Tyrants: Plato and the Contemporary Politics of Shame," *Political Theory* 32, no. 4 (August 2004): 468–94. For a view more sympathetic to the interlocutors, see John Beversluis, *Cross-Examining Socrates: A Defense of the Interlocutors in Plato's Early Dialogues* (Cambridge: Cambridge University Press, 2000).

11. Gregory Vlastos, "The Paradox of Socrates," in *The Philosophy of Socrates: A Collection of Critical Essays*, ed. Gregory Vlastos (Notre Dame: Notre Dame University Press, 1971), 16–17.

12. See Nehamas, *Art of Living*.

vinced that Socrates is being unfair with an interlocutor, we need to think deeply about why Plato presented him this way, given what we know about their relationship. In the end, this interpretation highlights the tensions and ambiguities in a dialogue in which the participants discuss political life in Athens; and although it would be unhelpfully anachronistic to believe that a text from ancient Athens could speak so directly to our deliberative projects, there are similarities between our current political climate and that of Plato's Athens worth examining. As long as we continue to rely on Plato's dialogues as a foundation of political theory, we should take care to acknowledge their complexity and use them as an opportunity to meditate on the problems we face in democratic deliberations. The ambiguity of the dialogue points directly at the difficulties of political deliberation, the misleading promises of sincerity and *parrhesia,* and the critical importance of developing our own judgment as an alternative to relying on assertions of sincerity.

Like our own straight talk, *parrhesia* was conceived as a radically democratic ideal, promulgated to allay Athenian fears of manipulative rhetoric. But it quickly became routinized and lost its provocative potential for democracy. Thought to be a safeguard against majoritarian dogmatism, *parrhesia* instead became an insistent "dogma of anti-dogmatism," a proclamation of independent thought used by speakers to assert their own authority.[13] While it was not identified as a rhetorical trope until the time of Quintilian, I believe that Socrates treated it as one, with all the loyal criticism he applied to other elements of Athenian democracy.[14] As Saxonhouse argues in regard to the tragedians' use of *parrhesia,* Plato's Socrates does not so much fulfill the ethic of *parrhesia* as "explore the ambiguities of this practice."[15] We can see the ironic phrasings of the dialogue as an ironic critique of the foundational and antipolitical claims of *parrhesia.* As presented by Plato in the *Gorgias,* irony can actually defuse tense deliberative situations, offering an alternative to Calliclean frankness. Of course, the dialogue and the interactions between the characters are extremely

13. I took this phrase from Jonathan Lear, who uses it to discuss an analysand's insistence of independence from the analyst. *Therapeutic Action: An Earnest Plea for Irony* (New York: Other Press, 2003), 218.

14. See Monoson, *Plato's Democratic Entanglements;* Euben, *Corrupting Youth;* and Christopher Rowe, "Democracy and Sokratic-Platonic Philosophy," in Boedeker and Raaflaub, *Democracy, Empire, and the Arts,* 241–53.

15. See Saxonhouse, *Free Speech and Democracy,* 129.

complicated, and there are many ways in which Socrates' irony seems need-lessly antagonistic; these moments also have something to tell us. Thus, I agree with John Beversluis when he argues that "the Socratic elenchus is neither wholly adversarial nor wholly altruistic."[16] Making a claim for iro-ny's contributions does not mean that it is not risky or that Socrates is a hero to be emulated. Yet it does help us appreciate that *parrhesia* is not necessarily a benefit, that irony might have an important place in a healthy democracy, and that the use of judgment (rather than universal rules) is critical to democratic deliberations. Moreover, making a place for ironic statements in politics does not mean that we are unable to make any posi-tive assertions or that "anything goes," but instead it is meant to temper our certainties with sustained intellectual engagement.

Instead of the frank speaker, we find in Socrates a character who plays with this ideal, subverting it on the surface, yet contributing to democratic ideals by forcing readers (if not the interlocutors) to learn to judge for themselves and rely less on teachers and leaders. Plato's Socrates responds to the co-optation of *parrhesia* by relying on incongruities in communica-tion to relay critique, rather than a straightforward consistency between words and meaning; Plato has created a character embedded in a particular context who, for example, flatters the least admirable interlocutors, requir-ing the reader's judgment to make sense of the situation. Though the dia-logues are marked by irony, Socrates does not seem to be engaged in an attempt to "fool" the audience (even as he remains unconvincing to many interlocutors and commentators). We should not place Socrates with more radical Sophists (or with Richard Rorty's contemporary liberal ironism), for the possibility of speaking a public truth remains a compelling ideal for him. In fact, an essential part of Socrates' irony is that he remains commit-ted to the search for truth despite his doubts that humans can grasp truth with certainty once they find it. This is what makes Socrates stand out among the figures of Western history—his capacity for both commitment and doubt. Yet even as democracy opens the way for and requires a Socrates, important tensions remain between his day-to-day discursive practice and the nature of democratic politics; exploring the ways in which democracy and Socrates resist one another also helps illuminate our own democratic prospects.

16. Beversluis, *Cross-Examining Socrates*, 35.

To Be "Ironic"

For philosophers and political theorists, the starting point for any discussion of Socratic irony lies with Gregory Vlastos. Vlastos's goal was to bring Socrates' "paradoxes, pushed to the margins . . . into dead center."[17] To accomplish this, he begins with a history of ancient *eironeia*. Vlastos relies on Quintilian's definition of irony: a figure of speech "in which something contrary to what is said is to be understood."[18] In early ancient Greek, the term indicated an intention to deceive. Yet with Socrates, Vlastos argues there is no such intention. According to Vlastos, when Socrates asks Thrasymachus to teach him, he mocks the interlocutor with no intention of deceiving him. Instead of duplicity, the point is humor, mockery, riddle. Socrates never discusses the nature of irony, yet it is a fundamental element of his work; he "changes the word not by theorizing about it but by creating something new for it to mean: a new form of life realized in himself . . . as innocent of intentional deceit as is a child's feigning that the play chips are money . . . though, unlike games, serious in its mockery . . . dead earnest in its playfulness."[19]

Vlastos also believes that Socrates' irony has another dimension; in certain cases, Socrates both means and does not mean what he says. If irony is to mean something contrary to what is said, should we not assume that Socrates does not mean that he is the only Athenian to practice the true political craft (*Gorgias*, 521d–e)? But if we were to assume such a thing, we would miss Socrates' other essential point, that the true political craft is something more complicated than governing and waging war, that it involves care for the soul. To account for this problem, Vlastos adds the category of "complex ironies," that is, statements in which what is said is meant in one way but not in another. This is how he makes sense of the apparent paradoxes in some of Socrates' most famous statements, for example, "I am not wise at all" (*Apology*, 21b). Socrates disavows that he has knowledge, and on one level, he means it—he knows nothing for certain.[20] Yet on another level, Socrates does not mean what he says, for he does have knowledge—the knowledge that comes with "justified true belief."[21] Vlastos argues that this form of irony can awaken understanding in the interlocutor and reader, whose job it is to decipher the irony.

Vlastos leaves us with two forms of irony—simple irony, which conforms to Quintilian's definition, and complex irony, which violates it, but better captures Socrates' usage. However, other commentators disagree. Alexander Nehamas argues that we should take Socrates' disavowals at "face-value," because to make too much of them as complex ironies robs Socrates of his strangeness and inexplicability.[22] If we were to rely on Vlastos's formulation, we risk assuming that ironists clearly know exactly what they mean; instead, "irony consists simply in letting your audience know that something is taking place inside you that they are not allowed to see . . . [leaving] open the question whether you are seeing it yourself."[23] This view highlights the mystery involved in irony; the meaning behind the spoken words often remains ambiguous. For Nehamas, uncertainty is intrinsic to irony, but the uncertainty of Socrates is best appreciated by believing that Socrates really means what he says (in contrast to meaning something on one level and not on another as with Vlastos). Similarly, Jonathan Lear writes that irony cannot consist in not meaning what one says: "Indeed, the irony becomes possible precisely because the speaker insists on holding onto what the words really do mean."[24]

While Nehamas and Lear provide an important correction to Vlastos, I disagree that irony always requires holding onto the meaning of words. If we are to take Socrates' disavowals at face value to preserve Socrates' mystery, haven't we actually removed a bit of the mystery, since we now know that he at least meant that much?[25] Instead, we may need to look beyond the spoken words to get a sense of whether a statement is ironic. Not all irony is verbal; it can also refer to characteristics of a situation; Nehamas and Lear seem to neglect several dramatic ironies, such as when Cephalus discusses the usefulness of wealth in old age in Book 1 of the *Republic*, only

21. Ibid.
22. Nehamas, *Art of Living*, 66–67, and *Virtues of Authenticity*, 102.
23. Nehamas, *Virtues of Authenticity*, 71–72.
24. Lear, *Therapeutic Action*, 68.
25. For Alexander Nehamas, Socrates' mystery seems to lie less in particular statements than in his entire life: Socrates "held that knowledge of *arête* is necessary for the good and happy human life. He disavowed that knowledge and the ability to communicate it. And yet he succeeded in living as good a life as anyone had ever done so far, in Plato's eyes as well as in the eyes of the tradition the two of them initiated. And he never let us know how that was possible." Nehamas, *Art of Living*, 67.

to later die a poor man. Moreover, I want to highlight the duality of Socrates' apparent flattery of interlocutors, which means at least opening the question of whether Socrates means or does not mean what he says. The playfulness of irony, which may depend on meaning the opposite of what one says, is worth appreciating, yet it is neglected when we purge the *possibility* of sarcasm from our conception of irony. What is interesting about Socrates in particular is that we do not know for certain whether he means exactly what he says; he rejects the dichotomy between sincerity and dissembling or sarcasm.

I propose that we adopt a plainer and more comprehensive understanding of irony. Such a description would allow Vlastos's simple and complex ironies to fall under the same umbrella and Nehamas and Lear's earnest ironies to remain ironic. Jill Gordon, motivated by similar objections, provides the useful alternative:

> Irony is an incongruity between phenomena within a dramatic context. The incongruity can be between things said, between actions taken, between words and actions, between what is said and how it is said or to whom or on what occasion, between what one says and what one looks like, between one's actions and the meaning of one's name, and so on. I choose incongruity because it allows the latitude necessary for understanding irony in a more complex and subtle manner than either (a) saying one thing but meaning another or (b) both meaning and not meaning what is said. Actions, behavior, modes of expression, thoughts, and words can all be incongruous.[26]

Thinking about irony as incongruity is a way to rescue it from excessive definition, as well as overuse. All these instances—from the authorial sarcasm of the *Get Your War On* cartoons, to Oedipus's fate, to Kierkegaard's questioning of Christendom—have something that leads people to call them "ironic." And that common element is that, in some way, things are said or done that seem incongruent with other things that are said or done. This description allows us to include both rhetorical and dramatic (or situational) ironies under the same basic heading, which is something that Vlastos's

26. Jill Gordon, "Against Vlastos on Complex Irony," *Classical Quarterly* 46, no. 1 (1996): 134.

definition does not explicitly accomplish (although he often relies on dramatic ironies to explain complex ironies). Meanwhile, the use of "irony" here does not necessarily include Rorty's liberal ironism, because it remains focused on "incongruity," rather than making a fundamental claim about the human condition.[27] It also alleviates the confusion about what exactly is ironic in Socrates' disavowal of knowledge or his claim to practice the political craft. In these cases, Socrates could really mean what he says, while his actions cause us to think again about what those words could really mean (since we know that he rarely participates in traditional Athenian political life). Meanwhile, we can safely call Socrates' flattery of his interlocutors ironic, since they are clearly unworthy of his praise.

A Mockery of Socrates

Through Socrates' irony and his subversion of *parrhesia*, Plato calls on Athenians to revisit the rhetorical tropes underwriting their democracy and to reengage with political life. A relatively recent addition to Athenian political ideology, *parrhesia* suffers from the same weakness as other defenses against the onslaught of potentially manipulative speech—it remains dependent upon those who use it. If Athens' citizens are to be accountable to one another and to the democracy, they must be able to explain themselves to others in a way that takes into account human complexity. Meanwhile, the potential for manipulation remains. Plato explores, and often tempers, these problems by critiquing *parrhesia* through Socratic irony. Moreover, we will see that irony can offer the psychological distance necessary to continue conversations that might otherwise end in silenced frustration, in addition to building community by calling some people into the conversation and awakening others to their outsider status.

At the same time, I want to be cautious about turning Socrates into a mouthpiece for contemporary democratic concerns. In many ways, Socrates remains antagonistic to democratic politics and an irresolvable mystery. But, as Melissa Lane argues, "Democratic readings can be developed beyond a simple assessment of whether someone (Socrates) was 'for' or 'against' democracy. By incorporating cultural complexities of the kind

---

27. Although these things may in fact be related in many instances; see Mara, *Socrates' Discursive Democracy*, and Seery, *Political Returns*.

sketched by the historical readings, democratic positions can be enriched in their self-understandings and in their understandings of Socrates alike."[28]

Athenians invoked *parrhesia* to counter the manipulative potential of public speech. Likewise, the *Gorgias* is rooted in Plato's fundamental concern with the same issue—how to mitigate a polity's vulnerability to men like Gorgias and Callicles. In the dialogue, Socrates attempts to determine what rhetoric is by questioning three practitioners: Gorgias, Polus, and Callicles. Gorgias, a foreigner in Athens on state business, has just given a presentation, which Socrates missed.[29] The men, along with a small anonymous audience, begin their own investigation into the nature of rhetoric. The discussion quickly moves to the more characteristically Socratic concern of what constitutes the good life. These two questions are related. If the goal of politics is to make people better, and rhetoric claims to influence politics by convincing people to act one way or another, then rhetoric has some influence on how people will choose to live. It is also worth noting that the events of the dialogue seem to span the Peloponnesian War, the period in which democratic deliberations break down in Athens.[30] Coincidentally, although this fact is contested, the dialogue is also often dated to 427—the same year of the Mytilinean Debate, a deliberation that makes clear the difficulties that come along with *parrhesia* as a political ideal (this is also about when *parrhesia* first appears in extant sources—Euripides' *Hippolytus* in 428).[31]

Socrates insists at the start on a discussion (rather than speeches) and claims that he "wouldn't be any less pleased to be refuted than to refute" (*Gorgias* 458a–b), setting rather Habermasian standards for the discussion (on the other hand, the terms of the debate strike others as highly confrontational, especially given the opening lines of the dialogue; what matters here, however, is Socrates' apparent openness and calmness in the face of argument). His constant insistence on questioning and being questioned is reminiscent of the Athenian *dokimasia* and *euthunai* discussed in the previous chapter; each discussant has a responsibility to explain himself to the satisfaction of the others present. Rarely content with their answers, he

28. Lane, *Plato's Progeny*, 42.

29. On the importance of Gorgias's status as a foreigner, see Euben, *Corrupting Youth*, 211. For more on the historical figure, see Scott Consigny, *Gorgias: Sophist and Artist* (Columbia: University of South Carolina Press, 2001).

30. Seth Benardete, *Rhetoric of Morality and Philosophy* (Chicago: University of Chicago Press, 1991), 7.

31. Wallach, *Platonic Political Art*, 181.

pushes Polus and Callicles to exhaustion. He argues that oratory is a "knack . . . for producing gratification and pleasure" (462d–e); it results in flattery, a state in which citizens are mollified rather than engaged in collective deliberation.[32] Such speechmaking in front of "a gathering" cannot achieve true teaching and can only "persuade." The danger, exemplified by Callicles, is that a speaker will use rhetoric to convince people of whatever is in the speaker's own interest. The analysis offered by this reading of Plato leads us to believe that philosophical discourse, exemplified by the Socratic dialogues, is the way to arrive at truth. Certainly, Socrates' comments, taken at face value, hold that rhetoric is a serious danger to human life, and exists in stark contrast to philosophy.

Yet Socrates does not follow his own method throughout the dialogue, nor does the dialectic (when it is there) succeed. Moreover, the very first words of the dialogue call these failures and tensions to mind: πολεμου και μαχης φασι χρηναι—to join in a war or battle. In many ways, the *Gorgias* is a story of deep failure in a context marked by conflict—the failure of leaders like Themistocles and Pericles, of Socrates, of philosophy, and of speech. Callicles, the native Athenian, remains unconvinced and unbridled. The dialogue weaves a picture of a community struggling with the temptations of power and the extreme difficulty of democratic imperatives. It highlights the deep tension between consensus and *agon* (struggle) in democracy and the difficulties of expressing this tension in language. The dialogue ends up showing us that only a democracy based on deliberation can handle these difficulties (however difficult the problems it poses may be); attempts to solve them for once and for all are more tyrannical than democratic. *Parrhesia* has failed to ensure truthfulness in speech, but in its own way, has contributed to the decline of democracy.

I begin with Socrates' use of sarcasm and mocking flattery. One of the most common complaints about the sarcastic ironist is that he mocks and insults his opponents into submission, much the same critiques leveled against ironists in our own democracy. More than any other form of irony, sarcasm seems most opposed to *parrhesia*. How could derisive flattery fit into a norm that calls upon citizens' sense of duty to speak the whole truth as they see it, facing danger courageously and refusing the enticements of pandering to the audience? Nehamas believes that there is an "essential

---

32. "Flattery" here refers to an intensification of dominant emotions; thus, not only direct praise but also references to the fears and dislikes of the audiences count as flattery. Thank you to an anonymous reviewer for this clarification.

connection between irony and superiority."[33] That is, "irony always implies that the ironist knows something that someone else does not and, at least for the present, cannot know. In all irony, therefore, there is an element of boastfulness."[34] For others, irony is the opposite of boastfulness; it is "the noble dissimulation of one's worth, one's superiority"—a more positive take on irony, to be sure, but no less undemocratic.[35] In democratic deliberations, in which participants are called to treat one another as political equals deserving of respect and dignity, and to reject deception, how can sarcasm contribute to the public good? But when put into a context in which *parrhesia* is perverted and democracy is threatened, Socrates' ironic sarcasm is a useful rhetorical strategy. To borrow James Boyd White's phrase, when words lose their meaning, as *parrhesia* had begun to do for the Athenians, the old ways of doing things are no longer effective.

When Callicles joins the discussion in the *Gorgias*, Socrates applauds his luck—he claims to have found a *basanos*, a soul against which he may test his own. Socrates tells Callicles that he fulfills the requirements of such a touchstone, having goodwill, *parrhesia*, and knowledge (487a). Unlike Polus, who is too timid to discard social conventions, Callicles tells Socrates what he believes he really thinks—that justice lies with the will of the stronger and that law has unduly stifled nature. Others may pay lip service to the "crowd pleasing vulgarities" of *nomos* or human law (482e), but Callicles, at least here in his own home and away from the *bema*, is willing to say what he believes and what he believes others believe as well but are too ashamed to admit.

At the same time, Socrates' praise for Callicles is incongruent with what we already know about Callicles. By the time Socrates makes these three claims about his personality, Callicles has already made clear that he does not in fact possess goodwill since he says he doesn't believe a word Socrates says (481b–c). He believes Socrates is playing the role of crowd-pleaser just as he criticizes others for doing (482d), is indulging in unmanly pursuits, and is avoiding adult interactions in favor of "whispering in a corner with three or four boys" (485a–e). Can such hostility contain goodwill?

Socrates says the evidence of Callicles' goodwill lies in the fact that he recently heard him give the same advice to his friends regarding philosophy (487d–e). But can Callicles, with his strategic use of people to fulfill his

33. Nehamas. *Art of Living*, 57.
34. Ibid., 49.
35. Strauss, *City and Man*, 41.

desires, be a friend to anyone? Is it possible to have goodwill toward others if you are intent on letting your appetites grow as large as possible and then fulfilling them? Also, the claim that Callicles has knowledge rests on Callicles' boast that he does and on his reputation in Athens for being well educated (487c); whether he truly knows anything remains to be seen.

As for Callicles' *parrhesia*, Socrates takes as evidence the fact that Callicles has claimed such a quality for himself and demonstrated it with his harangue of Socrates and philosophy (487d–e). Callicles claims to be a friend and aggressively criticizes Socrates' way of life; instead of frankness in the spirit of amiable cooperation, he appears to use claims of friendship to mask his hostility and justify his remarks. Thus, we see that claims and even attributions of goodwill do not ensure smooth deliberation. Callicles claims that the good life is one exempt from social conventions. But the bonds of friendship and democratic norms such as *parrhesia* are surely social conventions, so how could one trust Callicles' claims to be speaking as a *parrhesiastes*? *Parrhesia* is a social convention that involves the courageous exposure of a critical truth to a superior; but if Callicles is correct, then the superior can never be wrong because the world is defined in terms of his desires (or its desires—in the context of Athenian democracy, the superior might be seen as the *demos*). At the same time, if the goal is to fulfill all one's appetites with no regard for social convention, of course Callicles would invoke social conventions that are important to the weaker in order to conquer them.

That Socrates would accept someone's claim to *parrhesia* at face value should not be a foregone conclusion; instead, his description of Callicles should give us pause and raise the question of whether Socrates transparently means what he says. Is Socrates so full of goodwill toward Callicles that he gives him his full support? Does that mean that Socrates discounts Callicles' initial attack on his whole way of life? Is Socrates testing Callicles' frankness? Or is he saying something clearly untrue to draw our attention to the problems with *parrhesia*? Or is Socrates doing all this at once? Callicles does initially seem to lack shame and to speak frankly. It is not that he has or does not have *parrhesia*, but rather that the notion is complicated by someone like Callicles—an unknowledgeable person who draws on a democratic ethic in a strategic way, observing its form while subverting its intent. Moreover, Callicles later demonstrates his true conventionality and fear of the *demos* when he abandons his frank engagement with Socrates after the philosopher associates Callicles with the pleasure-seeking catamite. Callicles then answers only to fulfill argumentative consistency (495a–b) and to get the whole thing over with and to please Gorgias (501c–d).[36]

Rather than confirm Callicles' *parrhesia*, Socrates challenges him—demonstrating not only that Callicles will be unable to follow through on his claims to *parrhesia* and knowledge, but also showing that none of us really "tells it like it is." It is the ambiguity of Socrates' response that is compelling; we cannot know for sure what he is saying, and yet he is a character who constantly claims to want to understand what people really think. The common usage of *parrhesia*, as we see with Cleon or Callicles, designates a rights-bearing Athenian citizen who knows exactly what he means and who means one certain thing; there is no ambiguity in his responses to the world. In contrast, we do not know quite what to make of Socrates; does he care for Callicles or loathe him? By getting us to ask this question, the dialogue can push us to think about the ways in which all people retain a multiplicity of responses to the world, seemingly contradictory, yet unified in a single person (acknowledging this also requires acknowledging our own inability to fully understand the dialogue itself). It is often quite easy to condemn Callicles and side with Socrates. But Socrates also fails to give us a clear answer—does he justly condemn Callicles, offering a lesson to others? Are we meant to simply agree with Socrates, or is there room for other judgments? Or is Socrates an embittered and cruel old man, just trying to win an argument at any cost? Of course, this ambiguity complicates the political situation. How can we act if we cannot decide? Democratic politics is not *just* about talking and pondering. Through this aporetic move, however, we can perhaps temper our need for coherence without abandoning it and soften our own claims of rhetorical exemption (and thus superiority). By holding onto the ambiguity presented by Plato, we reinvigorate the activity of considering what Socratic meant for Athenian democracy, instead of just using Socrates' authority (or infamy) in support of our own positions.

Socrates' ironic comments on Callicles' character here draw attention to the difficulty and the potential of democratic discourse. Socrates seems correct when he claims that deliberative partners need knowledge, goodwill,

36. A "catamite" was the "passive" partner in anal sex, usually either the younger man in a pederastic relationship (who was expected to admit no pleasure from the encounter) or an adult male prostitute. Thus, there is also an implication that the type of person that Callicles has just praised is not worthy of citizenship.

and frankness in order to discover the truth about how to live. How can political life proceed in a climate of hostility, dissembling, and ignorance? At the same time, the desire for purity expressed by claims to *parrhesia* embodies an aversion to the confusion and complexity of political life. In this way, Socrates' irony—whether intended or not—here allows us a greater appreciation of the messiness of logocentric political life; in some ways, we are ineluctably located in a context marked by hostility, dissembling, and ignorance. This is not necessarily because we want this particular situation, but because social life remains fragmented, because our knowledge of ethics is forever incomplete, and because our own minds are often marked by multiplicity and opacity. Socrates' ironic sarcasm highlights these difficulties. Ironic statements can help lead us to a "consciousness of the inadequacy of language . . . by mocking or partially disclaiming one's own discourse, one disrupts the convention that implicitly holds that words carry intrinsic import."[37]

The *Gorgias* is infused with other instances of mocking irony. After Polus has rebuked Socrates twice for discourteousness (448a–b; 461b–d), Socrates is conspicuously deferential to the younger man, thanking him for his guidance (461d), praising him as "admirable" (461c–d), a "good friend" (461e, passim), imitating his rhetorical style (467c), and so on. If these comments are straight flattery, then Socrates does not improve Polus, but instead contributes to his self-satisfaction. If the comments are straight mockery, we should be concerned with their destructive qualities; you cannot expect the interlocutors to philosophize with you if you are snidely mocking them. But Socrates remains somewhere between these two options, evidenced by his own express rejection of flattery and his commitment to goodwill in conversation; he is using flattery ironically. Why? Ann Michelini points out that in the context of the competition accompanying Greek male social interaction, Socrates' irony may be the most socially sensitive reaction to the others' behavior. Polus has set the terms for the debate—aggressive, boastful, accusatory. Socrates disarms this through his own irony—his self-deprecation and flattery of others. Callicles continues this same dynamic with Socrates, supplementing it with claims of *parrhesia*, while Socrates maintains his ironic stance. "The ironist counters aggressive behavior but refuses to enter the conversation on the adversary's terms by responding in kind. . . . Socrates [shows] his good manners by

---

37. Seery, *Political Returns*, 181.

avoiding open confrontation."[38] Rather than a sign of Socrates' frigidity or cruelty, irony in this particular context may actually be a thoughtful, context-conscious response. While Foucault contrasts flattery with *parrhesia*, here we see flattery used in the service of criticism.

All of this is not to say that Socrates is not confrontational, but rather that he tries to reshape the standards of behavior that should accompany such confrontations between male Athenian citizens. In this case, irony addresses the rudeness expressed by Polus and Callicles in a way that provides enough social lubrication (and face-saving space) to allow the conversation to continue, while also criticizing the norms of Athenian masculinity. Plato does not present Socrates as ruthlessly "telling it like it is" without regard for social context (like the ethical purist described by Ruth Grant in *Hypocrisy and Integrity*). Socrates attends to his audience by recognizing their tactics and responding in a way that takes them, as individuals, into account. Polus's aggressiveness calls for some ironic flattery, and the boastful Callicles receives elaborate puns and sustained mockery. Perhaps as the politically ambitious native Athenian, Callicles requires this greater attention from Socrates—after all, his political decisions will affect all their lives in a much more immediate way.

Socrates' use of irony is deployed relatively elegantly in what could easily be a rather dull harangue of Gorgias, Polus, and Callicles. Through his ironic mockery, Socrates distances himself from his blunt interlocutors' aggression, deflating them without attacking them directly. Had he joined in on their terms, the encounter would have likely devolved into all-out verbal warfare. The interaction remains highly agonistic, but it does continue. Socrates provides an odd counterbalance of ironic civility to the increasingly tense discussion and minimizes the likelihood that Gorgias, the popular teacher of rhetoric (who is therefore in a position to also influence future democrats), will abandon the conversation. Instead, Gorgias keeps the discussion going, encouraging the interlocutors and claiming to take no offense at Socrates' criticisms of his "knack." Though Socrates fails to convince the one native Athenian in the group (Callicles), it is not clear that Socrates would have succeeded had he bowed to Callicles, addressing him more directly or in his own style. Instead, Callicles' version of *parrhesia* necessitates a move to ironic engagement. Callicles is supremely confi-

---

38. Ann N. Michelini, "ΠΟΛΛΗ ΑΓΡΟΙΚΙΑ: Rudeness and Irony in Plato's Gorgias," *Classical Philology* 93, no. 1 (January 1998): 51, 53.

dent and hostile. He has no respect for earnest care; his tolerance for Socrates lies in the fact that he believes that Socrates is playing with him, which challenges him to remain in the fray. But if Socrates had appropriated Callicles' rhetorical style, the discussion would have been a battle of wills, rather than a philosophical discussion. The dialogue remains fraught with conflict (as the opening lines of the dialogue suggest), but the drama plays out with a more complex understanding of the dynamics of deliberative engagement and judgment in the democratic context. Plato is careful to show the ways in which citizens like Callicles resist Socratic philosophy, remaining bound to their love/fear of the *demos* (see 481e). This resistance forces us to confront the frustration brought about by the commitment to open, (relatively) unforced argument as a way to resolve conflicting ideas about justice. We see the difficulties of the deliberative project, taking them into account so as to avoid both the cynicism that repeated disappointment brings and the blindness that bars us from seeing how the deliberations generate their own exclusions.

It also should push us to see the imperfection of Socrates; he comes off as punishing and sometimes cruel. Socrates may even be right, but his irony, which can be so fruitful in other ways, can also have a destructive edge. Like post-9/11 irony, Socrates' irony may be interpreted by others as much darker than it is here, but again like our contemporary scene, this risk may be necessary in the face of frank moralizing that claims unity where it does not exist or superiority where it remains undemonstrated. Tarnopolsky argues that the disruption of this false unity is critical; otherwise, " 'debate' becomes a reciprocal exchange of pleasantries, *such that neither party even has to endure the pain of having one's identity or ideals criticized by an 'other.' "*[39] She also argues that "for Socrates, *putting someone to shame is the very activity that first creates a potentially salutary discomfort and perplexity in the patient that is necessary for self-consciousness, self-reflection, self-criticism, and moral and political deliberation*" (emphasis in original).[40] While she and I differ in that I see mocking flattery as a central element of the dialogue (whereas Tarnopolsky sees a more earnest Socrates), the effects of Socrates' actions are the same, and these revelations are critical for the success of democratic deliberation—the thoughtful, often critical, weighing of different perspectives and options,

39. Tarnopolsky, "Prudes, Perverts, and Tyrants," 481.
40. Ibid., 478–79.

and the coming to judgments about them. Without these critical moments, there is a single (falsely) unified mass of citizens, in which all ways of life are equally valued, even that of the tyrant who would deny others their way of life if need be. We should also recall the competitiveness of Greek male social interaction. When we see Socrates being too rough, too cruel for our tastes, we should remember the bellicosity of his own environment. Perhaps the irony is not cruel at all, even as it remains confusing. Do we have good reason to believe that sincere pleading would have convinced the interlocutors? Why should we think Socrates would have seemed any less ridiculous to Callicles had he not engaged him in this matter?

The ironic mockery also reveals Socrates' debts to Athenian culture. There is a comedic element to his teasing and inversions in the *Gorgias*. Comedy in Athens developed alongside democracy and was a central forum for *parrhesia*.[41] On the comedic stage, poets criticized powerful figures, often coming very close to slander.[42] Their mockery of the powerful and famous reflected and shaped Athenian attitudes about such figures. Comedy, while not necessarily straightforward speech, provided the comedians a place to expose critical truths about the political arena. Comedy's laughter could forge community and release anxieties through its playfulness; at the same time, it could be used "consequentially," running the gamut from mild shaming to the destruction of reputations.[43] Thus comedy deepened the Athenian culture of accountability, both recognizing citizens' (especially powerful citizens') social embeddedness, as well as providing an outlet for dealing with this interdependence—the two critical purposes of democratic accountability.

While Plato often presents Socrates as critical of the comedic tradition in Athens, his dialogue draws on this tradition to complicate *parrhesia*. Socrates is seriously playful with Polus, and frustrates his seriousness and rude bluntness. Socrates' puns tease Callicles about his inability to deny either the *demos* of the Assembly or his lover Demos (481d–e); Socrates here both playfully and seriously channels comedic and potentially slanderous invective (*loidoria*) to point out Callicles' unmanly lack of self-control.[44]

---

41. See Henderson, "Attic Old Comedy," and Stephen Halliwell, "Comic Satire and Freedom of Speech in Classical Athens," *Journal of Hellenic Studies* 111 (1991): 49–70.

42. Halliwell, "Comic Satire," 54; Henderson, "Attic Old Comedy," 261, 265.

43. Stephen Halliwell, "The Uses of Laughter in Greek Culture," *Classical Quarterly* 41, no. 2 (1991): 282–83, 292.

44. Note the connection to gossip—a form of social policing—here. For more on the development of (and what would count as) *loidoria* and *diabole*, see Harding, "Comedy and Rhetoric."

This happens again when Socrates backs Callicles into a corner with his own arguments about the happy man and pleasure; the frank Callicles cannot admit that the life of the catamite is best, although his argument would seem to require such an admission (494e). At the same time, Socrates is not using invective in the traditional sense (although his statements call it to mind), because he does not claim that he is better than Callicles. In fact, Socrates states that he is like Callicles in that he himself cannot say no to his own beloveds, Alcibiades and philosophy. Instead, Socrates "attempts to defuse this zero-sum competition," while still speaking in ways that remain at least somewhat familiar to both interlocutors and ancient readers.[45] Although Socrates' mockery takes its toll on the conversation, it also extends Athenian mechanisms of accountability and the possibility of democratic discourse in a context marked by power inequalities and intense political ambitions. Socrates draws upon comedy—using puns, flattery, and invective—in innovative ways, exposing the inadequacy of naked *parrhesia* and the rhetorical complexity of deliberation.

In another parallel to the informal mechanisms of accountability in Athens, the silent audience of the dialogue calls to mind the *corona* of the lawcourts discussed in Chapter 2. Its presence transforms this private conversation about politics and rhetoric into a more public forum and helps ensure that the speakers will be held accountable for what they say in some way (most likely through gossip). Thus we have a dialogue indebted to Athenian culture, especially its mechanisms of accountability, but which also criticizes it. All the while, the ironic and comedic subtexts allow a certain distance that keeps the conversation from becoming too earnest and too fraught with emotion to continue at all.

Of course, the psychological distance that irony creates may come at a cost. Commentators have long viewed irony with suspicion, perceiving in it an inherent arrogance. This was especially true of the post-9/11 ironists in the United States. Meanwhile, Socrates' most memorable interlocutors remain suspicious of Socrates' intentions because of his irony and perceived mockery. The arrogance supposedly stems from the ironist's implicit claim to know something that her victim does not and, through the ironic remark, to flaunt that privileged information.[46] It creates suspicion and divides the audience into insiders and outsiders. But this view presupposes that a com-

45. Nightingale, *Genres in Dialogue*, 118.
46. Nehamas, *Art of Living*, 49.

munity somehow exists prior to the speech act, and that the ironist destroys that unity. There is no stable or comprehensive unity prior to a particular speech act; it is only through rhetoric that these communities are constituted. To presume that community already exists is to neglect the dynamism of social life. While we must have some shared values or meaning to communicate (otherwise, we have chaos), community remains a question, rather than a given. Individuals or groups bring communities into being, pulling people together for a moment in time. Sometimes the community is sustained over a period of time, but various fractures and differences always remain among members. Rather than creating differences, the ironist recognizes the assertion of a false community, sees differences that do in fact exist, and then calls those who also share that vision to join a momentary community of understanding. Like *Get Your War On* after 9/11, irony can disrupt erroneously assumed unity and create a new community along different lines. Through his irony, Socrates tries to create a community that could understand his criticisms of Athenian democracy as it was practiced by men like Callicles.

Critics also point out that irony is cruel—it thrives on the presence of an unknowing victim. Yet the victim, like Callicles, may deserve the mockery. Callicles is arrogant and tyrannical. He has no respect for democracy except as a means to his own satisfaction. Is democracy better served by allowing a Callicles to continue unchallenged? The idea that irony's victims are always unfairly ridiculed is spurious; some characters call for deflation, and irony is a less aggressive (and often more interesting) way than frank speech to deflate another's arrogance. It is also not necessarily uncaring—the arrogant are offered a way to save face by publicly taking the comments at face value. In any case, the community engendered by irony may be worth the potential risk; it is the task of judgment to decide. According to Wayne Booth, "We need no very extensive survey of ironic examples to discover—unless we are choosing the examples to dramatize the use of victims—that the building of amiable communities is often far more important than the exclusion of naïve victims. Often the predominant emotion when reading stable ironies is that of joining, of finding and communing with kindred spirits."[47]

Irony can also be more inclusive than a more straightforward form of

47. Wayne C. Booth, *A Rhetoric of Irony* (Chicago: University of Chicago Press, 1974), 28.

address. When Socrates tells Callicles, "My wonderful man, go easier on me in your teaching, so that I won't quit your school (489e), or calls him "wisest Callicles" (489c) or "my most excellent fellow" (515a), we do not know exactly what he means; this openness allows the reader to interpret the comment in a variety of ways, all of which may lead the reader or listener to listen more closely to the speaker. We get a hint that Socrates is ironic in his praise at 499b9, when he calls Callicles a *panourgos* (someone who is cunning or knavish). But to what degree Callicles is not an excellent fellow remains unclear; however, the alternative, "Callicles, you are a horrible fellow," would strike many as overly harsh and pedantic.

There is also little basis to reject irony as inherently arrogant. It is undoubtedly true that some people "get it" at a particular moment, while others may not. Understanding or drawing attention to irony is no more elitist than any other social practice that excludes some people—such as the use of statistics to make a point. In fact, the basis for inclusion and exclusion in irony's community may be less problematic than other, seemingly more open political practices. Indeed, as politics increasingly becomes a matter of technical expertise, citizens are more frequently called upon to judge between competing analyses of a problem that they lack the background to understand. Irony, however, often demands only that one employ one's basic intelligence to decipher the meaning, which is surely a more (although not fully) democratic exclusionary principle than specialized training. When used by a speaker, irony is a form; its qualities depend on its specific deployment. Of course it could be used to ridicule the uneducated and poor, but does anyone argue that Jonathan Swift wrote "A Modest Proposal" or *The Drapier's Letters* to serve the interest of Ireland's elite?[48] While a particular irony may not be understood by every listener, it is not necessarily elitist.

Nehamas is a bit skeptical of this community building; he believes that when we read Plato's dialogues, we are enticed to identify with Socrates, believing that we would know more than Socrates' targets.[49] For Nehamas, "Plato's irony is more disturbing than Socrates. It uses Socratic irony as a means for lulling the dialogues' readers into the very self-complacency it makes them denounce."[50] Surely many readers are struck by the apparent

48. See John Traugott, " 'Shall Jonathan Die?': Swift, Irony, and a Failed Revolution in Ireland," in *The Politics of Irony: Essays in Self-Betrayal*, ed. Daniel Conway and John Seery (New York: St. Martin's Press, 1992), 31–51.
49. Nehamas, *Art of Living*, 41, 43.
50. Ibid., 44.

buffoonery of some of the interlocutors—Callicles, for example. However, the aporetic moment remains to balance this danger, and it remains up the listener and reader to overcome their own arrogance.

I also believe that Socratic irony is too frustrating and complicated to assume that readers always identify with Socrates. While he is often presented as a hero of Western culture, he can also be annoying, punctilious, inflexible, rude—a boor. The Aristophanic Socrates does not surprise those familiar with Plato's dialogues; the criticisms may seem unfair, but they are not shocking. Instead of soliciting lazy agreement, Socrates' irony *can* disarm those who pay close attention, drawing us in to determine what he means. And when we do this, we are thinking for ourselves, practicing the judgment we need to exert to be democratic citizens. This ambiguity about Socrates' character is an integral part of the dialogues; it should stop the thoughtful reader or listener from complete identification with Socrates (or the other characters in the dialogues). Socratic irony, both in its mocking and more complex philosophical forms, can push the reader into the intellectual activity of judging (of course, it may also fail). Democracy is a logo-centric enterprise; it requires of its citizens vigilance and the ability to both submit to and supervise processes of accountability. This emphasis on thoughtful engagement is a critical part of a democratic education. According to Dana Villa, "Socrates can be said to put intellectual doubt at the heart of moral reflection; he makes such doubt the duty of any conscientious citizen . . . his energies are devoted to dissolving the crust of convention and the hubristic claim to moral expertise—the two things which stand in the way of thought and real moral reflection."[51]

This effort to lead others to think extends to the interlocutors in the dialogues as well. As Vlastos explains the process in his discussion of Socrates and Alcibiades in the *Symposium:* "What [Socrates] is building on is the fact that in almost everything we say we put a burden of interpretation on our hearer. When we speak a sentence we do not add a gloss on how it should be read. We could not thus relieve the hearer of that burden, for this would be an endless business."[52] If the interlocutor chooses to hear flattery rather than a comment on their arrogance or, at the very least, the possibility of irony, then Socrates cannot force this lesson. For interlocutors, particularly those chosen by Plato—like Alcibiades, Euthyphro, and

51. Dana Villa, *Socratic Citizenship* (Princeton: Princeton University Press: 2001), xii, 2.
52. Vlastos, *Socrates, Ironist and Moral Philosopher,* 41–43, 44.

Callicles—to grasp Socrates' meaning, they must arrive at this understanding themselves; any other method of instruction would be condescending and indicative of the larger problem. Plato's Socrates addresses the difficulties inherent in human communication by trying to improve the capacity of fellow citizens to deal with them.[53] At the same time, different techniques with different characters attest to the conscious practice of rhetoric in the dialogue.

We should also be wary of assuming that success with the interlocutors is the point of the *Gorgias,* which seems unlikely given the theme of failure throughout the dialogue. Instead, the dialogue here lays bare for the reader both the dangers of bluntness and the usefulness of irony. It is important to remember that the dialogues are stories, not transcripts of actual conversations. Thus, while Socrates may fail to educate many of his interlocutors, can we say that Plato has failed to educate us? Likewise, isn't there something to be learned from these failures in Athens? The text is not a face-to-face conversation, but an invented record of a conversation between several people and with witnesses, some written in by Plato (458c) and others existing through us. These two groups of witnesses may have been of more concern for Plato, and certainly should be for us—our students and citizens now matter more than Callicles.

Being one of irony's witnesses is certainly less intimidating than being one of irony's objects; the chances that one will get the point are obviously higher when one is not the "victim." And this appearance of irony in the world is certainly much more like the average contemporary citizen's relationship with irony. For example, *The Daily Show* is generally not mocking me or you, but the president or another political figure (when the show does mock the audience, we remain part of a large community of viewers and aren't individually and publicly singled out for criticism). Jon Stewart probably doesn't convince George W. Bush that he was wrong to invade Iraq ("Mess-o-potamia"), but success is to be found elsewhere, in the audience. The risks of insincerity are much greater on the interpersonal level when we discuss issues like love, family, ourselves. But in the decentered environment of mass democracy, we often discuss supercilious public fig-

---

53. I understand that the tradition of analytic philosophy holds that Socrates was trying to pin down the precise meanings of words in his dialogues. But I remain convinced that his usual inability to complete that task is a comment on language itself. Even when meanings and ideas seem to stabilize (i.e., the *Republic*), the text works against itself, again alerting us that something else is going on.

ures, and discuss them with a number of parties on a massive, public scale. The dynamics of irony shift with the addition of witnesses and the move to a medium (beyond interpersonal conversation).

Socrates as Rhetorician

It is not uncommon for readers of the *Gorgias* to see Socrates as a linguistic purist who disdains rhetorical flourishes and the ability of orators to persuade large groups. Socrates indicts rhetoric on the grounds that orators can speak persuasively on a subject they neither know nor care about. He accuses orators of being more concerned with flattery than truth (463b). Rhetoric so described exists in stark contrast to *parrhesia,* a courageous, critical, and truthful freedom of speech. In the end, proponents of this view argue, Socrates turns away from politics because the private life of the philosopher engaged in dialogue is the only arena in which *parrhesia* can be practiced.[54] Yet "critics who have assailed Plato's supposed rejection of discursive practical life have done so, at least in part, because of an excessive focus on Socratic *logos* narrowly understood . . . these criticisms are softened considerably when we begin to focus on Socrates' broader existential activity (*ergon*) in the dialogues."[55] That is, Socrates' apparent rejection of rhetoric requires that we ignore what he actually does in favor of a confident acceptance of what he says.

While Socrates was highly critical of the sophistic innovations, especially their practice of rhetoric, he was no reactionary hoping to return to the glory days of archaic Athens.[56] It is true that Socrates criticizes rhetoric, but that does not make him an unequivocal opponent of the practice; orators and comedians similarly disparaged the practice on a regular basis and were not necessarily considered opponents of either rhetoric or democracy. Socrates harshly criticizes the rhetoric practiced by Gorgias, Polus, and Callicles, but his own actions are thoroughly rhetorically conscious, complicating his criticisms. For example, if oratory is flattery, what are we to make of Socrates' overwrought politeness and praise of his interlocutors in the

54. See Monoson, *Plato's Democratic Entanglements,* and Foucault, *Fearless Speech.*
55. Mara, *Socrates' Discursive Democracy,* 16.
56. For more on Socrates' position between traditional authority and the innovations of Sophism, see Mara, *Socrates' Discursive Democracy,* chap. 2, especially p. 42. Also see Richard McKim, "Shame and Truth in Plato's *Gorgias,*" in *Platonic Readings / Platonic Writings,* ed. Charles L. Griswold Jr. (University Park: Pennsylvania State University Press, 2002), 39.

Gorgias? Socrates criticizes the poets and orators for persuading without teaching (454e–455a). Philosophers, by contrast, know the just, can give an account of it, and avoid using flattery to convey that account. But the problem here is that Socrates consistently claims not to know such things (*Gorgias* 506a–b; *Apology* 21b), and he seems to engage in flattery. He uses myths of the afterlife, ending the dialogue with a fearsome picture of judgment after death (*Gorgias* 523a–on). He jokes (447a–b; 449d–e; 461e). He acts effusively polite (467c; 469d; 470c–d; 489c; 515d–e). By the end of the *Gorgias*, Socrates dominates the discussion to comic effect, answering his own questions (505b–507c). This is not elenchus anymore—this is oratory (511d–513c; 517c–519e; 523a–527e), and it is filled with emotional appeals. At the end of the *Gorgias*, Socrates summarizes the supposed conclusions of the dialogue, few of which were actually satisfactorily resolved. These are not simple lapses in judgment on Socrates' part or in Plato's writing; rather, these practical subversions of his own *logoi* are a crucial part of the dialogue. At the very least, Socrates calls into question the lines between speaking the truth and flattery, between rhetoric and *parrhesia*. Why does Plato present Socrates this way? What do these subversions tell us about democratic deliberation and its relation to rhetoric?

First, Socrates' use of rhetoric acknowledges the Athenian love of skillful oratory.[57] As a central part of Athenian democratic culture, rhetorical ability was an indispensable skill in political life. Given the rise of teachers of rhetoric, the young man who wanted to influence political life in any way would be remiss to neglect his own oratorical skills. Socrates himself seems to keep up with developments in this field, having possibly read Polus's recent work on rhetoric (462b–c).[58] Socrates' statements also echo (or anticipate) motifs of Athenian oratory. He often claims a lack of skill in speech, which would become a trope by the fourth century (*Apology* 17a–18a; *Gorgias* 521e; 522e).[59] Plato's created interlocutors stress the danger he is in without this skill (*Gorgias* 486a–b; 521b–d); allusion to the danger in which a speaker finds himself was another commonplace theme by the fourth cen-

57. Monoson, *Plato's Democratic Entanglements*, 58.

58. Debra Nails, *The People of Plato: A Prosopography of Plato and Other Socratics* (Indianapolis: Hackett, 2002), 252. See also E. R. Dodds, *Plato's Gorgias: A Revised Text with Introduction and Commentary* (Oxford: Oxford University Press, 1959), 223.

59. Manin, *Principles of Representative Government*, 33; Hansen, *Athenian Democracy*, 308; Christopher Carey, "Rhetorical Means of Persuasion," in Worthington, *Persuasion*, 27–28.

tury.[60] Plato's Socrates is firmly embedded in Athenian culture—an important mark of the effective speaker: according to Socrates, "You mustn't be their imitator but be naturally like them in your own person if you expect to produce any genuine result toward winning the friendship of the Athenian people" (513b–c).[61] While the critiques are there, we should be careful about seeing a full-scale condemnation where the incongruity between *erga* and *logos* is so apparent.

The *Gorgias* also helps us consider the importance of context in speech. A *parrhesiastes* expresses the truth without regard for the listener, but Socrates does just the opposite. He chooses his words strategically, as we all do, even those of us who claim not to. "Such a strategic dimension . . . is, at a minimum, an aspect of any 'use' of language . . . to insist on the strategic dimension of language is to draw attention to the rhetorical quality of all speech, including truth-speak."[62] In a democracy, the choice to speak and to use certain words is precisely that—a choice, rather than some necessary and natural expression. Meaning hinges on context. Socrates seems sarcastic and teasing with Callicles in order to counter his aggressive hedonism; he quite possibly patronizes Polus as a response to the younger man's rudeness. But he takes a very different approach with his friend in the *Crito* when discussing his impending execution. Socrates' methods remain tightly intertwined with the particular personalities with whom he is involved. What is proper to his interactions with one person would not be proper with another. Linda Alcoff's work on the "problem of speaking for others" likewise notes that an engagement with the individual and her context can be an important component of political discussion: "When I acknowledge that the listener's social location will affect the meaning of my words, I can more effectively generate the meaning I intend."[63] In the context of the dialogue, this quality prompts the reader to ask *why this approach to this particular individual?* This helps to develop the reader's ability to engage with deliberative rhetoric, rhetoric that, to return to the

---

60. Carey, "Rhetorical Means of Persuasion," 27–28.

61. Of course, Socrates won the friendship of less than half his jury, calling into question his effectiveness. On the other hand, the split jury may indicate a fracturing of Athenian identity, rather than a failure of Socrates.

62. J. Peter Euben, *Platonic Noise* (Princeton: Princeton University Press, 2003), 28.

63. Linda Alcoff, "The Problem of Speaking for Others," in *Theorizing Feminisms: A Reader*, ed. Elizabeth Hackett and Sally Haslanger (Oxford: Oxford University Press, 2006), 83. (This version is slightly modified from Alcoff's earlier essay of the same title, "The Problem of Speaking for Others," *Cultural Critique*, no. 20 [Winter 1991–92]: 5–32.)

definition of deliberation offered earlier, helps us weigh competing options and judge between them.

In this way, Socrates demonstrates his care for the particular individual, often revealing a great curiosity about and knowledge of others (for instance, he knows that Callicles' lover is named Demos [481d–e], and has likely read Polus's recent work on rhetoric [462c]). He is attentive to their specific interests and psyches, tailoring his speech accordingly. He does not say everything on his mind, nor does he speak without taking into account what the audience is able and willing to hear. He engages the audience while also challenging their ability to understand. These rhetorical choices form a central part of Socratic practice. While a tension remains between his expressed goodwill toward some interlocutors and his apparently rough treatment of them, he is attentive, using different arguments and rhetorical styles with different characters. Moreover, "rough" treatment might be part of the individualized and context-driven response.

Interestingly, everyone in the *Gorgias* agrees that the masterful rhetorician can persuade people to take particular actions (456a–b). The disagreement lies in the fact that Callicles thinks Socrates is a fool for believing that a person would choose not to use rhetoric to protect himself and should willingly face punishment if merited (480a–481c). The battle is not over whether or not to banish rhetoric and democratic politics from the world, but rather about what sort of people should have influence in those realms.[64] And in Athenian democracy, the people decide who has influence—they can shout down a speaker, press charges against him, or vote for his proposals. Since the opportunity for manipulation will always be present, Socrates' irony helps prepare the interlocutors to confront rhetoric, learning to rely on their own critical capacities instead of leaders like Pericles or Socrates.

This irony also pushes the reader into the intellectual activity of judgment. Both Callicles and Socrates are identified with *parrhesia* in the *Gorgias*, and both of them seem to violate it in very different ways. One must be able to judge between the two, for they are in fact very different people and have very different ways of acting politically. Both Socrates and Callicles profess a commitment to *parrhesia*, to frankly discussing their views. But Callicles is unable to continue in the end (494e–495a) because he does

64. See also James L. Wiser, "Philosophy as Political Action: A Reading of the *Gorgias*," *American Journal of Political Science* 19, no. 2 (May 1975): 321.

not want to be seen as a catamite. He gives no ground, preferring instead to violate his earlier claims of frankness. Callicles will speak frankly when it serves his purpose; here, he uses *parrhesia* as long as he might still win the argument and not embarrass himself. Socrates too violates the formal dictates of *parrhesia*, mocking Polus (467b–c), flattering Callicles at the moment when he (Callicles) most obviously violates *parrhesia* (494e–495c), not clearly telling us what he really thinks. Socrates' indictment of rhetoric, coupled with his use of it throughout the dialogue, belies a straightforward commitment to *parrhesia*. But his violation of *parrhesia* serves a larger purpose than his own power in the democracy. He does not seem to care about his reputation or his status in Athens, making him a rather odd specimen of Athenian male. If we take Socrates' word for it, this effort is for the sake of caring for and improving both his fellow citizens and himself. In this case, the irony (and subsequent confusion and anger) may help to improve citizen judgment by inoculating them against false flattery and claims of goodwill. I do not mean to dull the edge of Socrates' irony here—too many interpreters have commented on it for it to be ignored. Yet this destructive edge seems necessary in certain contexts. Much like the ironist response to 9/11, Socrates' irony, while enervating to many, can also provide a cathartic moment for others, disintegrating veneers of agreement (it is important to keep in mind the multiple audiences of both the dialogues and contemporary democracy here). That is not to say that irony is always constructive, but only to make some room for it in an account of a healthy deliberative democracy.

Socrates' own use of flattery also shows us that the lines we draw between "us" (sincere speakers) and "them" (devious rhetoricians) may not be as stark as we had hoped. Socrates is known as a "gadfly," probing and pushing Athenians to examine their lives. But in the *Gorgias*, we see Socrates instead act as flatterer. He does this both directly—such as his questionable praise of the interlocutors—and less directly—such as when he closes the dialogue with an ominous story of the afterlife or when he seems to intentionally enrage the dyspeptic Callicles (thus intensifying dominant emotions). Instead, the difference between aiming "at what's best" and flattery is more complicated than a superficial reading of the dialogue might suggest. This juxtaposition hints that we can never be certain that we are challenging our audience, while our opponents flatter them, simply appealing to their emotions and fears. Our faith in the purity of our own motives and their rhetorical effects is part of the problem. However, the difference between the two, the difference between a Callicles and a Socrates, exists and is important. To find it we must use our judgment—for whether one hears flattery or a challenge depends on perspective and context.

Moreover, Socrates' irony, even (or especially) when it misleads, can help people appreciate that "all literal statements mislead."[65] That is, language can never fully capture what we believe; words map imperfectly onto the fullness of our experience. Some people, like great poets, excel at capturing the richness of life, using those same imperfect tools. But we should be wary of thinking we live in a transparent world that we can easily and simply describe. We make our statements contingently, hoping that we got it right for now. That does not mean we stop speaking—part of this irony is that we sustain faith in our ability to speak and to judge between different descriptions and speakers. This is an admittedly contemporary gloss on the dialogue's meaning, coming close to something like Rorty's liberal ironism. Yet Socrates' kind of irony remains different from Rorty's conception in important ways (not least of all because Rorty himself identifies Socrates/ Plato as a metaphysician); while Socrates professes to not know the truth and while Plato has written the character in such a way as to highlight the difficulties of communication, both author and character seem much more willing to commit to the *possibility* of truth and certainty than contemporary liberal ironists would be. At the same time, Socrates remains the champion of skepticism, rejecting many claims of knowledge. Negotiating between the differing interpretations of Socrates and the *Gorgias* (differences generated by the irony in the text) is the central activity for readers of the dialogues, which in turn helps develop the judgment critical for citizenship. Democracies require intellectually autonomous and strong citizens; faith in the capability of the average citizen was a "substantive [element] of the Athenian democratic self-image."[66] The dialogue lets us know that we fall short of the mental agility required of and praised by democratic citizens, because we value the wrong things—personal glory, material pleasures, life at any cost. This shortcoming is presented in a way that helps us develop our intellectual capabilities (rather than simply offering a blunt harangue of our deficiencies). When confronted with someone like Callicles, Plato uses irony to warn us against frankness that merely

65. Booth, *Rhetoric of Irony*, 275.
66. Monoson, *Plato's Democratic Entanglements*, 89–90.

poses as democratic *parrhesia*. His Socrates does not remove the danger of clever speech, but helps mitigate it: "The danger of a Kallikles is always there, in a society that—in principle if not in fact—allows any decision to depend on who happens to have spoken most persuasively at the time."[67] Meanwhile, we cannot simply rely on Socrates, for he too leaves us unsatisfied, with as many questions as answers.

The use of the dialogic form and various rhetorical modes also helps us to discern a greater variety of participant voices. Privileging Callicles' rhetorical style (purportedly the style of no style) would ignore a great many elements of Athenian rhetorical culture upon which Socrates, in contrast, draws—comedy, myth, the tropes of oratory. At the same time, given the anxiety about deceptive oratory in democratic Athens, the frank self-promoter—the person who unequivocally states his distaste for rhetorical conventions and boasts of his ability to tell the truth—finds himself at an advantage.[68] Meanwhile, the ironist performs; he chooses words carefully and seems to play a particular role, apparently masking his deeper intentions. Yet can speech be anything other than a performance? As Haiman notes, "Some modes of speaking may be thought of as masks which disguise the speaker's true self; politeness and irony come to mind. . . . We owe to Bahktin a profound rhetorical question: What makes us so sure that there is any mode of speech which is truly a 'face' and not just another 'mask'?"[69] By drawing our attention to the performative aspect of public speech, to the unavoidable distance between ourselves and what we say, we can better appreciate that all language, including the claim to frankness, is a convention and a performance. This does not mean we should not judge between different performances and different speakers, for the stakes of such judgments remain high.

Socrates as *politikos*

Perhaps the most obvious irony in the *Gorgias* is Socrates' claim that he is "one of a few Athenians . . . to take up the true political craft [*politike*

---

67. Rowe, "Democracy and Sokratic-Platonic Philosophy," 248.
68. Of course, this advantage is diminished if the audience can both identify someone like Callicles and appreciate that rhetoric is always a part of language.
69. Haiman, *Talk Is Cheap*, 111, 113.

techne] and practice [*epicheirein*] the true politics" (521d–e).[70] The statement is ironic because elsewhere (*Apology* 31d–e, *Gorgias* 473e–474) Socrates claims to have little experience with politics and Callicles berates him for preferring philosophy to politics (*Gorgias* 485a–486e). Yet Socrates means what he says. He continues: "This is because the speeches I make on each occasion do not aim at gratification but at what's best" (521d–e). Within the context of an investigation of the uses and value of rhetoric in political life, Socrates claims that he is the only true *politikos*[71] in Athens. His stated goal is to make his fellow citizens better through his constant questioning and nitpicking in private conversation. When Socrates spoke as *prytanis* (that is, as leader of the Boule when his tribe rotated into power), he says he made a fool of himself, indicating that he was not able to improve the citizens or the rather dire political situation (474a). He also refers to this event humorously here, even though it involved deadly serious events—Socrates' refusal to try the Arginusae generals as a group (see also *Apology* 32b). We see Socrates failing with the requirements of a more generalized, larger-scale discourse—and this time making light of it. Doesn't democratic political life at least require speakers who can do more than make fools of themselves on the public stage?

By presenting this puzzle, the *Gorgias* asks what it means to be a democratic speaker. Callicles is a speaker and a very adept one. He claims to be a man who does not shirk from explaining his convictions, regardless of social conventions (with one exception). Yet he is not democratic in his contempt for other people and his hope to manipulate his audiences to serve his own appetites (*Gorgias* 483a–484b). He loves the *demos*, yes; but although he claims to be fearless, he fears the power of the *demos* to reject him and to forestall that, he tells it what it wants to hear (481e). Callicles' self-confidence stands in stark contrast to Socratic irony; Callicles can appear as the *alazon* who knows all the answers, while Socrates often appears self-depre-

70. Some argue that Socrates here only means to signify his good intentions in politics by the use of *epicheirein* (read by some as "undertake" or "attempt"). The argument is that while Socrates may fail in the end, he is the only person in Athens who *attempts* to practice the true political craft and so may be excused from the criticism that follows here. Yet, as he elaborates his points about Pericles and donkeys, the argument is clearly results-oriented, rather than intentions-oriented. Also, see Vlastos, *Socrates, Ironist and Moral Philosopher*, 240, especially note 21, for more.
71. The Greek (*politike*) used by Socrates refers to things having to do with citizens. So rather than translate as the more familiar "politician," which brings along particular connotations of what politics involves (and thus closes off Socrates' irony), I prefer to leave the Greek.

cating and questioning. As Jonathan Lear points out, being something means actively living with the question of what it means to be that thing. "Irony is not meant for the esoteric to delight in, it is meant to help 'the vulgar' come to realize they already have a question, when before they thought they had the answers."[72] While Callicles claims to know how to succeed in politics and thus to be a good *politikos*, Socrates shows us a man deeply engaged with the question of what success is and what it would require, opening new possibilities for political life. Instead of inspiring absolute confidence in ourselves, democracy often requires that we remain open to new questions and new ways of answering the old ones, all without giving up on the whole endeavor. Otherwise, we cannot register the myriad claims brought about by our commitment to democratic accountability.

Democracy's promise is a promise we make to pay attention to one another. Our commitment to democratic accountability requires that we have communicable reasons for our actions and opinions. Irony's *aporia* can be therapeutic, and in a democratic setting fraught with rhetorical manipulators, such therapy is vital. In order to be democratic and accountable, we must first appreciate the complexity of those words. We must also appreciate the complexity of ourselves as democratic citizens, both loyal to and critical of our states. By pushing the question (rather than the presumed answer) of what it means to be *politikos* to the forefront, we renew democracy by imagining over and over again what it means to be democratic. Is being *politikos* running for office? Or writing a political blog? Serving as a juror in lawsuit against tobacco companies or attending a book signing for Ann Coulter or Michael Moore? We must judge each situation on its own merits. For example, during the late 1990s in the United States, the "deficit" became a bogeyman—the idea was that a deficit was inherently bad and should be avoided at all costs. And that view, when coupled with an economic boom, can make a lot of sense. But during a recession or other period of crisis, deficit spending—for education, for job training, day care, and so on—may be the better choice. Living with the question of how to be a democratic citizen is a risk, for we may sometimes get our answers wrong or find ourselves paralyzed by an inability to decide.

By claiming to be the one true practitioner of *politike* in Athens, Socrates has us consider what true care for citizens and citizenship looks like. We might think we know what a politician is, but Socrates' claim requires us

72. Lear, *Therapeutic Action*, 74.

to reconsider. In order to practice politics, we must first know what politics is, how political life is wrapped up in both private and public actions, and where we want to draw those lines. What is the *arête* of a *politikos* and how might that change over time? What is a democratic citizen? Is it someone who speaks with *parrhesia* at the Assembly? Is this sufficient? What does it mean after and during a war that fractures democratic identity? Only by asking such fundamental questions about our identities as citizens can we achieve the active engagement required of a democratic citizen.

The dialogue also contains Socrates' famous attack on revered Athenian leaders, most notably Pericles. Socrates claims that Pericles was a flatterer who did not make the citizens better people, but merely served their appetites (517a–c). As a result, Athenians were "wilder" after Pericles left office. The proof, Socrates maintains, is in the fact that the *demos* prosecuted Pericles for embezzlement. Yet this statement is problematic for two reasons. First, there is the obvious point that if Socrates has just described a test for political actors, he also fails this test, for the *demos* would later execute him. So something is out of order here. How could Socrates be a true *politikos* if he fails a test he himself devises? Second, when Socrates further elaborates on this test of those who practice the *politike techne*, he says to Callicles: "A man like that who cared for donkeys or horses or cattle would at least look bad if he showed these animals kicking, butting, and biting him because of their wildness, when they had been doing none of these things when he took them over" (516a–b). As Arlene Saxonhouse has shown in her analysis of the *Republic*, we should think twice before accepting Socrates' allusions to animal husbandry in the context of political life.[73] Humans are not animals; they have *logos* and therefore the possibility for democratic community. This also means they have the powers of self-creation and control—it is not necessarily the leader's fault that democracy falls short, but the citizens'. Perhaps Plato is not indicting Pericles but ridiculing the notion that people can or should be managed like farm animals.

Socrates' own actions also complicate the claim that leadership is like animal husbandry. It is relatively unproblematic to assert that Socrates hoped people would more closely examine their own lives, resolving the

73. Arlene W. Saxonhouse, "Comedy in the Callipolis: Animal Imagery in the *Republic*," *American Political Science Review* 72, no. 3 (September 1978): 888–901. See also Galen O. Rowe, "The Portrait of Aeschines in the Oration on the Crown," *Transactions and Proceedings of the American Philological Association* 97 (1966): 397–406, on the use of animal imagery as caricature.

conflicts between what they espouse and how they act. Yet it is not at all clear that he believes that the relationship between leadership and citizenry (as well as among citizens) should be without conflict. The Socratic dialogues are full of verbal combativeness, and Socrates urges his interlocutors to refute him. Plato presents Socrates as one who constantly questions traditional and sophistic conventions, calling himself a "gadfly." A gadfly is a long way from the obedient donkey above—in fact, the gadfly comes to Athens to "stir" up "a great and noble horse which was somewhat sluggish because of its size" (*Apology* 30e). So which is it? Why the contradictory portraits of the city? Like any large agglomeration, Athens is complex. While remaining the restless city described by the Corinthians in Thucydides' work, Athens has also grown complacent. In the *Apology*, Plato's Socrates hopes to renew the spirit of questioning that marks its democratic ideology and institutional practices into its day-to-day civic life. Instead of damning the particular leaders of Athens, perhaps Socrates' indictment of Pericles "constitute[s] a general warning against democrats relying too much on any leader."[74] The dialogue highlights a tension between two conceptions of democratic politics—one in which leaders must take responsibility for the character of the citizenry, and one in which citizens must take responsibility for the character of their leaders. The relationship is reflexive and often antagonistic; however, both must share the burden of making democracy work.

Instead of focusing on *politike* as a realm of leaders and masses, Plato here draws our attention to the individual, the particular, and the problem of leadership in a democracy. Socrates spends enormous amounts of time engaged in small discussion groups and talks disparagingly of his more public performances. Contrary to the focus on the individual in Plato's work, political life must also focus on the general and the group; this is one way in which Socratic discourse differs from political discourse. Moreover, the antipathy toward majoritarian politics exhibited throughout the Platonic corpus should give pause to those who might hold up the dialogues as a model for political deliberation. Yet Plato's criticisms here must be taken seriously; he shows us how democratic politics can resist the very advantages it creates for itself, drawing attention to the difficulties of collective life. While benefiting from the openness and freedom that democracy provides, the system often places its greatest trust in the least worthy. It grants

74. Euben, *Corrupting Youth*, 215.

power to frauds who shamelessly presume to speak for the entire community. It refuses to listen to those who do know. It takes critique as flattery. It won't quiet itself enough to experience *aporia*. Democracy is chaotic, self-satisfied, and marked by freedoms that can turn to shamelessness. Democracy drives Socrates to a private life.

But to concentrate only on Socrates' rejection of a more active citizenship disregards his claims to practice *politike* here, as well as the facts that he did fulfill his political duties when required, that he professed a clear commitment to the laws of Athens in the *Crito*, and that he explicitly endorsed free speech. We are left, then, with a person who practices *politike* by demanding a focus on the particular, while politics is usually concerned with the general. Socrates focuses on the individual because the individual citizen is the foundation of the meaning of all *politike*. Our political endeavors suffer when they forget this heterogeneity, thinking that people all understand the same comments in the same ways or that they have similar expectations of their own engagements with democratic political life. The generality of political life thus requires multiple and diverse ways of speaking and an even greater reliance on citizen judgment; attention to the particular is required in order to make way for the challenges of public life. As Stephen Salkever points out in his discussion of the *Menexenus*, "The ironical rhetoric of Plato's philosophical politics . . . is designed not directly to replace how politicians speak about the world but to incline them toward self-critical reflection about that way of speaking."[75] Because of the impossibility of *parrhesia* and the importance of judging between ways of speaking (as well as because of the mass character of our own democracy), we all must engage in this self-critical reflection on speech, learning to focus in on particular instances set against particular contexts—and judge.

Power and Consensus

For many, the suspicion that Socrates "love[s] to win" (*Gorgias* 515b–c) remains; we can never be sure of what we believe about this character. This is one of the most frustrating aspects of irony, regardless of whether Socrates employs it reflexively or not. Is he a benevolent guide or an ego-driven

---

75. Stephen G. Salkever, "Socrates' Aspasian Oration: The Play of Philosophy and Politics in Plato's *Menexenus*," *American Political Science Review* 87, no. 1 (March 1993): 141.

know-it-all? Is he sincere or sarcastic with his interlocutors? Does his lack of participation in politics signal a higher cause or a selfish desire to stay out of the Cave, gazing at the sun? According to Christopher Rocco,

> The *Gorgias* shows us the stakes involved in the struggle over who will set the terms of discourse, a struggle that suggests that the norms of society are decided politically as much as they are derived theoretically . . . the *Gorgias* asks us to consider whether Socrates truly seeks communicatively achieved understanding through the "unforced force of the better argument" or is simply a clever player in the endless game of domination . . . the dialogue resists both these alternatives, adopting an ironic stance toward the politics of truth that both projects Socratic dialogue as the ultimate arbiter of politics and contests that projection through the agonistic struggle between Socrates and Callicles.[76]

Like contemporary critiques of deliberative theory, this reading of Socratic discourse urges us to acknowledge that even a man almost wholly concerned with the meaning of "justice" is not above suspicion of being motivated by self-interest.[77] Perhaps it is a problem with democracy as a form of government, but we, like Socrates, must live with this uncertainty. Socratic irony pushes us to admit that transparency (of people's motives) may be an impossible goal. Humans remain embedded in particular power configurations, unable to retreat beyond all context to a pure state of self-understanding. We are often characterized by multiple and seemingly incompatible perspectives within ourselves; one may want to undertake a project for both the good of the city and for the honor and praise that will result. To require "pure" motives denies the complexity of the human psyche.

The dialogue also speaks to us about what constitutes success in politics and deliberation, because in many ways, the *Gorgias* is a dialogue about failure.[78] Socrates ultimately fails to improve either Callicles or the citizens of Athens. Both Callicles' hints in the dialogue (*Gorgias* 486a–b; 521b–d)

76. Christopher Rocco, *Tragedy and Enlightenment: Athenian Political Thought and the Dilemmas of Modernity* (Berkeley and Los Angeles: University of California Press, 1997), 22.
77. See, for example, Fontana, Nederman, and Remer, *Talking Democracy*.
78. James Boyd White, *When Words Lose Their Meaning: Constitutions and Reconstitutions of Language, Character, and Community* (Chicago: University of Chicago Press, 1984), 110.

and Socrates' failure to convince the Athenian foreshadow Socrates' later execution by the democracy. So how can irony benefit democratic deliberations when it leads to tragedy? What can we learn from these failures?

First, such failures call to mind the relationship between words and power. Callicles urges Socrates to take note of this relationship and to learn to defend himself with words, for democracy is not only logocentric, its words can be backed by force. What we say, what we argue about and for, can dramatically alter the lives we live. We are not simply "whispering in a corner" (485e). When viewed from one perspective, Socrates attempted to further the democratic potentials of his fellow citizens by pushing them to question the stultifying conventions of their lives. From another, he also antagonized and angered them, flattering them by adding to their own sense of superiority over the ridiculous and self-important philosopher. Who is Socrates to "teach" the Athenians? Who is any of us to teach anyone? We see with Socrates how such a self-appointed *euthunos* draws the ire of one's fellow citizens. Perhaps Plato felt that this irony—thought by many to be intentionally misleading as in the original Greek sense of the word—exacerbated the frustrations that led to his conviction and execution. On the other hand, perhaps Plato thought Socrates would have been executed much earlier were it not for his irony—the tumult of Athenian politics forced many other speakers to flee the city. Democracy is based on words, which are thought to be opposed to brute force. Yet, as Hobbes noted in *Leviathan*, physical force and language are intertwined. While language may remain ambiguous, it can have unambiguous, physical results. While these results are then in turn subject to words again through the creation of narratives to understand those events, we must also acknowledge that language can have profound and material consequences—whatever it ultimately means, Socrates was executed by the Athenian government.

Our democratic urge for equality does us a disservice in some ways. Knowing something that someone else does not does not necessarily imply boastfulness, but rather that the person you are talking to does not know everything. I imagine a feminist talking to a man with little experience with feminist perspectives. There are some experiences related to politics that she might have had that he has not. If he reacts with disbelief or a claim that she's being inappropriately partial, then perhaps irony is her best approach. For example, by ironically employing the conventions of male authority, the feminist can make herself heard while also criticizing the terms of the debate.[79] She can be both aggressively critical and offer some face-saving possibilities for her deliberative partner. And in the most basic sense, she is teaching him about the world (rather than just criticizing his lack of understanding), not because she necessarily assumes he is her intellectual inferior, but because he simply hasn't had access to these sorts of experiences or hasn't thought carefully enough about those he has had. Part of being a democratic citizen in a context of massive diversity may involve this openness to the "teaching" of others.

While words sometimes teach and sometimes lead to violence, other times they remain fragile and weak, as they are in the *Gorgias*. Callicles, the native Athenian and so perhaps the most important interlocutor, remains annoyed and unconvinced by Socrates at the close of the dialogue (although, as discussed earlier, the interlocutors are not the only relevant audience). Democratic deliberation does not necessarily ensure that we are understood in the way we hope to be, that others will come to the table, or that the best idea will carry the day. Assuming Callicles remains the power-hungry and arrogant hedonist, what can we take from this failure? Following Socrates' example, we can realize that while agreement may be impossible, the effort to find it is crucial to our democratic existence. To engage in deliberation only if consensus is possible sets us up for frustration and nurtures our authoritarian tendencies. We must embark on deliberations knowing full well that they may fail, all the while maintaining a deep and unjustified faith in the possibility of agreement. The potential for failure is part of the bargain. But in return we also receive the opportunity to exercise judgment and thereby, hopefully, improve our abilities to judge.

At the same time, a question about the extent of Socrates' failure remains, for we do not know what Callicles thinks later on in his life. True, his friend Andron became one of the Four Hundred in 411, but it is perhaps worth noting that Callicles was not a part of the oligarchy that seized power in Athens.[80] The dialogue fails, but how many people experience an immediate political and moral transformation? We often crave breakthroughs and dramatic change, but perhaps this is an unproductive way to view deliberation. While it may be transformative, we should not take the view that

79. See, for example, Sara B. Blair, "Good Housekeeping: Virginia Woolf and the Politics of Irony," in Conway and Seery, *Politics of Irony*, 99–118.
80. Callicles is often considered a fictional creation of Plato's; however, I read the biographical details included in the *Gorgias* with E. R. Dodds (*Plato's Gorgias*) and Debra Nails (*The People of Plato*), who maintain that he was, in fact, a historical figure.

unless each individual instance of deliberation produces immediate conversions, we have failed. Clinging to such a desired end imposes a perfect ideal on an imperfect world; we doom ourselves to disappointment by reducing human psychology and the power of the individual's previously held beliefs.[81]

Democracy contains a tension between responsibility to one's fellow citizens and the possibilities of democratic freedom. *Parrhesia* draws on an ethic of responsibility, calling citizens to be dutiful, brave, and truthful critics. We should tell each other what is on our minds, holding nothing back and, above all, refrain from manipulative and deceitful speech. At the same time, *parrhesia* also praises the intellectual independence of the individual. The *Gorgias* shows us that freedom, creativity, and opacity are all elements of democratic community of speech. Socrates does not tell the interlocutors everything on his mind. It remains difficult to discern whether and how he means what he says—is he sarcastic or earnest? His peculiar irony is both—and there's the difficulty. Socrates' strangeness demonstrates the unknowable interior life that exists for each of us. It's not that the ironist is, in Purdy's words, "all spin, all the way down," but that we all retain an interior life that refuses public transparency. Outside the Assembly, Socrates tries to strip down his interlocutors in order to see them divested of their worldliness and public personas. But he most often fails—they are left annoyed by the exercise, and Socrates is left dissatisfied. Moreover, Socrates himself remains a mystery to all those around him. Even in the private sphere, and in a Socratic dialogue where the particular is most clearly catered to, the urge for transparency is never satisfied. Why doesn't Plato give us stories of Socratic success? And why the reverberations with Athenian mechanisms of accountability?

Perhaps Plato is trying to show us that this need for complete transparency is at least partially misplaced, even while a just life is a critical foundation for healthy politics. How can we expect such transparency in public life when Socrates fails to achieve it in private (and especially when that failure is so fruitful and fascinating)? While democracy is based on accountability, which demands answers from citizens, it also entails an essential respect for this freedom from complete transparency. Authoritarian political systems demand control over the minds of individuals—there are no

81. See also James H. Kuklinski, Paul J. Quirk, Jennifer Jerit, David Schweider, and Robert F. Rich, "Misinformation and the Currency of Democratic Citizenship," *Journal of Politics* 62, no. 3 (August 2000): 790–816.

secrets from the state. Democracy must withstand this urge to strip citizen's souls naked in public, for otherwise we risk erasing the freedoms that democracy provides. Distance and opacity are not inherently dangerous for democracy; instead, they can be ways of maintaining one's sanity in situations where authority demands unity and transparency. This does not mean that democracy should not encourage interpersonal and self-examination, but rather points to the limits of such examinations. It also offers us a chance to see the benefits that might come from disregarding the dictates of *parrhesia* or sincerity in favor of the potential for psychological space, the destruction of false communities and the rebuilding of others, and the development of judgment that irony can provide.

At the same time, Socrates, especially when juxtaposed with Callicles, is seen by many as the dutiful, brave, and honest critic that Athenian democracy needed. Foucault and Monoson believed that Socrates fulfilled the role of *parrhesiastes*, appropriating the ethic for philosophy and leaving the world of democratic politics behind. In contrast, I believe that Plato's Socrates can move us to think about the dangers of *parrhesia* for democratic politics in a way that draws our thoughts to the unavoidable tension between the need to speak and hear the truth and the difficulties of doing so. The irony of *parrhesia* is that it is not the best way to encourage one's fellow citizens to value the truth above all. The use of irony, long considered deceptive, is specifically deployed by Plato's Socrates to awaken people from their stupor and take control of their political lives. Although this stance is fraught with risk, perhaps in our own political life—where we praise "straight talkers" yet remain largely disengaged from politics—we should hope for great ironists, rather than celebrate irony's death.

CITIZEN JUDGMENT AND MYTH IN THE *REPUBLIC*

The *Gorgias* is ironic until the very end. There, Socrates discusses the possibility of failing at politics, of being called up in court and being at a loss to explain himself, "for I'll be judged the way a doctor would be judged by a jury of children if a pastry chef were to bring accusations against him" (521e). Because he apparently lacks rhetorical skill, Socrates claims that Callicles is right about Socrates' inability to defend himself in Athenian courts.[1] Socrates explains to Callicles that this prospect does not trouble him nearly as much as the possibility of being unjust: "For of all evils, the ultimate is that of arriving in Hades with one's soul stuffed full of unjust actions" (522e). Socrates goes on to offer a "very fine" *logos* "showing that this is so" (523a, 522e). The account he gives is a story (*muthos*) about the three gods of the dead, Minos, Rhadamanthus, and Aiacus. After finding themselves too often fooled by the adornments of humans' lives—fancy clothes, good reputations—they now judged one's naked soul, stripped of social refinements. If the soul is unjust, that is, if "everything was warped as a result of deception and pretense, and nothing was straight, all because the soul had been nurtured without truth," the judges send the soul to Tartarus for punishment (525a).

Socrates offers Tantalus, Sisyphus, and Tityus as examples of those pun-

---

1. The irony is that Socrates does not seem to lack rhetorical skill—he is often capable of being persuasive—but that either he lacks a desire to use that skill in a certain way (that he associates with most orators) or that his jury lacked a willingness to entertain arguments about the good.

ished for the wickedness they committed while alive. Meanwhile, the "philosopher who has minded his own affairs and hasn't been meddlesome in the course of his life" goes off to the Isles of the Blessed (526c). Socrates then sums up the arguments of the *Gorgias:* that it is better to suffer injustice than to commit it, that flattery is always to be avoided, and that rhetoric must be used to support what is just (527b–c). He acknowledges that the story he has just told might seem like old-fashioned superstition and that it "wouldn't be a surprising thing to feel contempt for it if we could look for and somehow find one better and truer" (527a). But, in the end, Socrates calls on the interlocutors to use it as a guide. Tellingly, he repeatedly calls the tale a *"logos"*—a valid explanation, not just some fairy tale, even though he acknowledges the oddity of ending with this particular *logos.* Once they have used the myth as a guide and practiced *arête* together, "if we think we should, we'll turn to politics . . . when we're better at deliberating than we are now" (527d).

After his relentless indictment of rhetoric, Socrates ends with a long speech, a summation of the points that his interlocutors have refused to accept, and a myth about souls "covered with scars" (525a). Is Socrates trying to scare Callicles straight? Is it an admission that his interlocutors have no capacity to truly understand and must rely on unfalsifiable myth? Is it just a Platonic flourish to make the dialogue exciting? Does Socrates tell the myth (especially the bit about the treatment of the philosopher after death by the gods) as a way to remind or convince himself that the sacrifices of this life and his eventual execution are worthwhile?[2] Set against the context of the critique of rhetoric in the *Gorgias*, this recourse to a story seems odd. Why can't Socrates convince us through frank argument? Does myth contribute to frankness or undermine it? Doesn't it leave those who use it unaccountable for what they say?

This chapter addresses these questions. I begin by outlining the threats myth can pose to political communication, moving on to a consideration of the particular character of myth in ancient Athens and in the *Republic* and its relation to *parrhesia*. At that point, I examine the meanings of Socrates' indictment of the poets, the Myth of the Metals, and the Myth of Er. I show that instead of shoring up traditional authority and inegalitarian social arrangements, Socrates' mythmaking challenges the authority of tra-

2. Of course, it is questionable whether Socrates is "meddlesome" or not; according to his own description in the *Apology*, he annoys, rouses, and reproaches his fellow citizens (30d–31a). So another question: is the dead philosopher described by Socrates really Socrates?

ditional (and hegemonic) discourses in Athens. In this way, myth becomes a democratic and thought-provoking practice, aimed again at improving citizens' faculty for political judgment. I argue that Socrates' use of myth in the *Republic* specifically highlights the literary qualities of all speech, including frank argument; the inseparability of rationality and emotion; and the multiple perspectives that make up our shared political reality. Given these points, political judgment—that is, the ability to reflect and choose—is key. As I noted in the introduction, judgment is how we come to understand who we are, what we want, and how to get it; it is intimately tied to discourse, because deliberation is how we clarify those things. Political judgment (or *phronesis*) is inexact. It has no universal rule or set of universal rules that could cleanly direct decision making: instead, "It allows us to comport ourselves to the world without dependence upon rules and methods, and allows us to defeat subjectivity by asserting claims that seek general assent. In this way political reason is liberated, and the common citizen can once again reappropriate the right of political responsibility and decision making that had been monopolized by experts."[3]

The Dangers of Myth

What is it about the use of myth in politics that makes us so uneasy? When we think of ourselves as citizens of a deliberative democracy, we tend to consider ourselves to be rational, realistic, and pragmatic. (I think the case can be made that even those who don't think of democracy as particularly rational think of *themselves* as such.) Those who think mythically are bound by their cultural heritage or ideology, doomed to think in untruths. When we call something a "myth," we are saying that it is not true. But part of the trickiness of myth is that rather than being simply untrue, myths are often instead unverifiable. At the very least, a myth is held to be true by some particular audience, leading those who do not share that faith to believe that those who do have been deceived, either by another person, tradition, or their own ignorance. Myths are stories about moral precepts, transformations, the beginning or the end of the world, the afterlife, foundings, the origins and fundamental characteristics of peoples, higher beings,

3. Beiner, *Political Judgment*, 2.

or important public figures (heroes, founders, saviors).[4] The myth is often traditional, but does not necessarily have to be (as we see with Socrates' mythmaking).

In his discussion of national myths and liberal nationalism, Arash Abizadeh identifies four types of myth: *myth-as-lies, myth-as-embellishment, myth-as-omission,* and *myth-as-story.*[5] In the first three forms, Abizadeh argues that myths often contain false historical truth claims, which is the basis of their ability to provide a collective identity. He argues that if a myth relies on untruths to justify a collective identity, it will be incompatible with the practices of liberal democracy (which he conceives of as deliberative). Yet for other authors, myths remain constitutive parts of national memories; they help create states by providing a coherent narrative of a common past, often selectively omitting details and embellishing others. Responding to David Miller's argument in *On Nationality* that myths provide a valuable social integrative function regardless of their untruth, as long as they are subject to open discussion, Abizadeh argues in return that the critiques that would arise during debate inevitably rely on claims about the myth's truth or untruth. For Abizadeh, the problem is that the first three forms of myth—*myth-as-lies, myth-as-embellishment,* and *myth-as-omission*—leave little room for citizens to critique existing social relations that are legitimized by the untruths of the myths. While the myth may provide social cohesion and a sense of shared historical identity, myths often authorize unequal and oppressive social relations. It is only the exposure of the myth as a false belief about history that enables the marginalized to contest the dominant discourse and find redress. The debate cuts to the heart of what we find disturbing about myth in politics—"The assumption must be that speakers make insincere truth claims in order to persuade *others* of historical facts that would be socially useful to believe."[6]

In a deliberative democracy, we celebrate the power of speech to ensure democratic accountability. Democratic accountability presumes equality; and as equals, we are expected to offer true accounts to one another. In contrast, the use of myths implies inequality—someone is telling someone else a story that is either untrue or impossible to verify, and the audience

---

4. Christopher G. Flood, *Political Myth: A Theoretical Introduction* (New York: Routledge, 2002), 41, 157–58.
5. Arash Abizadeh, "Historical Truth, National Myths and Liberal Democracy: On the Coherence of Liberal Nationalism," *Journal of Political Philosophy* 12, no. 3 (2004): 297–98.
6. Ibid., 299.

is expected to accept it as foundational truth. Moreover, the narrative quality of myth often strikes us as too emotive; the imagery and the situatedness of the story draw people in, perhaps too seductively, causing them to believe something that they would not if they were behaving rationally. Myths are often told with pedagogic intent; but who in a democracy has the authority to teach his or her fellow citizens? Are there figures in whom we place so much trust that we are willing give them that kind of power? What prevents someone from resorting to myth to avoid teaching verifiable truth? We are right to be wary of myth in the political realm. We are right to assume that people use myth as a substitute for rational thought. Myths help simplify complex political situations; in fact, myths often take the political out of politics by providing certain and unambiguous answers to questions.

Abizadeh's scheme of myth contains a fourth type, however, and here is where things get complicated. *Myth-as-story* is a "historical narrative undergirding a collective identity [that] can be called mythical in the sense that it is understood by the collectivity's members in literary terms."[7] Here, myth is acceptable because it is an allegory of founding and is understood by the members of the collectivity as such. Instead of historical truths, *myths-as-story* transmit ethical or moral truths; they reveal what sort of ethical persons the actors believe themselves to be. Although not noted explicitly by Abizadeh, these myths also make historical truth claims; the difference is that the collectivity understands those claims as literature, not history. These myths are not merely taken for granted, but are open to discursive contestation, shaped by the citizens. Yet how do we differentiate between these four types of myth? What designates a myth as *myth-as-story*, instead of the other undemocratic types? As Euben asks: "When and with what consequences is an invidious contrast established between members of cultures who are deemed prisoners of their myths, and more rational societies that possess their culture rather than being possessed by it? How have such distinctions constructed views of agency and contrasts between those capable of autonomous thought and action, and those who, lacking reflective consciousness, are fated to live as they do?"[8]

This difficult problem underlies the terrain of this chapter. Do Socrates and Plato differentiate between the types of myth? What do we learn about

---

7. Ibid., 298.
8. Euben, *Platonic Noise*, 6.

the qualities of myth along the way? Can myth be used in ways that promote citizens' intellectual capacities, rather than hindering them as commonly presumed? A look at the use of myth in the *Republic* can help us to
begin to consider these questions, but we first need to understand how
mythmaking contrasts with *parrhesia*.

Parrhesia and Mythmaking in Athens

Perhaps even more so than irony, mythmaking seems the antithesis of *parrhesia*. As discussed in Chapter 2, *parrhesia* was a response to the concerns
regarding truth and truth-telling in Greek society. But prior to the development of philosophy and *parrhesia*, truth and truth-telling were the province of the mythmakers, who at that time were poets (thus, myth in archaic
Greece was a type of story about sacred matters told by poets). According
to Martha Nussbaum, the poets were accepted as the "central ethical think-
ers and teachers of Greece."[9] The notion of truth-telling in place during
this period was quite different from the one that would develop by the fifth
century B.C.E.: "Greek mythology, whose connections with religion were
very loose, was basically nothing but a very popular literary genre, a vast
realm of literature, mainly oral in character—if, indeed, the term 'literature' can be applied when the distinction between fiction and reality had yet
to be made and the legendary element was serenely accepted."[10] In Homer,
"mythos is felt to denote a special category of speech that carries implications of power and efficacy and is related to the special powers of the creative poetic word."[11] Myth was something that was worthy of
remembrance, not necessarily factually true or false. Our own categories of
evaluation—fact versus fiction, belief versus disbelief—do not map onto
this context well. Instead, the more appropriate criterion would be the ethical truth of the myth—does the myth reflect the ideals to which the Greeks
and Athenians aspired?

The Presocratics, with their rejection of mythology and interest in scientific explanation, thus saw the poets as rivals to be dealt with before they

9. Martha Nussbaum, *The Fragility of Goodness: Luck and Ethics in Greek Tragedy and
Philosophy* (Cambridge: Cambridge University Press, 1986), 12.
10. Paul Veyne, *Did the Greeks Believe Their Myths? An Essay on the Constitutive Imagination* (Chicago: University of Chicago Press, 1988), 17.
11. Kathryn Morgan, *Myth and Philosophy from the Presocratics to Plato* (Cambridge:
Cambridge University Press, 2000), 18.

could continue with their own project. There was no such thing as "mythology" until philosophy named it in an attempt to work out the categories of factual truth and falsity and to appropriate mythology's status as authoritative and truthful for itself. It is through early philosophy's critique of myth that the standards for philosophy were developed.[12] Thucydides, the chronicler of the hyper-sincere Cleon, was especially interested in dispelling the power of myth in Athenian politics, as his refutation of Herodotus's story of Harmodius and Aristogeiton demonstrates: "For men accept from one another hearsay reports of former events, neglecting to test them" (1.10). Instead, he offers an alternative mode of discursive accountability based on the important of democratic openness.[13]

Alongside these intellectual developments, we see the development of new civic concepts, namely *parrhesia*. Intuitively, myth appears to differ from *parrhesia* in important ways. First, myth's relation to truth as an objective, verifiable reality is ambiguous at best. Ancient Greek myth designated authoritative ethical discourse, rather than traditional tales or *pseude* (lies). It structured moral behavior with a sure system of various threats and rewards. Myth therefore made a rather dramatic claim to a sort of truth. However, myth as it came to be understood by the philosophers was an untruth—one that, when posing as truth, could do violence to the actual truth. To identify a myth, philosophy aims, as we often do now, to demonstrate that important parts of the narrative are unproven or untrue. But this is a difficult proposition. As I have discussed, when myths deal with the supernatural, they are not necessarily untrue (but rather unverifiable). And if the myth is powerful, then believers are unlikely to be swayed by evidence—the grounds for falsification will not be agreed upon. This can have a stifling effect on deliberations. While the *parrhesiastes* has a potentially verifiable relationship to this truth, the mythmaker cannot provide evidence outside of personal revelation, authoritative text, or tradition.

Second, because it consists of stories told across generations and because it usually focuses on moral lessons, myth tends to be conservative. Walter Ong, following Eric Havelock, posits that while oral repetition does lend itself to variation because of its lack of textual stability, it is limited to variations of relatively set themes because it relies on oral transmission.[14]

12. Ibid., 28–29.
13. Arlene Saxonhouse, "Democratic Deliberation and the Historian's Trade: The Case of Thucydides," in Fontana, Nederman, and Remer, *Talking Democracy*, 83–84.
14. Walter Ong, *Orality and Literacy: The Technologizing of the World* (New York: Routledge, 1988).

Add to this the fact that myths transmit long-standing community moral codes from one generation to another. In this sense, it is unlikely to be critical or dangerous, as *parrhesia* has to be.

Third, the very character of myth is contrary to *parrhesia*. It is always a created story, and therefore a rhetorical ornament. Myth is a figurative mode, which draws on metaphor and symbolism, while *parrhesia* is a claim to transparency that holds the promise of plain and true meaning. It also draws on affective language, most often invoking ideas of pleasure and pain to affirm its message.[15] Emotional pulls, like the threat of great suffering in the afterlife, are often a crucial part of myth's persuasive power. The style is not transparent; in this way, it seems to violate the autonomy of the listener. Furthermore, "since myth is slowly but surely transformed at each stage of its transmission, it eventually accumulates a certain number of disparate elements which seem to be so many incoherencies, whether shocking or simply ridiculous."[16] Because of its odd relation to "truth," and because of its sentimental character, we often assume that the listener is meant to simply digest and follow the strictures contained in the message. As Luc Brisson puts it, "Whoever is persuaded by the myth surrenders his liberty, for he is led, without being fully aware of the fact, to modify his behavior according to a system of inherited values."[17]

Myth in the *Republic*

These characterizations of myth lead one to wonder what relationship mythmaking can have to democratic accountability. We should take the Popperian fear of myth very seriously: what if someone uses myth to construct a totalitarian regime? What if we are deceived about the most important things in our shared life? What if we are emotionally manipulated into policies that harm us or other people? Because myth makes a positive, substantive contribution (in contrast to irony's apparent negativity), it seems to be both more alluring and more dangerous.

But myth is not the only form of speech that can be dangerous in the "wrong" hands. All speech is subject to the problems of power inequalities and deception. The problem with *parrhesia* is that it claims exemption from

15. Luc Brisson, *Plato the Mythmaker* (Chicago: University of Chicago Press, 1998), 10.
16. Ibid.
17. Ibid., 9.

such human constraints. Its realism can be as seductive as the realistic fantasy of myth. The mixture of truth and untruth, emotion and rationality, that is at the heart of myth can be a component of all language, even seemingly frank argument. The multilayered deployment of myth in the *Republic* calls on us to recognize this. At the same time, *parrhesia* poses the threat of singularity; when we are told a *parrhesiastic* truth, the room for other perspectives is often eliminated. Like irony, myth's place in our deliberations cannot be determined prior to a specific contextual engagement, just as *parrhesia*'s cannot. The point is to do our thinking ourselves. In certain contexts, like Socrates' use of myth in the *Republic*, myth can draw attention to this point. Moreover, the myths in the *Republic* are not just a meta-discourse on deliberation; they also make substantive comments on the state of Athenian democracy. Given the threat of political chaos in Athens at the time, the callipolis, the ideal city of the *Republic*, is at once a positive vision of political perfection and a critique of that same vision.[18] The *Republic* offers a positive vision, while also undermining some of its most famous and disturbing critiques of democracy, through the ironic use of myth. Thus, the mythmaking of the dialogue extends Socrates' ironic stance toward the world.[19] It is seriously playful and playfully serious; Socrates claims to be "playing," but the group discusses the most important matters—justice in one's soul (*Republic* 504d).[20] Although the discussion is about death and the immortality of the soul, there is also a comedic subtext, as Saxonhouse has shown in her exploration of the animal imagery of the dialogue.[21] Moreover, this comedy can serve a very serious purpose: "Laughter demolishes fear and piety before an object, before a world, making of it an object of familiar contact and thus clearing the ground for an absolutely free investigation of it. Laughter is a vital factor in laying down that prerequisite for fearlessness without which it would be impossible to approach the world realistically."[22] Through its currents and eddies—its

18. J. Peter Euben, *The Tragedy of Political Theory: The Road Not Taken* (Princeton: Princeton University Press, 1990), 38.

19. See Mara, *Socrates' Discursive Democracy*, and John Evan Seery, "Politics as Ironic Community: On the Themes of Descent and Return in Plato's *Republic*," *Political Theory* 16, no. 2 (May 1988): 229–56.

20. For more on the "play" of the dialogue, see Mara, *Socrates' Discursive Democracy*, 20–21, and Bernard Freydberg, *The Play of the Platonic Dialogues* (New York: Peter Lang, 1991).

21. See Saxonhouse, "Comedy in the Callipolis," 888–901.

22. M. M. Bakhtin, *The Dialogic Imagination: Four Essays* (Austin: University of Texas Press, 1981), 23.

serious playfulness, its tragic idealism—the *Republic* generates an urge to think and a capacity for judgment.

Such a view of the *Republic* immediately seems at odds with standard interpretations of Plato's most famous work. There are generally two sides to the debate. In the first camp, there are those who read the *Republic* as a dangerous utopian statement of Plato's political theory, epistemologically motivated by a world of Forms (*eide*) that alone provide true and certain knowledge. The callipolis described by Socrates is a serious proposal; it is a hideous blueprint for true justice, achieved only when the city is ruled by philosopher-kings who tightly control poetry and use noble lies to maintain the docility of the rest of the population. This view of the *Republic* can be found in the work of Karl Popper, Martha Nussbaum, and others.[23]

In a second, anti-utopian camp, readers find a dialogue that works so strenuously against itself that it can only be a warning against philosophy's involvement in politics and against the possibility of achieving true justice in the political realm. They reject a strictly literal reading of the dialogue and instead find that the historical context, dramatic elements, and ironies of Socrates undermine the positive vision offered. While the specific accounts vary, Leo Strauss, Allan Bloom, and Mary Nichols offer examples of this type of interpretation.[24]

Yet a third way is possible. This approach to the *Republic* asks why Plato presents these two possibilities together. Why is he so detailed in his thinking about the callipolis and seemingly committed to the Forms, yet includes so much evidence for rejecting that vision? What should be made of both his idealism and the ways in which he seems so different from Platonists? Because Plato offers relatively few resources for resolving the tension between these two compelling versions of his work, and because these controversies have led to so many vigorous intellectual debates through history, it seems to me that the *Republic* itself is one of the "summoners," described by Socrates as something that is both itself and not itself and thus "awakens understanding" (524d).[25] By considering something that is two

23. Karl Popper, *The Open Society and Its Enemies: Vols. 1 and 2* (Princeton: Princeton University Press, 1971); Martha Nussbaum, *Plato's* Republic: *The Good Society and the Deformation of Desire* (Washington, D.C.: Library of Congress, 1998).

24. Leo Strauss, *City and Man* and *Persecution and the Art of Writing* (Chicago: University of Chicago Press, 2004); Allan Bloom, *The* Republic *of Plato* (New York: Basic Books, 1991); Mary P. Nichols, *Socrates and the Political Community: An Ancient Debate* (Albany: SUNY Press, 1987) and "The *Republic*'s Two Alternatives: Philosopher-Kings and Socrates," *Political Theory* 12, no. 2 (May 1984): 252–74.

25. Thanks to Susan Bickford for the discussions that led to this point.

dichotomous things at once, the soul calls on understanding to judge whether the thing considered is one thing or two separate things. By doing this, we learn to ask abstract questions—not only "what the big is and the small is" (524c)—but also what justice is. In this way, the *Republic* thus is not simply a story about justice and the Forms, but rather a story about the practice of judgment in a democracy caught up in the turmoil of the Peloponnesian War that helps, in turn, to develop the judgment of its readers.

Censorship, Poetry, and Democracy

On its surface, the *Republic* is a discussion of justice in the human soul; in order to determine what that entails, Socrates and his interlocutors agree to analogize from the individual soul to the city so that they have a larger image to study. The dialogue then describes an ideal city, governed by guardians, in which three divisions of citizens (the guardians, the auxiliary guardians, and the workers) do their own jobs and defer to the rational power of the Forms (*eide*), which are comprehended only by the philosopher-kings. The philosopher-kings tightly control stories and poetry so that they only transmit messages that can develop the virtue of the citizens; when needed, the philosopher-kings can tell "noble lies" to the citizens in order to maintain order. The poets were to be turned away, banished from the city because, as Socrates asks, "Shall we carelessly allow the children to hear any old stories, told by just anyone, and to take beliefs into their souls that are for the most part opposite to the ones we think they should hold when they grow up?" (377b–c).

Because myths were transmitted through poetry in ancient Greece, Socrates' apparent indictment of the poets in the *Republic* is an important element of the complicated relationship between philosophy and myth presented in the dialogue. In addition to Socrates' banishment of the poets from the callipolis (377b–c; 386a–392a; *passim*), Socrates proposes to "also tell poetry that there is an ancient quarrel between it and philosophy" (607b). To our modern ears, this sounds reasonable, but to the ears of ancient Athenians, it would have seemed absurd; philosophy was a newcomer and thus an ancient quarrel would be impossible, if not inconceivably arrogant on the part of philosophers.[26] The dialogue is suffused with criti-

26. Nightingale, *Genres in Dialogue*, 60.

cism of the mythopoeic tradition, beginning early in the second book when Socrates criticizes the way that poets praise justice; that is, they recite frightening and misleading stories of the afterlife (363c–e), they make the just life seem burdensome (364a), and even praise injustice (365d–c).

So it is odd that Socrates makes so many references to poets and dramatists to support his points (404b–c; 414c; 441b; 453d; 457b; 466c; 468c–d; 501b; 444d; 446e; 563b–c; 566c–d; 590a). Mythic poetry can apparently corrupt the callipolis, but is integral to the discursive community presented by the *Republic*. Like the democratic city that contains all types of speech (557b–c), Socrates uses all styles of speech to make his points in the *Republic*. He quotes the archaic poets not only to criticize them but also to build his ideal city; Socrates relies on the old poets even after he banishes them. Socrates' critique of poetry, full of multiplicity and tension, alerts us to an irony. Socrates does not exclude poetry in favor of philosophical discourse; rather, he blends genres: "By entering into the mode of intertextuality, Plato transgresses the boundaries of both his own genre and the genres that he targets. Plato's use of intertextuality, in fact, is *about* boundaries. Or to be more precise, intertextuality allows Plato to explore the boundaries of this new activity he calls 'philosophy'—the boundaries of a unique way of living and of thinking."[27] To intervene in the dominant discourse (the mythopoeic tradition), Plato's Socrates remains inside that discourse to some extent, exploring its boundaries in search of a place for an alternate way of thinking about Athenian society. Socrates tries to co-opt some of the authority of the poets, but in doing so acknowledges the power of tradition and the epic poets who told myths within Athenian culture. Similarly, Socrates reflects the sophistic rejection of traditional authority—and subverts it. He knows that traditional morality is useful in limited ways— Cephalus does not seem to be an evil man, and Glaucon has a commitment to justice (even if tenuous), while the Sophist Thrasymachus seems unhinged throughout Book 1. While criticizing unreflective acceptance of traditional authority, Plato's insertion of poetry at so many points in the *Republic* demonstrates his awareness of the influence of the historical environment on the person. Our cultures shape our psyches. As Socrates has "the laws" pose the question to him in the *Crito*, "We have given you birth, nurtured you, educated you, we have given you and all other citizens a share of all the good things we could" (51c–d). The culture of Athens is

27. Ibid., 12.

constitutive of who Socrates is; he can't discard poetry but instead continues to rely on it. He can draw on this shared history precisely because it is
shared, even as he criticizes and helps to reshape it.

Furthermore, Plato's admission of poetry into the discursive community
of the *Republic* (and in the voice of his teacher) complicates what is usually
seen as Plato's pure rationalism. The *Republic* presents the tripartite division of the soul, which is properly ruled by reason; rightly or wrongly,
Plato has often been criticized for elevating reason above the supposedly
irrational emotions. But the use of myth and poetry in the *Republic* also
demonstrates his awareness of the *intertwining* of logic and emotion. The
danger of poetry is precisely its ability to stir the soul, calling on listeners
to identify with the hero or tragic figure. That is why Plato presents an
argument for controlling the messages of the poetic tradition. At the same
time, his inclusion of poetry challenges the idea that he banishes the emotions from the good psyche. Instead, he suggests that emotions can inform
the properly rational person.[28] Socrates' use of poetry suggests that mythic
poetry actually fulfills a deep need that cannot be eliminated from the soul.
The *Republic* attracts us through stories that alternatively inspire or
frighten us, giving us a reason to stick with the arguments; it thus helps
interlocutors and readers to want to care about the discussion. It leads us to
action by directly stirring the emotions, which work in tandem with reason
(just as theoretical argument appears alongside poetry in the book itself).
While he certainly stops short of the kind of valuation of the emotions we
see in Aristotle, Plato is more aware of the complex relation between reason
and emotion than the more seemingly Platonic characterization of the tripartite soul ruled by reason suggests. Making a serious argument for justice
requires speaking in ways that acknowledge this complexity. Humans are
not creatures of pure reason; they are more like Cephalus—kept awake at
night by childhood stories for fear of dying with injustice in one's soul.
Emotions are an important part of making the sort of moral and ethical
judgments that help define political life. Acknowledging this intertwining
is important for our own political life. Correspondingly, both contemporary
political theory and neuroscience have demonstrated the importance of
emotion in decision making; awareness of this fact can help mitigate unde-
served faith in both pure rationalism and pure emotivism.[29] George Lakoff's

28. For more on how emotions form an important component of rationality, see Hall,
"Recognizing the Passion in Deliberation."

29. See, for example, Barbara Koziak, *Retrieving Political Emotion:* Thumos, *Aristotle,
and Gender* (University Park: Pennsylvania State University Press, 2000), and Joshua D.

work in cognitive linguistics also demonstrates that political life revolves around metaphorical understandings and that ignoring the moral, mythic, and emotional dimensions of politics is self-defeating.[30]

We must also be careful of our own modern reactions to Socrates' criticism of the poets. Of course, his argument smacks of censorship and undemocratic limits on our most precious freedoms. But we already accept limitations on certain kinds of speech and choices.[31] As Julius Elias puts it, "His attack on the poets . . . is a critique of the effects they have on the public, and . . . no modern society, including the most temperate, has hesitated to place constraints where those effects are soon to impair the rights of others and, more broadly, the public interest."[32] Moreover, there are some undercutting currents here. He allows poetry, but only good poetry. The good man will only imitate good and moderate men and will refuse to seriously present himself as anything but a good man, "unless it's just done in play" (396e). The good man can narrate about bad things and people, but will not imitate them (396d–e). Here it seems that rather than banishing poetry and theater, Socrates proposes to banish all evil characters, unless they are only described (not personified by an actor) and described as obviously bad men, unworthy of imitation in real life. "We ourselves should employ a more austere and less pleasure-giving poet and storyteller" (398a–b); while the clever and thoroughly imitative storyteller is to be honored, he should be sent from this city (398a). But the line above about "play" makes it less clear what acceptable circumstances are for this poor sort of imitation, especially given that Socrates says elsewhere in the dialogue that he is only playing (536b–c). Furthermore, what sort of imitation is going on in the *Republic* itself? It is not simply a casual story; it is a pseudo-transcription of an evening of discussion—more like a play with both good (Socrates) and unworthy (Thrasymachus) men. And while Thrasymachus is not always presented in the best light, he is still a developed, and in many ways, sympathetic character. He is not obviously evil. His frustrations in Book 1 are likely ones felt by other observers of Socrates, including modern readers. By the close of the dialogue, his volatility has

Greene, R. Brian Sommerville, Leigh E. Nystrom, John M. Darley, and Jonathan D. Cohen, "An fMRI Investigation of Emotional Engagement in Moral Judgment," *Science* 293 (2001): 2105–8.

30. Lakoff, *Moral Politics*, 19, 41.
31. See Nussbaum, *Plato's* Republic, especially 20–28.
32. Julius Elias, *Plato's Defense of Poetry* (London: MacMillan Press, 1984), 215.

disappeared, replaced by a more balanced disposition. Moreover, the dialogue is written as if Socrates were narrating the whole scene to someone who was not present; in a sense, Socrates is playing all the parts in his recitation, including that of Thrasymachus. While the *Republic* was meant to be read, not recited, unlike the poetry of the period, its similarity to the imitative and narrative work of earlier ethical texts should not be dismissed.

Socrates' test of the good poet offers another irony. He poses a question: "If Homer had really been able to educate people and make them better, if he'd known about these things and not merely about how to imitate them, wouldn't he have had many companions and been loved and honored by them?" (600c). The test of the good poet is how well he is loved, indicated not by his reputation or some objective test, but by how his companions treat him. Socrates goes on to describe a suffocating love—they "clung to them tighter than gold and compelled them to live with them in their homes . . . followed them wherever they went" (600e). Furthermore, the failure of the poets is compared to the success of Prodicus and Protagoras, the latter of whom is elsewhere parodied by Plato's Socrates. This claim should cause us again to reconsider Socrates' apparent disdain for Homer and Hesiod. While we know that Socrates was beloved by his friends, he shunned the constraints of such suffocating friendship—he refuses to claim a role as their teacher, he shames his friends for crying before his execution.[33] Socrates was willing to give up the friendships of his mortal life for a higher civic and moral duty; he seems more like Homer than his criticism would lead one to believe. Moreover, as I discussed in Chapter 3, his elenchus often seemed to end in failure. Add to this Socrates' frequent reliance on epic poetry and the echoes of the mythological motifs of that tradition, and his criticism of the poets appears much more complicated and less hostile than it first seems. Of course, for most people, it is not the banning of the epic poets but other practices that make the callipolis so unpalatable—namely, the Myth of the Metals and the handing of the judgment of stories over to the elite "gold race."

The Myth of the Metals

On its face, the Myth of the Metals seems to be entirely at odds with an emphasis on the importance of individual judgment and democracy; as the

---

33. Even as the *Republic* shows the importance of emotion, we again see the doubleness and "frigidity" (to use Vlastos's words) of Plato's character here.

founding myth of the callipolis, it appears to legitimate authoritarian politics. What is surprising and interesting about the appearance of the Myth of the Metals in the *Republic* is not that it necessarily exposes Socrates and Plato as authoritarians or aristocrats, although that element is there. Rather, the story draws on Athenian traditions and myths of the period to draw readers into a complex literary landscape that ultimately emphasizes the critical importance of individual political judgment. As part of a larger work focused on problems of truth, political organization, and justice, and presented in dialogue form with various characters marked by their own histories and conflicts, the dialogue leads readers to develop skills useful for political judgment—what is the context here? Who is this person and what do I know about him or her? Do I share this belief? Is it an acceptable claim? According to whom?

We hear the Myth of the Metals near the end of Book 3, after the group has discussed the role of stories and lies in the city. No one in the city is allowed to lie (389b), poets must only describe the gods as virtuous (389a), actors and storytellers can only imitate good men (396c–d), and the poets can use only "noble" harmonic modes and rhythms (398e–399b). The city is to be governed by guardians who have been tested "more thoroughly than gold is tested by fire" (413e) to make sure that there is no chance those who protect and lead will lose their true convictions. Socrates proposes to devise a "noble lie" to ensure that the guardians and citizens protect the city as fiercely as possible, yet remain gentle to one another and obedient to the rulers.

Socrates says that it's a "Phoenician story which describes something that has happened in many places. At least, that's what the poets say, and they've persuaded many people to believe it too" (414c). Socrates immediately points out that the story has not been told in Athens and it "would certainly take a lot of persuasion to get people to believe it" (414c). Given such a contradictory introduction, it is unclear whether the myth is believable or fantastic; nonetheless, Socrates proceeds as if the story is a ludicrous one. He hesitates, acknowledging that once the interlocutors hear the story, they will understand why it is so unbelievable. Glaucon pushes him to tell the story and not fear the reaction of the audience; although he does not use the word itself, he counsels Socrates to speak with *parrhesia*. Socrates does not know how people can be made to really believe the story he is about tell, or how he will even find the nerve to tell it. He then proceeds to tell a pastiche of two Athenian origin myths with a bit of Theban mythic history thrown in, myths often repeated to the Athenian citizens, quite familiar and unextraordinary to any Athenian listening.[34]

The myth actually consists of two parts. First, Socrates says he'll try to persuade everyone in the city that their life up until that point had been a dream and that they had actually been reared inside the earth. Thus the citizens would treat the land as their mother and "defend it as their mother and nurse and think of the other citizens as their earthborn brothers" (414e). In the second part of the story, the citizens are told that the gods who made them mixed various metals into each person—gold, silver, or bronze and iron. Those with gold are to rule the city, those with silver are to be auxiliaries, while the remainder of the population, the bronze and iron citizens, will be workers and farmers. In the first part of the myth, the story of Athenian autochthony is retold. The ideas of Athenian autochthony were complex, stemming from an autochthonous founder (either Erichthonios or Erichtheus) who sprung from the ground, but extending over time to apply to all Athenian citizens.[35] Athenians claimed to be naturally native, in contrast to the Spartans, who were seen as immigrants in their own land. According to official discourse, Athenian citizens were born in the earth, even though they would have been quite aware of the existence of their human mothers and fathers. Like them, Socrates is quite aware of his own parentage: "I am not born 'from oak or rock but from men, so that I have a family" (*Apology* 34d). I propose that instead of wanting the citizens to *really* believe this story, Socrates is drawing attention to what the Athenians already believed. The story *has happened* to them.

So why the pause? Why Glaucon's incredulity—"It isn't for nothing that you were so shy about telling your falsehood" (*Republic* 414e). Is Socrates also pointing out how ridiculous it is for the supposedly intellectually strong Athenians to believe such things? By presenting a familiar Athenian myth in this way, Plato draws our attention to how strange it is that Athenians, knowing full well their own personal histories, can be said to believe something like this for civic purposes. Perhaps Socratic mythmaking serves as an indirect elenchus here. On another level, however, perhaps Plato is

34. For more on the Theban elements of the myth, see Kateri Carmola, "Noble Lying: Justice and Intergenerational Tension in Plato's *Republic*," *Political Theory* 31, no. 1 (February 2003): 54–55.

35. Nicole Loraux, *Born of the Earth: Myth and Politics in Athens* (Ithaca: Cornell University Press, 2000), 17. See also for a discussion of the implications of autochthony on women's position in Athenian society.

also pointing out that the citizens of the callipolis do not need to literally believe this story any more than the Athenians already really believe that they came from inside the earth, rather than from their human mothers' bodies.

The actual content of the story is also worth consideration. The myth is most commonly assumed to provide a call to the citizens of the city for unity. Myths of autochthony would be most recognizable to fifth-century Athenians in the form of funeral orations (*epitaphios logos*). This genre of speechmaking, which would have been all too familiar to Athenians in the midst of the Peloponnesian War, often drew on autochthony as a way to justify the sacrifices made and to mitigate the pain generated (Monoson has demonstrated the importance of funeral orations for Athenian democracy).[36] This is precisely what Socrates seems to hope the myth will do— lead to strong, unified citizens ready to defend the land as if it were their own common mother. The prevention of murderous civil strife certainly seems to be an almost overwhelming concern of Plato's, understandable given what he witnessed over the course of his own life. But Plato has Socrates critique the same myth in a proposed funeral oration in the *Menexenus*.[37] Moreover, as we will see, positive images of diversity among the citizens are another important part of the story told in the *Republic*. First, however, we should consider the remainder of the myth—the division of the citizens according to metals in their souls.

The pairing of the story of autochthony with this second part seems odd because autochthony was one reason for political equality among Athenians, while the division of citizens legitimates political inequality.[38] Because of the second part, the entire myth is often assumed to legitimate an authoritarian society ruled by the "best." But the second part of the myth, like the story of autochthony that precedes it, echoes Athenian culture in ways that call a straightforward reading of the myth into question. First of all, the Myth of the Metals recalls Hesiod's *Works and Days*.[39] Like the Myth of the Metals, *Works and Days* splits humanity into several metallic races—gold, silver, bronze, and iron. Socrates later makes an explicit refer-

36. See Monoson, *Plato's Democratic Entanglements*, chaps. 3 and 7.

37. For more on the importance of the *Menexenus*, as well as its relation to the *Gorgias*, see Salkever, "Socrates' Aspasian Oration."

38. Loraux, *Born of the Earth*, 34.

39. Hesiod, *Theogony and Works and Days* (Oxford: Oxford University Press, 1988). Hereafter referred to parenthetically as *WD*.

ence to the fact that the races are both "Hesiod's and your own" (546e). Rather than define various groupings of human beings alive today, Hesiod identifies the gold race of men who "lived like gods, with carefree heart, remote from toil and misery" (*WD*, 40). The gold race died out, becoming *daimons* (supernatural beings), and was succeeded by the silver race. The silver race was arrogant and unrestrained, eventually destroyed by Zeus for their lack of respect for the gods. Then came the bronze race, so violent and war-loving that they destroyed each other. This group was followed by the heroes, and then by the current group of humans, the iron race, destined to toil and finally to be destroyed for their myriad faults—"They will cease to respect their ageing parents . . . one will sack another's town, and there will be no thanks for the man who abides by his oath or for the righteous or worthy man" (*WD*, 42). Like Athens during the later Peloponnesian War, Greeks will turn against one another, unwilling to justify their actions, calling good bad and bad good.[40] Hesiod laments his own status as a member of the iron race: "Would that I were not then among the fifth men" (*WD*, 42). The gold race enjoyed the most perfect human existence— free from want and worry, while the iron race is tragically susceptible to human flaws—jealousy, arrogance, deception. The nostalgia for an earlier and more perfect time was a common motif in Athenian discourse, and was parodied not only in the *Republic* but also by Socrates' contemporary Isocrates.[41]

There are multiple echoes of Hesiod's story in the *Republic*. Like Hesiod's gods, Plato must wipe the slate clean to implement the callipolis (501a; 540e–541a). All those too imprinted by the current state of things are exiled (540e–541a) (which then obviates the question of how to get people to believe the story), while any imperfect or illegitimate children are left to die (460c). In both works, the story of the ideal society is intertwined with violence and destruction.

Plato's myth is also told within a larger work (*Republic*) that recalls Hesiod's in certain ways. Brothers play prominent roles in both works— Hesiod's poetry is addressed to his lazy brother, who desires success with-

---

40. The contrast with warring Athens and Callipolis is made clearer in 469b–471c, where Socrates describes the proper rules of conduct among Greeks, which should be more like that between family members than true enemies.

41. For more on Isocrates' parody, see Harding, "Comedy and Rhetoric," 206. The *Phaedrus* alludes to both such nostalgia for the past (250d) and to Socrates' relationship to Isocrates (278e and 279b). For more on Athenian nostalgia, see Hansen, *Athenian Democracy*, 297.

out working for it. Glaucon (and perhaps Adeimantus) is not lazy, but desires a sort of easy success—sure knowledge of how to succeed in politics. Glaucon is willing to follow Socrates' argument a bit too easily—"That's my opinion anyway, now that I hear it from you" (530b)—while Socrates tries to push him to move forward on his own—"You won't be able to follow me any longer, Glaucon" (533a). Like Hesiod, Glaucon laments his distinctly human existence, wishing instead for the transcendence that accompanies gold status. Like Hesiod's gold race, the gold souls of the callipolis will become superhuman *daimons* at death (469a). Socrates claims a sort of divine inspiration (that only directs him negatively), yet he still requires his particularly arduous brand of philosophy to live. No one, including Plato's teacher, can escape the toil of being human. The separation of the human and the divine was one of the great themes of tragedy in ancient Greece, and Plato reiterates this familiar theme here in the *Republic.* The juxtaposition of Socrates' mythic picture and Athenian literary tradition should throw the straightforwardness of the telling of the myth into question. As humans, we cannot return to the age of the gold race, content and peaceful. That too is a myth, a dream of a divine and impossible existence.

Thus the Myth of the Metals would not have sounded completely foreign to Athenians. It would be one way to understand the need for civic unity and the human inability to exert control over others' destructive behavior. After telling the story, Socrates doesn't belabor the point but says, "Let's leave this matter wherever tradition takes it" (415d). He and Glaucon doubt whether they could convince people that the story is true, but perhaps it would take hold after a generation or so. The citizens alive now would compare the story to their own experience and not believe; but the distance provided by time might make the story believable, just like Hesiod's story of the creation of humanity or Athenian autochthony. But the stories remain falsehoods, incredible ones that the interlocutors cannot understand how anyone might actually believe. Except that they (sort of) believe such things themselves. Socrates' ambivalence frames the story—it might have happened (he doesn't firmly deny that it has or hasn't), and he wants to move on once he's told it. The episode is not one of serious conspiracy or planning. Instead of placing himself as a staunch proponent of aristocracy, Plato here manipulates the existing discourses in democratic Athens to criticize the current state of Athenian political life.

If the noble lie is not a straightforward myth intended for social control, what is the point? Part of what's interesting about myth is that it often contains a kernel of truth. What is true about the Myth of the Metals? According to Cole, metaphors were more common for the ancients than abstractions; and autochthony was one way of rephrasing as metaphor the problem of civic unity.[42] Funeral orations and the Panatheneum, two occasions at which the myth of autochthony often played a prominent role, served to solidify the bonds of friendships and loyalty that kept the polis intact. Given the enormous effort it took to enact Athenian democracy, it should not come as a surprise that the polis went to great lengths to keep the city unified. Cleisthenes' reform of the *demes* (based on location—soil—rather than familial relations), the *dokimasia* prior to one's acceptance as a citizen, and the mechanisms in place to punish or exile those who disrupted the unity of the polis were formal mechanisms meant to maintain civic solidarity. Autochthony is the myth that complements these practices.

At the same time, Plato, through Socrates, recognizes the limits of civic solidarity. The proposed callipolis is intensely unified and organized along homogenous lines, and the second part of the myth provides an image of undisrupted social control. But the community that discusses the callipolis—Socrates, Glaucon, Thrasymachus, Adeimantus—remains heterogeneous and boisterous.[43] At the same time, this discursive community will come to an end, with the interlocutors soon trying to kill one another in real life.[44] Like Oedipus's inability to recognize difference and similarity, the *Republic* is itself a dramatic telling of the problem of recognition in a political context. Differentiation remains and is crucial to the city, yet also poses a threat to it. Socrates himself differentiates between individuals—he is attracted to specific individuals, he has a family.[45] And while power may not be spread evenly in this discursive community, Socrates invites everyone to talk, to philosophize—everyone is encouraged to be a ruler of themselves. The city remains composed of distinct individuals, yet these individuals must remain bound together somehow. The differentiation that

42. Cole, "Oath Ritual," 228.
43. See Nichols, *Socrates and the Political Community.*
44. Nussbaum, *Fragility of Goodness*, 137.
45. See Nichols, "The *Republic*'s Two Alternatives." Also, Socrates' statements in both the *Republic* (544d) and the *Apology* (34d) invoking Homer's "born from rock or oak" passage, as well as his doubts about Euthyphro's universalizing in *Euthyphro*, point to a person who is not at all sure about collapsing all familial distinctions. See Arlene Saxonhouse, "The Philosophy of the Particular and the Universality of the City: Socrates' Education of Euthyphro," *Political Theory* 16, no. 2 (May 1988): 281–99.

exists in Athens—the democratic city full of all types of speech—is the city that allows Socrates to exist for seventy years, but one in which speech has also begun to lose its meaning. Athens is a city worshipping new, foreign goddesses, making deals with old enemies—the civic identity has begun to unravel; but it is also a city that takes its vitality at least in part from its openness and its diversity. Tradition is respected both no longer and too much. By presenting this particular pastiche of traditional myths—one myth that simultaneously celebrates and criticizes the foundations of civic unity, one recognizing and warning against dreams of godliness and total similarity—Plato pushes Athenians to think about the tightrope between these various poles. Civic unity can be achieved through violence if necessary—the Thirty, with their scrutiny of the citizenship rolls and violent purging of the city, are an obvious example. Likewise, putting the "best" people in charge may be a wonderful idea—and certainly is more analogous to contemporary representative democracy—except that it also turns out to be a dangerous fantasy when pushed too far. The problem of diverse groups of people living together in a polity remains, only exacerbated by violent attempts to master it.

It is also important to remember that the myth is a *lie*, explicitly presented as such. But it is also a lie in that it misrepresents the solution to the political problems facing the Athenians. While the myth appears to settle disputes about the meaning of equality for Athenians, it concomitantly obliterates politics from civic life. The falsity is especially clear when we consider the events surrounding Plato's writing of the piece—the rule of the Four Hundred and the Thirty—solutions to the problem of equality that Plato has seen fail. Moreover, the myth reiterates its own falsity and fragility. It claims a cultural product—education—as a natural outcome of mythical birth, eliding the great lengths to which people both inside the callipolis (the philosopher-kings) and outside (the interlocutors in the dialogue) go to develop their judgment. We also find that the myth, for all its violence and force, is, at best, a fragile solution to the problem. It does not provide the secure foundation for the callipolis that is hoped. The auxiliaries must be protected from all sorts of things, including drunkenness (403e), Corinthian *hetairai* (404d), and precious metals (416d–417b), because they could so easily forget their training and take to lives of vice. Socrates and his interlocutors admit that the elites are painstakingly created through strict training, rather than simply born of good stock (gold or silver). Thus, even an allegorical understanding of the myth as an ethically true description of the inequalities between people cannot suffice as a way to build an ideal state—there is no way to discern among the souls early on since their goodness turns out to be a matter of training. Later in the *Republic,* the Myth of Er will prompt more doubt about the Myth of the Metals and its message of inequality, for here we see the deep failure of the callipolitan education—that is, habit without philosophy would lead former guardians to choose tyranny over justice (619c–d). These lies and failures of the Myth of the Metals provoke unease with Plato's proposed solution, as well as with some of Athens's own mechanisms of civic solidarity. This response to the text can, in turn, serve a useful function, leading interlocutors and readers to reject the seemingly obvious solutions to such problems.

The Myth of the Metals also draws attention to the importance of myth and narrative for civic life. While Plato questions the Athenian belief in such stories, he also acknowledges the importance of stories for the development of judgment. Story takes into account our rational and emotional needs, which are never really distinct from one another, by (potentially) providing a moving narrative that calls on the reader or listener to engage the story. This engagement was part of the beauty of the Athenian theater.[46] Plato echoes this, devising stories that do not stand independently from their context, but which should be read as responses to the particular history and context of the polis. Myth can also set up the emotional connection by which we can begin to value things. For example, both the unease and the deep love of Athens provoked by the Myth of the Metals may help Athenian citizens commit more fully to the practices of civic accountability and individual judgment needed to ensure the quality of the democracy.

The narrative quality of myth provides needed attention to the particularities of human contexts. Thomas Heilke argues, in reference to Thucydides' work, that theoretical knowledge is insufficient for practical political life: "We require not only theoretical exposition, but narrative. That is, we require stories that integrate, contextualize, illustrate, and illuminate in those specific ways that theoretical analysis cannot."[47] The *Republic* itself is a story, designed to help readers develop practical skills and knowledge about politics, to draw them into a conversation about justice, just as we see happening with the interlocutors.

Returning to the problem of *myth-as-story,* we can also see that the

---

46. See Monoson, *Plato's Democratic Entanglements,* chap. 4.

47. Thomas Heilke, "Realism, Narrative, and Happenstance: Thucydides' Tale of Brasidas," *American Political Science Review* 98, no. 1 (February 2004): 136.

myth has a *paideiac* function. While only children believe stories in a straightforward way (378d–e) and Socrates points out the difficulty of getting adults to go along with his plans for mythmaking in the callipolis, the *Republic's* subtext is that stories have a deep and lasting effect on the human psyche. Consider Cephalus's fears of death: "When someone thinks his end is near, he becomes frightened and concerned about things he didn't fear before. It's then that the stories we're told about Hades, about how people who've been unjust here must pay the penalty there—stories he used to make fun of—twist his soul this way and that for fear they're true" (330d–e).

One function of the Myth of the Metals is to help alleviate this confusion. Jonathan Lear analyzes the discussion of poetry in the *Republic* and argues that its problem, for Socrates, lies in people's inability to recognize it as allegory.[48] Myth can teach, but the children (and adults) who take stories of gods and monsters literally miss the deeper meaning of the myth, as well as the fact that it has a deeper meaning. The situation is not remedied because it is impossible to reshape the early psychic effect of the myth by telling the person "it's just a story." The work was completed in childhood before the person could recognize the myth as a myth. Lear points to Cephalus's fears of the afterlife in his old age. Even though he knows the stories of Hades are not literally true, he cannot sleep at night for fear. Likewise, the problem in the Cave is that those who have not been turned around will persecute the others when informed that the images on the wall are only representations, not actual objects. Lear interprets the Myth of the Metals as a remedy to this problem. For him, the Myth of the Metals is a protophilosophical discussion meant to instill in hearers an ability to understand allegorically. The myth involves explaining to people that all their experiences thus far in life have been a dream: "I'll first try to persuade the rulers and the soldiers and then the rest of the city that the upbringing and the education we gave them, and the experiences that went with them, were a sort of dream" (414d). For the first generation, the myth is not really believed (415c–d); they recognize it as allegory, much like the interlocutors. Yet this recognition takes place amid fundamental disorientation about the nature of life; for Lear, this disorientation hinges on the theory of Forms, that is, people think the objects of their lives are the real

48. Jonathan Lear, "Allegory and Myth in Plato's *Republic,*" in *The Blackwell Guide to Plato's* Republic, ed. Gerasimos X. Santas (London: Blackwell, 2006), 25–43.

thing, not imitations of the Form. We do not, however, have to rely on the Forms to see this disorientation. While the first generation would recognize the Myth of the Metals as allegory, the Platonic irony here is that for those same citizens, the confidence that comes with recognizing the allegory as such would perversely limit their ability to see all the other ways in which they remain "captured" by their myths.[49] Likewise, the myth as Platonic irony here can be "a means for lulling the dialogues' readers into the very self-complacency it makes them denounce."[50] Both we and the interlocutors believe ourselves to have knowledge, lacking the self-awareness that we remain deeply ignorant.[51] In the interlocutors' case, they remain ignorant that they, as Athenians, already believe myths like the ones they would tell to the ignorant of the callipolis. Plato's inclusion of this myth, written in this particular way, should provide a warning to those of us who think we, of course, get it.

Lear also shows the result of the Myth of the Metals on subsequent generations of the ideal city. Here, the effect is less disturbing:

> Even as a surface story, the myth begins to teach the child to be hermeneutically suspicious of the other myths he has heard in childhood. After all, it's all been just a dream up till now. Thus one can think of the Noble Falsehood (told in childhood) as itself beginning to inculcate the capacity to recognize allegory as such. For it is an allegory told to us when we cannot recognize allegory as such but which *right on its surface* tells us that the other allegories we've already heard (and by hypothesis have not yet recognized as such) are really only dreams. In that way, the Noble Falsehood embeds an anti-fundamentalist message about all other myths: none of them should be taken literally.[52]

The myth then is a subtle critique of that childlike state in which the Athenians are currently living. Mythmaking in the *Republic* has a liberating and antifundamentalist message: trust no story as gospel truth. The Myth of the Metals can thus be seen as myth-as-story, designed and told

---

49. See the discussion of Platonic irony in Nehamas, *Art of Living*, 41–43, 45.
50. Ibid., 45.
51. For a similar argument regarding modern interpreters of Plato, see Michael L. Frazer, "Esotericism Ancient and Modern: Strauss Contra Straussianism on the Art of Political-Philosophical Writing," *Political Theory* 34, no. 1 (February 2006): 33–61.
52. Lear, "Allegory and Myth in Plato's *Republic*," 33.

to improve the citizens' capacities to treat all myths as myth-as-story. It is an attempt to teach a loyal skepticism of tradition and an appreciation of the ability of traditional cultural resources to transmit allegorical ethical truths, which remain up for discussion, even if Glaucon seems to accept the stories with minimal reservation. It is crucial to remember here that Plato created these characters (even if they are based on actual persons); he presents Glaucon's ready acceptance of the myths and plans for the callipolis as a form of Platonic irony, a reflection of our own ready willingness to feel superior to the "mob," those who would believe such silly stories.

At the same time, the telling of the Myth of the Metals is not a call to abandon myth or a complete condemnation of its effect on society. It also casts light on the role of culture and the power of story in political life. Socrates finds traditional poetry so dangerous not only because of its power to keep Cephalus up at night, but because the ethical messages of something with that sort of power should be carefully crafted, not the result of old moralities left unexamined. As rhetoricians have long argued, our language choices shape our moral choices by structuring our sense of the acceptable, of power, of fearsomeness, and so on; this, in turn, has profound effects on political life. By falsely dividing communication into the frank and the affective, we try to ignore something that nevertheless continues to influence deliberation—the various rhetorical effects of all speech, including the frank styles. Meanwhile, the particular emotive aspects of myth and story are not necessarily bad—they entertain, they can form a cultural legacy, they educate.

While distinct from myth, frank speech has its own emotional pull— after the dissatisfying abstract elenchus of Book 1 (which is one type of frank speech, in that it seems to lack rhetorical ornament), Glaucon believes that Thrasymachus has given up too easily, "charmed by you as if he were a snake" (358b). Socrates highlights the fact that the gulf between "reasoned argument" and the stories that here appear as myth may not be as great as we imagine (that is not to say that the differences in content do not matter). Instead, Plato's juxtaposition of the two modes underscores the point that all arguments should be recognized as charming stories, allegories that contain truth, narratives constructed by speakers to explain how they see the world. No argument is a complete or transparent map of our world and experience; certain details are omitted, others are highlighted, and the accounts—even the most "objective" and "frank"—reflect an ethical worldview. This is not to collapse the distinct effects of myth in the *Repub-*

lic with the effects of frank argument. But the danger of *parrhesia* is that it often denies that it also has this quality. It refuses to admit engaging in the sort of inspirational work of figurative modes. By denying what it in fact provides in some way, frank speech can leave us bored and disconnected, yet confused about the cause of our alienation from politics. Socrates' use of myth draws attention to the literary elements of human communication. By locating these criticisms of discourse within a story (the *Republic*) that contains stories, Plato devises his own *paideiac* text to inspire and develop the critical judgment of citizens, a capacity integral to the practices of democratic accountability. Without such a capacity, citizens cannot distinguish between "mere rhetoric" and rhetorical aspects of communication.

The noble lie, like an allegory, contains some kernel of truth. The Myth of the Metals in this specific deployment within the *Republic* is a call to an allegorical understanding of the bonds of civic unity amid differentiation. The goal of the *Republic* is to find justice in the human soul; the jump to the city is an attempt to think analogically, one which has too often been unquestioningly assumed to be meant earnestly and unproblematically. The various races of the Myth of the Metals are another iteration of division of the soul, told in a story form for "those lacking keen eyesight" (368d). How are we to be so sure that Plato intends the story as an opaque lie to be told in a truly ideal city given these echoes and incongruities? We are perhaps too quick to see hierarchies, passivity, and ignorance, when instead the *Republic* presents a narrated story of a dynamic discussion of the ways that myth shapes our commitments and lives. Like Socrates' interlocutors, we succumb to the temptation of superiority.

While it is important to be on guard against *myth-as-lies* and the dangers of factual untruths, we too often assume that the people who believe such things lack the agency to think for themselves and to actively contribute to the political life of the community. Yet we can think of examples in our own familiar setting. As Abizadeh notes, many Christians and Jews read Old Testament stories regularly and celebrate them in religious ceremonies.[53] However, those who do not share their faith do not necessarily think of all Jews and Christians as prisoners of false belief, as citizens with no understanding of the "true" facts of history. Instead, religious narratives of the past can provide cultural identity and ethical teaching (in addition to

53. Abizadeh, "Historical Truth," 297.

the historical truth it provides for some). For most believers, they are not "mere" stories, cynically discarded and trotted out for show; they are deeply important to their identities. Yet they are not necessarily uncontestable; this depends on the norms of the particular religious community, rather than on the fact that they are religious narratives.

While not a myth, considering the Allegory of the Cave alongside the mythmaking of the *Republic* can help us understand the purpose of myth in the dialogue. Like the Myth of the Metals, the Allegory of the Cave is used to demonstrate to people that many of their beliefs have no firm grounding. (This is not necessarily a problem—in Socratic fashion, it is a problem only when one thinks the foundations are secure.) Their beliefs are dream-like, their situations cave-like. The Allegory here is explicitly identified as an imaginary example to aid understanding: "Compare the effect of education and of the lack of it on our nature to an experience like this: Imagine human beings living in an underground, cavelike dwelling, with an entrance a long way up" (514a).

The explicitness with which the imaginary example is presented—it is not a story to be literally believed—reiterates the message of the myth, but without some of myth's more disturbing seductions. The appearance of the Allegory of the Cave alongside other myths in the *Republic* is Socrates' attempt to get his interlocutors to understand the allegorical nature of all such stories about justice and civic life. Juxtaposed with the Myth of the Metals and the Image of the Divided Line that immediately precedes it, the Allegory of the Cave is another attempt to understand Socrates' various arguments about knowledge, the duties of citizenship, and the difficulties of persuasion. These attempts are presented in different discursive modes, drawing attention to the partial and ultimately incomplete justifications for being just.

According to Socrates, "The power to learn is present in everyone's soul" (518c), even though the "majority cannot be philosophic" (494a). What is required is an individual turning of the soul, not simply a transfer of knowledge from teacher to a group of students, for there is no single answer that the teacher can pour into the student's head. This turning requires engaged and independent students. The problem is how to inspire people so that they care to learn. Early in one's education, this happens through music and poetry—with these subjects, one develops the habits necessary to continue on with education (522b). The Allegory of the Cave stirs people to learn, while also acknowledging the difficulties of the process.

Allegorical understanding comes with time—we are not born into it. Like-wise, the Allegory comes after the Myth of the Metals; we are moving forward in our own capacity to judge along with the movement of the dia-logue.

The Myth of Er

Like the *Gorgias*, the *Republic* ends with a myth. The Myth of Er is a response to the story of Gyges' ring from the start of Book 2; it is a story to counter another story. The Myth of Er claims that even if committing injustice improves one's material comforts on earth and no other person knows about it, one will still "pay" for injustice. Socrates tells the story of Er, a soldier sent back from the dead to report to those still living about the afterlife. (There is an echo of Homer and his story of Alcinous, again demonstrating how Plato drew on Athenian cultural traditions.)[54] In this story, Er sees the wicked paying tenfold for their earthly crimes. He also sees souls who are about to return to Earth choosing from various model lives—animals, heroes, tyrants, private citizens (617d–618b). It is here "that a human being faces the greatest danger of all. And because of this, each of us must neglect all other subjects and be most concerned to seek out and learn those that will enable him to distinguish the good life from bad and always to make the best choice possible in every situation" (618c). Because we will each have the choice of our next life's model, the good citizen who does not understand why he is good and who just happened to live in a just polity (i.e., the bronze and iron and silver people of the calli-polis) has no insurance against making a bad choice in the afterlife. It is not enough to be good, but one must understand the reasons for being so. Hence the need for philosophy. But if philosophy is so necessary, why does Plato end the *Republic* with a myth? The deployment of a myth at the end of such a long meditation on justice strikes many readers as peculiar—and much has been made of why Plato chooses to use a myth here. Is it a hedge against false belief for those who remain unconvinced? Is it a rhetorical flourish?

According to Luc Brisson, myth is used in the dialogues to convince those incapable of philosophy; it is "the discourse of and for the other."[55]

54. See Seery, "Politics as Ironic Community."
55. Brisson, *Plato the Mythmaker*, 11, 87.

Accordingly, one could argue that the Myth of Er occurs at the end of the *Republic* to make sure even those who failed to understand philosophical argument cannot praise injustice. Brisson discusses how Plato came to recognize the importance of persuasion based on the prospect of pain or pleasure and that the problem was not necessarily myth but the fact that philosophers did not control its fabrication and interpretation. In this view, myth is not an intricate component of philosophy, but a substitute for those unable to appreciate the "true" form of intellectual understanding. Myth is presented as a substitute for evidence. Yet this explanation of Socrates' use of myth too easily explains away his recourse to it. It also overlooks Socrates' religiosity; this is a man who seems to seriously believe in his *daimon* and who claims to believe many myths himself. That is, Socrates is not motivated to philosophize solely because of "rational" and fully explicable reasons. Socrates himself might then be "the other."

John Evan Seery argues that a Big Lie may in fact be necessary, but goes further to point out that all explanations of justice are necessarily humanly constructed accounts, crafted imperfectly to explain something for which precision and certainty are impossible goals.[56] "The book on the whole, up to this point . . . holds out the suggestion or promise that we can be exposed to enlightenment. The problem is, the book further suggests, we have to do it mostly ourselves."[57] The *Republic* is an invitation to study, not simply a picture of justice. Here we see the *Republic* as a "summoner," rather than a transparent exposition. The intention behind Socrates' use of myth is not as clear as Popper would have it; his relation to "truth" is ambiguous; he violates the model of the "rational" philosopher. He invites criticism for deploying myth. In these ways, his juxtaposition of myth and philosophy encourages the reader to consider the textual authority in a way that the philosophy alone could not. The *Republic* is full of different explanations of justice—mathematical (587c–588b), abstract (Book 1), mythic (Myth of the Metals, the Myth of Er), and allegorical (Allegory of the Cave). No single explanation is sufficient or firmly convincing. According to Bernard Freydberg,

> This attitude, clearly manifest in relation to myths, is also present
> in relation to all elements of the dialogues. It can be characterized

56. Seery, "Politics as Ironic Community."
57. Ibid., 243.

quite simply as the willingness to take something up respectfully and inquire as to its meaning and significance, whatever its source. It is not only the stance when faced with the charm of myths, but is the posture toward virtually all of the (normally considered) philosophical issues in the dialogues, e.g. the theory of forms, metaphysical and moral intellectualism, the immortality of the soul, and above all the ultimate worthiness of the *logoi* regarding each of these.[58]

At the same time, the stories and myths that one hears may have a deeper effect than we recognize. It is such stories of the afterlife that keep Cephalus awake at night. While Socrates sometimes mocks our willingness to believe, he himself believes in many stories, he loves to listen to them, he repeats myths he has heard from various sources, including foreign ones. Myth may be a way to soothe the misology that is the danger of the persistent state of ignorance in which we find ourselves; it is a way to fall in love with words and knowledge again, even after all the trouble they cause and their false promises. Myth explicitly recognizes the connection between our rationality and emotions—they are intertwined in us, just as they can be in myth.

Of course, the content of the Myth of Er is likely to provoke anxiety, for we find the familiar templates for living the good life called into question yet again. But the discomfort can be a partner to judgment, prompting us to reject the easy answers provided by tradition or good luck. In this way, emotional responses are an integral part of intellectual activity (rather than its opposite). The danger is that those experiencing the anxiety will reject judgment and instead demand certainty, resentful of Socrates' seeming obfuscations. But the dramatic arc of the *Republic* suggests that continued engagement can temper that anger and need, as we see the interlocutors become more comfortable with the seemingly endless investigation. At the same time, Glaucon's openness to questioning becomes a reliance on Socrates; he's going along, waiting patiently for the answer (in contrast to Thrasymachus's earlier anger or Glaucon's own early demands for answers). Yet the risk of choosing an unjust life pattern is ever present, as Socrates points out to Glaucon while recounting the myth: "It seems that it is here, Glaucon, that a human being faces the greatest danger of all" (618b–c). Perhaps

58. Freydberg, *Platonic Dialogues*, 25.

this is Socrates' final warning to Glaucon: start judging for yourself, damn it! The risk is daunting; Socrates counsels judgment rather than daring, again tweaking standard Athenian responses to such dilemmas. Thus the need for a new education in judgment, to "distinguish the good life from the bad and always to make the best choice possible in every decision" (618c–d).

The myths of the *Republic* also demonstrate that discussions often require the use of narrative elements to present the full picture. Arendtian storytelling offers an instructive parallel (again, myth is a category of story dealing with foundational or sacred matters). Although it is not literally true, myth, like story, is a human artifact that offers a relatively coherent narrative, organizing reality for the audience. Lisa Disch presents Hannah Arendt's mode as an alternative to the objectivist project, one that brings assumptions to the surface, acknowledges the situatedness of politics, and promotes engagement between text and reader.[59] It does not come from a privileged point of view, but from an acknowledged particular perspective. While myth writ large could be considered an attempt to speak as a final authority that rejects partiality, we can see it here as a tool used self-consciously to draw attention to problems of authority in speech and the importance of recognizing the various perspectives of any single problem. Myth often has characters and places that are meant to seem real. Discussion moves from abstraction to recognizable description. Politics becomes something we live (or can imagine living), not just conceive or compute.

Furthermore, the importance of what is typically thought of as philosophically extraneous ornament (myth, for instance) is highlighted by this interpretation. Standard interpretations point out that myth and story are more interesting and hold an audience's attention better than abstractions, as if we could do away with the myths in the *Republic* if only we had more mature interlocutors and readers. But for Arendt, certain events, as well as certain audiences, require a move outside conventional rhetorical modes. When writing about the Holocaust, Arendt consciously chose to use certain literary devices; otherwise, the event itself remained incomprehensible.[60] Furthermore, that the Nazis were so effective at remaking reality for the German public shook Arendt's faith that barbarity based on lies could be

59. Lisa Disch, "More Truth Than Fact": Storytelling as Critical Understanding in the Writings of Hannah Arendt," *Political Theory* 21, no. 4, (1993): 665–94. See also Young, "Communication and the Other."
60. See Disch, "More Truth Than Fact."

combated simply with exposure to the truth. Instead, she wanted to tell the story of totalitarianism in Germany in such a way that "does not compel assent but, rather, stirs people to think about what they are doing."[61] Because she did not view the Holocaust (or any political event) as a necessary result, this effort required the use of her own moral judgment. She uses story, hyperbole, and other devices to tell the history because this event could not be written about in any other way. An attempt to give a strictly "rational" interpretation would be disingenuous (not to mention ineffective); emotion and the moral judgments leading to emotion must already be bound up with the story.

At the same time, "reality" does not consist simply of one person's critical understanding of the myriad facts available. According to Arendt (and as I will elaborate further in Chapter 5), "The reality of the public realm relies on the simultaneous presence of innumerable perspectives and aspects . . . only where things can be seen by many in a variety of aspects without changing their identity, can worldly reality truly and reliably appear."[62] That is, the multiple perspectives of individuals *constitutes* the shared reality in which politics takes place. The use of both abstract argument and myth in the *Republic* helps us appreciate the multiple perspectives that constitute our reality; not only is there no Archimedean point of view from which to see reality, there are various modes of discussing that reality.[63] By appreciating the multiplicity of the *Republic,* we are better poised to appreciate the multiplicity of the actually existing democratic city. I do not mean to say that all perspectives are somehow equal or that we have no way to discern among competing views and facts. But accepting that some things are facts and others are not, or that some things are ethically appealing and others repugnant, should not tempt us into a belief that there are necessary and singular descriptions of those same facts and values.

Whether or not you agree that Plato and Socrates believe in the importance of diversity in modes of expression, the variations in mode of the *Republic* itself give us some relief from the sometimes stultifying force of frank speech. The latter form often leaves scant room for others in a discussion. Book 1 of the *Republic* leaves everyone dissatisfied, including Socrates, and Thrasymachus has not been convinced, only silenced, once he finds

61. Quoted in ibid., 671.

62. Hannah Arendt, *The Human Condition* (Chicago: University of Chicago Press, 1998), 57.

63. For more on this subject, see the work of Richard McKeon.

himself logically and rhetorically outmaneuvered.[64] The recuperation of argument and discursive accountability in the *Republic* requires recourse to other modes (although to draw a stark dichotomy between philosophy and myth would be to miss the point). Multiple ways of speaking are not only possible, but necessary. When understood as story, mythic speech is more open to disagreement and questioning than frank speech. Because they are not literal and because they often exist alongside a number of alternative versions, myths-as-stories can avoid the literalism that makes frank speech so dangerous for deliberation. It does not mean that we accept every story entirely, either, because they are obviously not exactly compatible; instead, this multiplicity helps us understand the nature of human social life. According to Wayne Booth,

> How do we manage to take all this seemingly conflicting "wisdom" seriously, without falling into absurd contradictions? We do so . . . both by acknowledging that all statements of truth are partial (these poetic claims are not unique in their partiality), and by embracing the very plurality that from other perspectives may seem threatening. We not only recognize that there are many true narratives; we celebrate multiplicity, recognizing that to be bound to any one story would be to surrender most of what we care for.[65]

At the same time, it is important to also recognize the dangers of narrative. Myth is story, and stories, as Socrates point out, can be too convincing. We may forget that a myth is but one story among many; indeed, we may even mistake it for a source of historical truth. As Disch puts it: "We believe that we have gotten to the facts of the matter when those facts can be recounted in story form. A well-told story produces this conviction by seeming merely to follow from events."[66] Coupled with the claim to sacred truth involved with some myths, the seduction can seem total. For some readers, myth becomes reality, and the fact that it was produced by human minds is forgotten. The imagery becomes too powerful, and we fail to remember that the story only offered one way to see the world. So there is

64. Mara, *Socrates' Discursive Democracy*, 40.
65. Wayne C. Booth, *The Company We Keep: An Ethics of Fiction* (Berkeley and Los Angeles: University of California Press, 1988), 344–45.
66. Lisa Disch, "Impartiality, Storytelling, and the Seductions of Narrative: An Essay at an Impasse," *Alternatives* 28 (2003): 264.

a tension here—a tension that cannot be erased, but must be confronted in each situation anew. Judgment is the key.

If we were to claim that narrative is necessarily and always "better" than abstract argument, we would give too much credit to those who would draw a dichotomy between the two. Of course, we can often superficially recognize one or the other; there are certain stylistic elements that separate them. They may share some of the same functions for different listeners, but they are also capable of accomplishing different things (especially in the context of the *Republic*). This was Arendt's attraction to storytelling. But myth and zero-degree tropes are more similar than we often acknowledge. Mathematics has its own *eros,* as does an action film, or a mythic story of political founding; we may be aesthetically attracted to algebra, or we may be attracted to poetry—each style and form has its own pull and audience. We do ourselves a disservice when we forget that "we were only playing and so [speak] too vehemently" (536b–c), sure of the authority of our discursive style. People identify with Plato's Socrates as philosopher-king or as ironist or as mythmaker, when we need to remember the ways that each role is bound up with the other.

The juxtaposition of myth and philosophy in the closing of the *Republic* forces us to consider the ambiguities of both genres. Both types of speech—abstract argument and myth—are alluring in their own ways, and the democratic citizen must be capable of dealing with both. Rather than opposites, myth and frank speech can be similar; for different individuals, one or the other may have unquestioned authority. The juxtaposition of myth and philosophy in the *Republic* gets the reader to think about textual authority in a way that abstract philosophy alone could not. Kathryn Morgan argues for an appreciation of this multivocality; myth and philosophy are not as inherently different as commonly thought. She critiques views in which myth simply adds interesting details to dry philosophy or takes up where philosophy ends. Instead, she reads philosophical myth as a style that "stands for and exaggerates the problematic aspects of language."[67] It draws attention to the difficulty of discerning true speech at all; myth leads us to ask if language is adequate to the quest for truth, for if the world of appearance is unstable, then so is language.

Morgan also argues that the changes in perspective entailed in Socrates' use of both forms is crucial to this task. The nesting of myth in philosophy

67. Morgan, *Myth and Philosophy,* 2.

forces the serious reader to question where on a myth-philosophy contin-
uum one stands at almost every point, reinforcing the idea that a stark
binary between the two is misleading. The effort calls on one's reason—a
philosophical endeavor—and, again, draws attention to issues of textual
authority. This attention is crucial. It destabilizes the connection between
truthfulness and truth claims by disrupting the unquestioned authority of
either style of speech. It forces those engaged in philosophy to deal with
problems of literary convention, removing the pretense of complete (and
good) transparency in speech. In these ways, myth again serves as a summoner, a call to judgment.

We most often read the myths as tools of deception, yet the manner in
which myth is deployed in the dialogues actually works against such an
interpretation.[68] If no authority can be trusted completely, then the listener
must exercise his or her own judgment concerning the material being presented. The memorization of analytical arguments is likened to reliance on
myth; it is not adequate to a democratic community founded on *logos*. In
the context of Socrates' criticism of the poets and the rhetoricians, it is a
warning against those who would claim to know the truth. It is not Socrates' own knowledge, or science, or even his daimon that can give people a
glimpse of this Form. By denying his own authority to transmit truths, yet
continuing his search for them, Plato's Socrates is acting as the antirealist.
Through this use of multivocality and the incongruity between the *logoi*
and *erga*, Socrates helps develop that capacity for judgment that citizens
need and mitigate reliance on the false certainty provided by both myth
and *parrhesia*. The Myth of Er makes plain this need for judgment; in turn,
judgment can help sustain a democratic character that neither panders to
nor claims complete autonomy from social convention.

How does "judgment" work? What is its relationship to politics? Isn't it
distinct from philosophy (and thus how does Socratic philosophy move us
toward it)? Standard views point to Socrates' discussion of the Divided Line
and the invisible world of Forms as the basis for philosophical knowledge.
In contrast, "judgment" concerns the world of appearances and things
about which we can deliberate—the *political*.[69] But philosophy as it is practiced in the *Republic* is not made up of a silent gaze on *eide*; the possibility
of a world of Forms is offered, but Socrates' own discussions follow a very

68. See, for example, C.D.C. Reeve, "The Lies of the Rulers," in *Philosopher-Kings: The
Argument of Plato's* Republic (Indianapolis: Hackett, 2006), 208–213.

69. Thanks to Jill Frank for helping me think through this problem.

different philosophical pattern. There may be universal first principles (such as a definition of "justice"), but Socrates never satisfactorily fills in the content and claims to remain ignorant of that content (although he does seem to live a just life). So even if there is a "philosophical judgment" distinct from "political judgment," the *Republic* tells us that the path to both is strikingly similar (especially since our understanding of both types of propositions remains tentative). Philosophy as we see it practiced in the *Republic* is a process of examination and as such may be closer to "political judgment" than to "Platonic" understandings of philosophy. Whether it is fully distinct from philosophy or not, the judgment described here requires a commitment to questioning everything, whatever the source. But the point is not necessarily endless talk (although endless talk is one result); the point is that we *choose* interpretations of reality, some equal, some better, some worse. One single story is not necessarily the only good one (again, this does not mean that there are not bad ones or that they are all equal). We must choose how to live and what to value. These choices are never certain; they form part of one's ethical background, the core values that frame one's life. We may choose to believe things we cannot prove or see for ourselves. These choices carry responsibility in any case. Neither Thrasymachus nor Cephalus pass muster because they rely too much on either one's freedom or one's embeddedness in culture; instead, one must judge for oneself, while tempering the tyrannical desire for complete autonomy. A belief in justice, grounded in the force of a human tradition celebrating justice, roots citizens. But the belief and tradition must be one that is practiced, discussed, and debated.

The *Republic* as Myth

Not only can we read the individual myths of the *Republic* to gain a better understanding of Plato's efforts to instill a type of judgment in his readers, but we can examine the *Republic* in its entirety. The Myth of the Metals and the Myth of Er are actually embedded in a larger *muthos* that sounds many of the same tones. Viewing the book in this way also allows us to better see the Arendtian aspects of the *Republic*, that is, its ability to "stir people to think" without providing certain answers. Like the "summoner," Plato's work offers multiple perspectives at the same time and calls on us to negotiate this terrain. To bring these multiple perspectives to light, it is useful to look at the *Republic* in its historical context.

The dating of the dramatic action of the *Republic* has long been problematic.[70] The dialogue appears to be assembled from several original texts, and any definite dating creates anachronisms. Generally speaking, the action takes place sometime between 432 and 404 B.C.E.; the Peloponnesian War has begun. Moreover, the *Republic* was written after the most cataclysmic events of the war—the plague, the disastrous Sicilian Expedition, and the oligarchies of the Four Hundred and the Thirty. While we may not know exactly when the action is supposed to take place, we do know that the period was one of great tumult in democratic Athens.

Because of this disorder, the setting of the *Republic* could signify either a loss of Athenian identity or assertion of it. It opens with Socrates recounting how he went down (*kateben*) to the Piraeus to see the Festival of Bendis with Glaucon (327a). Bendis was a Thracian goddess, probably imported to Athens to woo help from a Thracian king in the war against Sparta.[71] So there they are in the Piraeus, the center of the democratic resistance against the oligarchic Thirty, honoring the goddess of a foreign monarchy. Has Athens so lost its moral grounding that it is willing to forget its own heavenly patrons and look for military aid wherever it may be found? Could this be the same people that Pericles describes in his Funeral Oration as Athenians that "advance unsupported into the territory of a neighbor, and fighting upon a foreign soil usually vanquish with ease men who are defending their homes" (2.39)? And does this mean that *Republic* criticizes an already corrupt city by presenting an ideal one?

Perhaps. But the Piraeus also signifies Athenian openness. It is the seaport, the place where foreigners enter the city, where foreign ships bring outside goods and ideas to Athens. And this openness is a central part of what makes Athens great; again, according to Pericles, "We throw open our city to the world, never by alien acts exclude foreigners from any opportunity of learning or observing . . . we are the school of Hellas; and I doubt if the world can produce a man . . . graced by so happy a versatility as the Athenian" (2.39–41). When Socrates recounts his visit to the Piraeus, he says: "I wanted to say a prayer to the goddess" (327a). He does not seem critical or disdainful of the festival, but rather interested and respectful (or perhaps he is engaging in some mocking irony?). As Plato presents him here, Socrates is a model Athenian, curious about the world around him

70. For discussion, see Nails, *People of Plato*, 324–26.
71. Ibid., 324.

and wanting to see how the festival processions are carried off by both the Athenian and Thracian contingents. Rather than demonstrating the corruption of the city, perhaps the festival that opens the dialogue is a celebration of the *xenophilia* of Athens. So we are left with ambiguity from the start. What is Plato trying to accomplish with this particular setting?

The characters in the dialogue offer more context. After accosting Socrates and forcefully persuading him to join their company, they then meet the wealthy *metic* Cephalus, who is performing sacrifices. It is here that they begin to discuss justice. Socrates asks Cephalus about old age and its burdens. Cephalus seems to represent the old morality; Socrates characterizes his (Cephalus's) belief about justice as "speaking the truth and paying whatever debts one has incurred" (331c). Cephalus's wealth, it seems at the time, will allow him to die having paid his debts, made the proper sacrifices, and without having to cheat or lie to people. But Plato is setting up an irony: Cephalus later dies a ruined man, his son Polemarchus executed.[72] So is Cephalus doomed to be unjust because he has pinned his plans on his money instead of philosophy or citizenship? Is traditional morality useless? How does the father's religious practice affect the life of his son, Polemarchus, later forced to drink hemlock by the Thirty? Moreover, what does Polemarchus's presence as a *metic*, especially one whose name is derived from the Greek word for "war," mean for the discussion of civic unity in the dialogue?

Meanwhile, perhaps Thrasymachus represents the new teachings about justice. He is a visiting foreigner and is presented as Plato's stereotypical Sophist: he celebrates the boundlessness of power and the apparent ability of rhetoric to achieve it. Like the tyrannical man described by Socrates, Thrasymachus has discarded the old ways in favor of self-serving ideas about justice: "The old traditional opinions that he had held from childhood about what is fine or shameful . . . are overcome by the opinions, newly released from slavery that are now the bodyguard of erotic love and hold sway along with it" (574d). In Book 1, he is unaccountable and a danger to those around him. Like Athens during Thucydides' Melian Dialogue, Thrasymachus at first sees no need to explain himself and no binding reason that he should bargain with those weaker than he. Thrasymachus's character echoes the dangers in which Athens finds herself at the close of the war—ruled by brutal and self-indulgent oligarchs, unaccountable, and filled with false speeches.

72. Seery, "Politics as Ironic Community," 231.

162 THE POLITICS OF SINCERITY

Plato's brothers Glaucon and Adeimantus are two of the few "true" Athenian citizens in the dialogue. Glaucon plays the more prominent role in the dialogue; here is a young man who is eager to learn and apply his learning to the city. He wants autonomy, certain political answers, and plans to implement them; thus, many commentators read Glaucon as a threat to be contained.[73] He claims to share Socrates' faith in justice, but he cannot explain why (358c–d). Without firm conviction, Glaucon could become tyrannical: his portrait of the appeal of Gyges' injustice is convincing enough "to throw [Socrates] off the canvas and make [him] unable to come to the aid of justice" (362e). Like Oedipus, Glaucon craves both the freedom of living without boundaries (his name recalls Homer's Glaukon, who refused to explain his origins)[74] and the comfort of certain answers (it is Glaucon who presses Socrates for exact details about the social system of the callipolis, 450b–d). Glaucon is a member of the Athenian aristocracy, groomed for political power, and he seems to readily agree to Socrates' most revolutionary social plans in Book 5. When detailing the "three waves," it is Glaucon that Socrates refers to, hypothetically, as "their ruler" (458c–d), and it is Glaucon who wants to know exactly how to bring the callipolis about (471c–472d). Yet he is unlike the Thrasymachus of Book 1. He retains hope that there is a better way than either old or new moralities; that is, a better understanding of justice than unreflective acceptance of tradition or its complete rejection in favor of personal power. The *Republic's* drama revolves around Glaucon's confrontation with the problem of justice. Socrates' repeated failure to explain define justice to Glaucon's satisfaction should draw our attention to how insisting on such a definition can itself be dangerous and authoritarian. The *Republic* becomes less about justice than about the cultivation of a capacity for judgment suitable to the quest.

In addition to the particular historical moment and characters involved, the *Republic* also takes place in a particular discursive context. While *parrhesia* is explicitly mentioned only once (557b) and while the usage appears to be negative, the ideal of *parrhesia* forms a discursive background to the dialogue.[75] Socrates and the interlocutors attempt to practice *parrhesia*; they push each other to say the truth, to confront their opinions forcefully, free of deceptive intent, and with no care for the ridicule or contempt that might

73. See Gerald M. Mara, "Politics and Action in Plato's *Republic*," *Western Political Quarterly* 36, no. 4 (December 1983): 609, and Carmola, "Noble Lying," 40.

74. Carmola, "Noble Lying," 48–49.

75. See Monoson, *Plato's Democratic Entanglements*, chap. 6, especially pp. 165–78.

arise (345b; 367b; 368b–c; 414c–d; 426a; 449b; 473c; 507a; 509c; 516c–518; 536b–c). This is *parrhesia*, even if it remains unnamed. The negative reference to *parrhesia* (557b) is not to *parrhesia* per se, but to democracy's inability to discern between true and false speeches.[76] In a democracy, "isn't the city full of freedom and freedom of speech [*parrhesia*]? And doesn't everyone in it have the license to do what he wants? . . . Then I suppose that it's most of all under this constitution that one finds people of all varieties" (557b–c). The problem is not that the speeches are necessarily bad in a democracy, but that the city has all sorts of speeches, and the people are not able to identify the good ones. Monoson argues that "Socrates used this term [*parrhesia*] to enlist Athenian attachments to the ideal in order to reduce his interlocutors' suspicions of philosophy" and to get them to recognize the importance of philosophy for politics.[77] Without philosophy and its call to judgment, the city remains vulnerable and subject to the dangerous influence of those who would abuse *peitho* (persuasion) and manipulate the public.

But because the citizens are so accustomed to freedom, "if anyone even puts upon *himself* the least degree of slavery, they become angry and cannot endure it. And in the end, as you know, they take no notice of the laws, whether written or unwritten, in order to avoid having any master at all" (563d–e). Philosophy and political judgment could be seen as forms of slavery in a figurative sense, because they imply acknowledgment of some authority. This "slavery" ironically frees a person from the tyrannical impulses of the soul that has neither democratic judgment nor tradition— the "Thrasymachian" soul, so to speak. According to the dialogue, "Extreme freedom can't be expected to lead to anything but a change to extreme slavery" (564a). The danger is that "democracy, dismissing the unifying *eide*, means that nothing and no one is imprisoned in a form. Socrates extends this even to the level of language; in a Thucydidean twist, words unconstrained by definitions take on multiple meanings."[78] But even Athenian democracy must have some limits, or it will cease to be democratic.

At the same time, the lack of limits in Athens also allows Socrates to be Socrates. Without the freedom of Athens, without this "finest or most

76. Ibid., 173–75.
77. Ibid., 166.
78. Arlene W. Saxonhouse, "Democracy, Equality, and *Eide*: A Radical View from Book 8 of Plato's *Republic*," *American Political Science Review* 92, no. 2 (June 1998): 279.

beautiful of constitutions . . . like a coat embroidered with every kind of ornament" (557c), Socrates' practice of philosophy would likely have been prohibited sooner. Only Athens is the "School of Hellas." Philosophy was banned in Sparta, the city most often described by Athenians as a negative reflection of themselves. And while the democracy would ultimately put an end to Socrates, he was condemned by a small majority of his jurors at a very old age. Moreover, when the Thirty took control of Athens, Critias and Charicles briefly banned the teaching of the "art of words," supposedly to curtail Socrates in particular.[79] Socratic questioning is inconceivable under another type of regime, not least of all because the practices of demo-cratic accountability—that is to say, *dokimasia* and *euthunai*—lay the groundwork for Socrates' incessant questioning. So we again find textual tension—two visions of one context.

For all Athens's glory, the *Republic* shows the city as a *polis* in great danger. The traditional ways have been disrupted, the Sophists' revolution is pushing further and further, and the war with Sparta has divided the *demos*. Athens is a city of *parrhesia*, but one without the critical capacities necessary to replace the old moralities with something different from Thra-symachean desire and power. As Socrates asks: "Is there any greater evil we can mention for a city than that which tears it apart and makes it many instead of one?" (462a–b). In contrast to Socrates' usual emphasis on the particular and individual, we see here the importance of transforming the self into a member of a community through judgment.[80] To move back from the precipice of tyranny and dissolution, Athenians must develop these capacities for political judgment. To develop that capacity, Athenians must understand the limits of *parrhesia* and how our own perceptions of reality can be incomplete and misleading. Thus, they could learn to better, in Ron-ald Beiner's words, "appraise particulars without dependence upon rules or rule-governed technique," and find "release from the confines of private subjectivity since we can [I would add must] support our judgments with publicly adducible reasons or grounds."[81] Only through judgment can we form community without relying on the false hopes of mythic unity (as seen in a surface reading of the Myth of the Metals).

These currents and counter-currents of the *Republic* should push us to

79. Nails, *People of Plato*, 110.
80. For a related argument in terms of *phronesis*, see Hariman, "Prudence in the Twenty-First Century," 303.
81. Beiner, *Political Judgment*, 8–9.

think more deeply about any single and definitive interpretation of the work. The callipolis in words is built within this context of disintegration *and* greatness. Even if the words and actions of the dialogue did not contradict themselves as they often do, we should think twice about the ultimate meaning of the *Republic,* for the context in which Plato was writing is marked by extreme complexity—democratic and tyrannical, oligarchic and unwise, free and enslaved, traditional and innovative. Like Arendtian storytelling, the search for an "ultimate" meaning is quite at odds with my point here—the *Republic* challenges the reader to reflect on the difficulties of democratic speech, to continue deliberations, and to accept the lack of a settled position. When Plato's Socrates criticizes democracy, I believe he means it, but his criticism does not equal a complete rejection of citizenship in favor of philosophy. As Dana Villa argues, "For more than two thousand years the Western philosophical tradition has insisted upon the Platonic distinction between the philosopher and the citizen, elevating a *tension* to the status of an ontological difference."[82] Criticism and deeper reflection demonstrate engagement; Plato would not engage if the subject— democracy, rhetoric, mythic poetry, Thrasymachus, Glaucon—did not matter.

Accountability in the *Republic*

When Glaucon and Adeimantus reached adulthood in the real democratic city of Athens, they were able to address the Assembly. Glaucon did this to ill effect; not knowing what he was talking about, he was dragged from the *bema.*[83] To address the Assembly ideally required intellectual strength, courage, and a sense of shame. One must know when to speak and when to listen. The pride of addressing the Assembly must be tempered by political judgment. To quote Foucault from Chapter 2: "*Parrhesia* is a kind of verbal activity where the speaker has a specific relation to truth through frankness, a certain relationship to his own life through danger, a certain type of relation to himself or other people through criticism . . . and a specific relation to moral law through freedom and duty."[84] When one invokes *parrhesia,*

---

82. Villa, *Socratic Citizenship,* 299.

83. Robert W. Wallace, "Law, Freedom, and the Concept of Citizens' Rights in Democratic Athens," in Ober and Hedrick, *Demokratia,* 106.

84. Foucault, *Fearless Speech,* 19.

one brings a particular claim to one's speech. But when *parrhesia* becomes a trope, as is quite understandable given its appeal in a society fearful of deception and verbal manipulation, it becomes chatter. The fearlessness implied by *parrhesia* can become that of the tyrant, groundless, seeking out victory without listening or questioning or regard for the costs to democratic deliberation. While democracy contains all sorts of speech and its freedom—that is, its lack of limits—help define it as democracy, a persistent tension exists: to get the kind of discursive accountability needed to succeed, democracy requires the voluntary acceptance of a type of intellectual rule. The *Republic*'s mythmaking acknowledges our existence as a complex, needy, autonomous, and diverse people bound together in a political community. It is highly critical of power exercised in the absence of a thoughtful weighing of perspectives or options, deployed only in the service of more power. The *Republic* also helps develop our ability to treat myth-as-story not as "mere" story, but as constitutive and nourishing allegories, which require reflection.

At the same time, we cannot completely avoid the possibility of deception in politics. While its effects can be mitigated, we cannot prohibit others from trying to manipulate speech if they desire to do so. Democracy is defined by its freedom from such control. The problem becomes how to equip citizens with the intellectual tools and courage to throw shameless speakers from the *bema*, while at the same time encouraging citizens to listen to critical speeches that they don't necessarily want to hear. The *Republic* helps to do this, while also acknowledging the limits of such an endeavor. It presents a variety of images of justice; these myriad metaphors offer something for everyone—the mathematical minded, the abstract thinker, the story-lover, the traditionalist—while also exposing them to other styles. In each case, the individual is encouraged to care for his own capacity to judge. Reading the *Republic* calls on our intellectual capacities, pushing us to identify what is good about any particular speech based on the deep context. We learn that our rationality is intertwined with our emotions—that the two dimensions of our personality are inseparable and that intellectual judgment is a matter of understanding and harmony rather than banishment. We begin to understand that all speech contains its seductions and risks. The variety of metaphors for justice helps us understand how a variety of perspectives is crucial to any attempt at a full description of human experience and needs. Appreciating these points can lead to stronger citizens, more able to confront the challenges of human political endeavors.

At the same time, the possibility of failure is ever present; we may never learn to differentiate between types of myth. We may take our stories too literally. This potential for failure does not mean that we should retreat from political life. It is, however, a cost of being political beings, hopefully mitigated by our love of this world, of our own Athens and the Laws.

The processes of accountability in Athens—the *eisangelia, dokimasia, euthunai, ephesis, graphe paranomon, antidosis,* jury service, ostracism, and even social gossip—were institutions that served as a check on human failings. But they also required judgment to be useful to the democracy. Bringing spurious charges against a fellow citizen caused dangerous distractions from the affairs of a democracy already threatened from many quarters. Of course, not bringing charges or speaking out could be similarly dangerous. Listening to the wrong speakers or following the loudest counsels was likewise destructive. The members of a real democracy are all different and experience reality differently. These differences lead to the cacophony of democratic deliberation; there is an infinite variety of speech. Sincerity and *parrhesia* are meant to help us sort out that cacophony and make better judgments. Yet they are too simple to really capture what we want in democratic accountability because they limit the room for judgment by blinding us to important alternative possibilities. Instead, our openness to the cacophony can be a critical part of our democratic experience, one that, when coupled with judgment, strengthens democracy. The multiple messages of the *Republic,* and the tension between these messages, helps us to understand this.

The *Republic*'s multiplicity makes it a summoner, a thing that awakens understanding. The *Republic* itself is a myth, a story that contains both true and untrue bits, leaving the sorting to us, threatening us with frustration and misology. In these ways, it reflects the political world in which we live. The dialogue is also about *parrhesia,* speaking courageously and truthfully. But like myth, *parrhesia* can also be an amalgam of fact and fiction. The appeal of a discourse beyond power, beyond emotion, fixed only by rationality, is, like the philosopher-kings, alluring. But set in the context of the *Republic,* we can also see that they are dangerous hopes.

Of course, we do not want to give up on the importance of factual truth in politics. We want to be able to hold one another accountable. If all speech may be mythic and ironic in its own ways, and judgment is crucial for discerning the usefulness of a particular utterance, what are the criteria for this judgment? Up to this point, the discussion has focused on trying to dislodge the unquestioned place of sincerity in deliberation, using Plato's dialogues as a way to examine the complexities of this problem. But once we appreciate the problem and probe deeper into the rhetorical context, what should we look for? Why not look for an authentic sincerity that seems to underlie apparent divergences from the ideal, like irony and myth-making? Haven't I collapsed false sincerity (like Machiavelli's or Cleon's) with the possibility of true sincerity?

These last two chapters emphasize the strangeness of Plato's Socratic dialogues and Socrates' role as *parrhesiastes*. Socrates fails the strict test of a frank speaker; his irony and his mythmaking cast suspicion on him—so much so that he is eventually declared an enemy of the city. Most commentators, from Habermas to Foucault, would argue that one's consistency and intentions are the key to this problem. While the Athenian jury executed Socrates, we think we would likely know better, able to judge his words smartly, alongside his remarkable consistency in action over time. Thus, the idea is that we should try to figure out Socrates' true intentions—why don't I just lay out the criteria by which irony and mythmaking can be judged as sincere and well-intentioned? Chapter 1 also called into question the usefulness of sincerity as a predictor of democratic quality, as well as our ability to judge it in people. These last two chapters then further elaborated these arguments, urging us to rethink our praise of Socrates as either a model *parrhesiastes* or a deliberative authoritarian, as well as detailing how the dichotomies between sincerity/insincerity and truth/myth are appealing but false. Thus, my hesitation to provide such criteria. Moreover, we should take seriously the effort that the Athenians put into trying to figure out and establish Socrates' "true" motivations for his efforts in Athens; surely, many of those who convicted Socrates believed that they saw through Socrates' assertions and into his corrupt and corrupting true self. But there are other reasons as well. In the next chapter, I offer a deeper explanation of why the search for one's *true* intentions is a dangerous distraction from the very necessary and very difficult task of political judgment.

BEYOND SINCERITY: TRUTH, TRUST, AND JUDGMENT IN DEMOCRATIC LIFE

At the close of 2004, U.S.-led efforts in Iraq seemed bogged down in bad news; the number of U.S. and Iraqi causalities crept steadily upward, revelations of torture in both Iraq and the U.S. base in Cuba continued to surface, while prewar assumptions about the military capabilities of Iraq and its connections to al Qaeda had been shown to be false. As the situation worsened, criticism of U.S. defense secretary Donald Rumsfeld mounted. The secretary was seen as indifferent to the troops on the ground, ignoring officers' advice, misjudging troop strength, and offering a pseudo-scientific (and ultimately false) explanation when asked why personnel carriers had not been outfitted with protective armor ("It's essentially a matter of physics. . . . It's a matter of production and capability of doing it").[1] Amid the controversy, reports surfaced that Rumsfeld had used an "autopen" to sign the condolence letters sent to families of dead soldiers. Once this came to light, polls showed that a majority of Americans wanted him to resign, and Senate leaders from both sides of the aisle called on President Bush to replace him.[2] Rather than explain why Rumsfeld's miscalculations and errors did not warrant his resignation, President Bush defended Rumsfeld's heart and inner thoughts: "I know Secretary Rumsfeld's heart. I know how

1. AP, "Controversy Continues Over Rumsfeld Armor Question," December 9, 2004. In response, military contractors told reporters that they could increase production, but had not been asked or paid to do so.

2. AP, "Bush Defends Embattled Rumsfeld as 'a Caring Fellow,'" December 20, 2004; AP, "Bush Defends Rumsfeld, Says He's 'Doing a Fine Job,'" December 20, 2004; AP, "Rumsfeld Passionately Defends Himself," December 23, 2004.

much he cares for the troops."[3] Bush explained, "I have heard the anguish in his voice and seen his eyes when we talk about the danger in Iraq and the fact that youngsters are over there in harm's way."[4] What seemed to matter most was that Rumsfeld meant well—his sincerity was impeccable as far as Bush was concerned. Considering that the public seemed to be most outraged at the autopen revelation (rather than the torture scandals or prewar intelligence failures), this move was the most effective response to a public obsessed with sincerity. The result, however, was to marginalize discussion of Rumsfeld's performance and command of the facts; the quality of his intentions and the character of his soul were, according to the commander-in-chief, the most important criteria by which to judge his performance.

Unfortunately, the following year gave us no shortage of examples of the obsession with personal sincerity in politics. When nominating Harriet Miers, for a seat on the U.S. Supreme Court, President Bush closed his introduction by stating, "I've known Harriet for more than a decade. I know her heart."[5] A few months later, FEMA director Michael Brown asserted his sincerity amidst the post-Katrina controversies: "I got to tell you, in all sincerity my heart goes out to those people, and I am determined, absolutely determined, to speed this thing up, make this thing work and get the aid to those people."[6] However, rescue and recovery efforts in New Orleans continued to stall; Bush eventually removed Brown from the post. Meanwhile, rapper Kanye West proved that administration opponents were similarly concerned with what goes on in politicians' hearts. Speaking at a televised Hurricane Katrina fundraiser, West complained, "George Bush doesn't care about black people."[7] First Lady Laura Bush responded with an assertion of goodwill: "I mean I am the person who lives with him. I know what he is like, and I know what he thinks, and I know how he cares about people."[8] This obsession with sincere intentions is not limited to the

3. AP, "Bush Defends Embattled Rumsfeld as 'a Caring Fellow.'"
4. Ibid.
5. Office of the White House Press Secretary, "President Nominates Harriet Miers as Supreme Court Justice," October 3, 2005, http://www.whitehouse.gov/news/releases/2005/10/20051003.html/ (accessed January 10, 2006).
6. Michael Brown, interview on Nightline, ABC News, September 1, 2005, http://www.dallasnews.com/sharedcontent/dws/news/katrina/rescue/stories/090305dnnatkattrans.1f527f23.html/ (accessed January 10, 2006).
7. CNN, "First Lady: Charges That Racism Slowed Aid 'Disgusting,'" January 9, 2005, http://www.cnn.com/2005/POLITICS/09/08/katrina.laurabush/index.html/ (accessed January 10, 2006).
8. Ibid.

United States. In Britain, Tony Blair has been the most outspoken advocate of his own good intentions; according to David Runciman, "One of the things that has united all critics of the war in Iraq, whether from the left or the right, is that they are sick of the sound of Tony Blair trumpeting the purity of his purpose, when what matters is the consequences of his actions."[9] Meanwhile, "he has not shirked from the questioning the motives of his opponents, from the wicked Saddam, to the malicious French, to the self-serving Tories, to the cynical media."[10] When popular discourse focuses on the quality of actors' innermost intentions and whether or not they are "good" people, it is not surprising that attention to actual governance takes a back seat.

This move to interior moral qualities is an integral part of hyper-sincere modes of speaking. By invoking one's sincerity, even in a coded way (for example, using folksy grammar or by making fun of intellectuals or the French), we learn to perform truth-telling, all the while claiming to have removed performance from politics. We move politics from a discussion of policies and actions to a discussion of true intentions and authentic goodwill. By refocusing attention on the actor's supposed authenticity, speakers circumvent issues of fact and ethics.[11] Politics becomes a display of intimacy, rather than a discussion of public matters, and the political realm is marked by melodrama and mistrust.[12] It seems that in the thirty years since Richard Sennett first criticized these tendencies in *The Fall of Public Man*, the situation has not changed very much:

> In modern politics, it would be suicide for a leader to insist: forget about my private life; all you need to know about me is how good a legislator I am or executive I am and what action I intend to take in office. Instead, we get excited when a conservative French President has dinner with a working-class family, even though he has raised taxes on industrial wages a few days before, or believe an American President is more "genuine" and reliable than his

9. Runciman, *Politics of Good Intentions*, 33. See also Sullivan, *Conservative Soul*, 170.
10. Ibid., 42.
11. Thomas Frank argues, and I agree, that this has been one of the basic tools of the "backlash" conservatism in recent years. See Frank, *What's the Matter with Kansas? How Conservatives Won the Heart of America* (New York: Metropolitan Books, 2004), especially chap. 10.
12. For more on this tendency, see Alan Wolfe, *Does American Democracy Still Work?* (New Haven: Yale University Press, 2006), chap. 2, especially p. 37.

disgraced predecessor because the new man cooks his own break-
fast.[13]

Political theorists extolling the importance of sincerity in political deliberation and denigrating rhetoric exacerbate the problem. Both popular and academic discourse lauds this personal transparency, encouraging people to not
just *appear* in public, but to authentically *be* who they *really* are.

Chapter 1 detailed the dangers of sincerity for political deliberation, con-
centrating specifically on contemporary manifestations of hyper-sincerity.
By centering politics on the moral interior of political actors, the emphasis
on sincerity can stifle democratic deliberation. What is left to discuss in the
face of such trustworthy men? Because the discourse ethics advocated by
some deliberative democrats highlights the sincerity of speakers, deliberative theory currently offers no satisfactory way to critique this phenomenon. At the same time, there are strong reasons to search for an ethic that
could guide deliberations and ensure the accountability of speakers. As we
see in both ancient Athens and the contemporary scene, institutions of
accountability coupled with widespread citizen equality provide the foundation for democracy by offering us a nonviolent and relatively cooperative
way to deal with our interdependence. The question then becomes how to
conceive of an alternative that offers the possibility of democratic accountability *and* a way to critique hyper-sincerity, while also rejecting the impossible demand for interior transparency that would effectively end political
judgment.

In the previous chapters, I argued by that by returning to ancient Athens
and Socrates' place in it, we might find a distant mirror that would help
unsettle our own presuppositions about the character of democratic speech.
Chapter 2 began constructing this mirror by examining the Athenian
mechanisms of accountability, paying special attention to its logocentric
focus and the place of *parrhesia* within it. I concluded Chapter 2 by looking
at the ways in which *parrhesia* was tamed, becoming a cliché of Assembly
debate that served to shut down deliberations. Chapters 3 and 4 examined
the Platonic Socrates' response to the taming of *parrhesia*. While the culture of democratic accountability remained an important force that pushed
Socrates and interlocutors to continue discussion, it also became apparent
that Socrates subverted *parrhesia* in various ways. Chapter 3 began the task

13. Richard Sennett, *The Fall of Public Man* (New York: W. W. Norton, 1974), 25.

of filling out this characterization of Socrates, showing how his use of irony critiqued the type of *parrhesia* embodied by Callicles in the *Gorgias,* while encouraging the interlocutors to join in a discussion marked by diverse rhetorical styles. At the same time, Socrates' irony reminds us both of Socrates' own failings and the difficulties of deliberative projects. Chapter 4 extended this analysis to include Socrates' mythmaking in the *Republic.* Socrates highlighted the literary qualities of all discourse, as well as the role of tradition and emotion in political discussion. Rather than serve as a justification for lying or an exemption from *parrhesia* when dealing with "inferiors," Socrates' mythmaking in the *Republic* acknowledges the fundamental importance of a diversity of perspectives for democracy, which can be threatened by the claims to authority evoked by certain usages of *parrhesia.*

These two chapters pointed to an alternative way, one grounded by a commitment to democratic accountability that is also capable of responding to the (mis)appropriation of a democratic ideal like *parrhesia* or sincerity. Instead of a straightforward commitment to *parrhesia,* we see in the dialogues a need to confront the difficulties of deliberation from *within* discursive practices, rather than attempting to ground them from without. Still, Plato's Socrates cannot answer all our questions. We see little decision-making in the dialogues—the need for political judgment remains circumscribed, limited by the fact that we are witnessing private conversations about politics among a small group of acquaintances and friends. With the exception of the *Apology* and the *Crito,* Socrates and his interlocutors do not face decisions with immediate political effects. Moreover, while the parallels between Athens and the contemporary scene can be striking, the context is radically different. There is no television, no Internet, no hundreds of millions of citizens from diverse backgrounds, no reliance on representation. While we may gain insights into politics from the dialogues, they cannot offer a sufficient model for our times. Finally, while I have challenged some aspects of this view, Plato's Socrates retains a focus on the interior life that might still inadvertently encourage the politics of sincerity (even as the dialogues highlight the difficulties inherent in such a practice). While the dialogues may be, in Gary Shiffman's words, "formidable cognitive therapy,"[14] this is largely *pre-political* work—that is not to say that

14. Gary Shiffman, "Deliberation versus Decision: Platonism in Contemporary Democratic Theory," in Fontana, Nederman, and Remer, *Talking Democracy,* 110.

this individual soul-work is not critical to the success of the polity, but that it cannot be a complete model for how to deliberate in public settings.[15]

Thus, the dialogues never fully answer the question at hand: how are we then supposed to talk and listen to one another in our own democracy? If one's sincerity shouldn't be a political question, does that leave the political arena full of hypocrites and liars? I am not saying a politician's commitment to truth is irrelevant. I am saying that emphasizing sincerity as a critical ideal is a poor way to judge the quality of our discourse. Like the Athenians, we can too easily fall prey to the sort of pandering that we hoped our ideals would help us avoid. Moreover, the danger of psychological and physical violence that has often accompanied searches for the "authentic" person is deeply worrisome.

I argue here that an Arendtian political ethic provides a better alternative to the sincerity ethic, retaining the focus on the legitimating function of discourse in democracy, while also highlighting individual judgment and citizen plurality. It enriches our understanding of deliberative democracy by helping us appreciate that we have nothing more than appearances on which to rely when it comes to politics and by valuing the unpredictability of human action and ever present possibility of new beginnings. Arendt's vision of politics also pushes us to continuously solicit the active presence of others, without whom we can have no sense of reality, highlighting the tension between "thinking for oneself" and living with others in a democracy, a tension only confronted—never resolved—through judgment. By pushing the realm of appearances to the fore and counseling against a search for hidden true intentions, a more Arendtian approach may help alleviate the deleterious effects of clichéd hyper-sincere speech, as well as the citizen apathy and cynicism that marks the contemporary scene.

The Political Stage

"For us, appearance—something that is being seen and heard by others as well as by ourselves—constitutes reality."[16] What makes Hannah Arendt especially appealing for the problem at hand is her emphasis on the realm

---

15. For more on these criticisms of Socrates, as well as arguments against them, see Villa, *Socratic Citizenship*, chap. 1, especially pp. 52–55.

16. Arendt, *Human Condition*, 50; henceforth cited as *HC* in the text.

of appearances for politics.[17] In her view, political life should focus only on this arena—the public one, the one in which action takes place in the presence of others. Arendt divides human activities into three categories—action, work, and labor. Democratic politics at its best is action, which includes both speech and what we more commonly think of as action; it reveals our "unique distinctness" (*HC*, 176), while labor and work relate to the facts, respectively, that we are biological entities who require attention to our physical being and beings who create artificial things to make our existence more pleasant and permanent (*HC*, 7). In action, we have freedom from our animal nature and are able to create history and culture. In contrast to the massive political apathy many of us feel today, politics for Arendt is, as it was for Aristotle, the only realm in which we can be truly human: "The actual content of political life [is] . . . the joy and gratification that arise of being in company with our peers, out of acting together and appearing in public, out of inserting ourselves in the world by word and deed, thus acquiring and sustaining our personal identity and beginning something entirely new."[18]

As Arendt makes clear, political identity does not really exist prior to action. It is through action that we both create and reveal who we are. The self-revelation of action is not the whole of our existence—we also have an interior life, as well as a private life at home (and that possibility should give us solace when we end up not liking the way we acted or appeared to act in public). But the self-revelation of action is wholly constitutive of our public selves. People who never have the opportunity or desire to act live a shadowy, not quite fully human existence. Overwhelming concern with one's private life—even something we usually consider relatively noble, like concern for one's own family—had disastrous consequences in Arendt's view, empowering Himmler to turn a nation "of job holders and family men" into the Third Reich: "Nothing proved easier to destroy than the privacy and private morality of people who thought of nothing but safeguarding their private lives."[19]

Action also differs from other human activities in that it is marked by

17. See also Mark Warren, "Democracy and Deceit: Regulating Appearances of Corruption," *American Journal of Political Science* 50, no. 1 (January 2006): 160–74.
18. Hannah Arendt, *Between Past and Future* (New York: Penguin Books, 1977), 263; henceforth cited as *BPF* in the text.
19. Hannah Arendt, *The Origins of Totalitarianism* (New York: Harcourt Brace Jovanovich, 1973), 338; henceforth cited at *OT* in the text.

unpredictability and spontaneity. It stands in contrast to the sort of conformism that Arendt saw encroaching on political life in the mid-twentieth century. Living in this state, we are prone to the sort of shallow and selfish thought that Arendt believed marked the "family man" of interwar Germany, demonstrated most dramatically in the insulation from "thinking attention" provided by Adolph Eichmann's "clichés, stock phrases, adherence to conventional, standardized codes of expression and conduct."[20] Paradoxically, "straight talk," considered the opposite of clichéd speech, has become a sort of conformity-inducing norm in the contemporary political landscape. Precisely because Arendt is correct and we cherish uniqueness, we proudly tout our ability to transcend stifling community norms and tell it like it really is. But these ideals have been so thoroughly assimilated into popular culture that they are now used to sell the most banal products and ideas to people either eager to demonstrate their "X-tremeness" or else resigned to the co-optation that has taken place.[21] The historical context that gave rise and meaning to the ideal of sincerity in politics—in the U.S. case, the particular history of political theory, the upheavals of the 1960s, Watergate, the decline of ideological, party-based politics, to name just a few factors—is obscured, while assertions of sincerity become paramount and the current context of hyper-sincerity is elided. Everyone wants to be unique, and we have learned very well how to present ourselves as such; it has become a predictable response to the world. *Parrhesia* functioned in a similar way in Athens—a clichéd mode of asserting one's unique and courageous commitment to the truth.

Discourse ethics, which would ideally be used to critique shallow sincerity, fails on several counts. First, the categories don't map well. Can we take a claim of sincerity at face value? Given our psychological complexity, can we ever really know such a thing about ourselves? And even if we could identify sincerity in ourselves or others, it might very well turn out to be a poor heuristic—do we have solid evidence that personal sincerity leads to better political judgments or leadership? Second, as Chapter 1 demonstrated, invocations of sincerity can narrow the range of discourse and cut deliberations short. Finally, the norms of discourse ethics can become akin to the sort of thing that Arendt warns against—predictable and normalizing

20 Hannah Arendt, *The Life of the Mind: Thinking, Willing* (New York: Harcourt Brace Jovanovich, 1977), 4; henceforth cited as *LOM* in the text.
21 For a variety of examples, see Thomas Frank, *The Conquest of Cool* (Chicago: University of Chicago Press, 1998).

constructions that insulate political judgment from the actual world. Seeming violations of the ethic can instead serve as actions that transcend the ethic; we see this especially in irony (which was viewed as intentional deceit by many of Socrates' observers; that is, action's unpredictability can also lead to misunderstanding). Instead, Arendt urges us to direct our judgment away from the interior and back to the properly political—the realm of appearances. We must judge each act anew, based on a rich understanding of the context, rather than presumably universal assumptions. But, again, why not use the language of "sincerity" to describe this contextual response? To return to our opening example, doesn't the disconnect between Rumsfeld's statements and efforts reveal his true intentions? He said the Defense Department could not arm the vehicles any faster because of the laws of physics, but he was proven wrong by several military contractors who said that the Department of Defense just hadn't asked or paid them to go any faster—it looks to some like Rumsfeld lied. So why shouldn't we speak of his true intentions?

Behind the Mask

There is still one more danger of sincerity, which is highlighted by Arendt's work: the distraction away from public matters and the disturbing focus on the individual's interior life in politics. Arendt confronts this danger by emphasizing the importance of masks and theatricality for politics. For Arendt, political life takes place on a metaphorical stage on which we both present our unique selves and in which we try to make ourselves understood to the others without whom we could have no fully human life. But the presentation of the political self should not be confused with the idea that one is somehow revealing her *true, real* self for all to see; although the public realm is integral to a fully human life, Arendt did not subscribe to the idea that a stage was where one could *really* be real, expressing one's deepest self. It is performative but not expressive.[22] We engage our identities, yet politics somehow does not become a fierce battle of core identities. Instead, Arendt offers us a way to reject the dangerous politics of sincerity, celebrating the stage of politics and the masks that offer us a public *persona,*

---

22. Dana Villa, *Politics, Philosophy, Terror: Essays on the Thought of Hannah Arendt* (Princeton: Princeton University Press, 1999), 110.

and rejecting the idea that a "real" person behind the mask is *politically* significant (even while that inner self informs one's public actions). While Plato's work highlights the difficulties of making a sincerity/insincerity distinction, Arendt goes further and helps us appreciate that, because of its focus on the interior, the question of one's sincerity is not a properly political one.

In *Between Past and Future*, Arendt writes: "The performing arts . . . have indeed a strong affinity with politics. Performing artists—dancers, play-actors, musicians, and the like—need an audience to show their virtuosity, just as acting men need the presence of others before whom they can appear; both need a publicly organized space for their 'work,' and both depend upon others for the performance itself" (*BPF*, 154). It is not so much that performance is a metaphor for political life, but rather that politics is a sphere of performance.[23] Politics takes place as a (relatively) organized human activity and requires the presence of others; we come to the stage of politics in order to appear before others. By appearing, we construct a public *persona*, revealing a part of ourselves. We neither take on some presumed and foreign identity, nor are we exposing some deep inner core of ourselves for all to see. Instead, politics takes place somewhere between these two poles. Through action, we construct a public identity; the enabling device is the *persona*, empowered by political equality. Arendt traces the legal *persona* back to the Greek theater: "The mask as such obviously had two functions: it had to hide, or rather to replace, the actor's own face and countenance, but in a way that would make it possible for the voice to sound through."[24] The mask of politics does not deceive or conceal; it protects the actor while allowing his or her voice, not that of an imposter or a substitute, to sound through. For example, while we may believe all people are created equal, this is neither self-evident nor universal, according to Arendt; it is something we enact through politics and law (*BPF*, 246–47). The mask is what enacts those rights, while protecting the private person:

> The point was that "it is not the natural Ego which enters a court of law. It was a right-and-duty-bearing person, created by the law, which appears before the law." Without his *persona*, there would

23. For more on the relationship between performance and public life, see Erving Goffman, *The Presentation of Self in Everyday Life* (New York: Anchor Books, 1959).

24 Hannah Arendt, *On Revolution* (New York: Penguin/Pelican Books, 1977), 106; henceforth cited as *OR* in the text.

> be an individual without rights and duties, perhaps a "natural man"—that is, a human being or *homo* in the original meaning of the word, indicating someone outside the range of law and the body politic of the citizens, as for instance a slave—but certainly a politically irrelevant being. (*OR*, 107)

Why does the natural person behind the mask need protection in the first place? What is wrong with a politics of sincerity in which people appear as they really are, not acting but being? Arendt addresses this in her discussion of the French Revolution and Terror. She argues that Robespierre and the Jacobins placed their political faith in the will of the people rather than political institutions (*OR*, 76). The general will (a lá Rousseau) was to guide the state; thus, any wills that were not identical to the *volonte generale* were suspect. How to find such deviation? It is here that Robespierre's search for hypocrisy and purity began: "Thus, his problem was where to detect a common enemy outside the range of foreign affairs, and his solution was that such an enemy existed within the breast of each citizen" (*OR*, 78). Society was seen as a corrupting influence, one that led humans away from their natural goodness in the state of nature. In a pre-social state, humans were authentically compassionate and their inner motives pure. Robespierre's mission became to search hypocrisy out and purge the impure from France, which led to horrible violence and social instability. "It was the war on hypocrisy that transformed Robespierre's dictatorship into the Reign of Terror . . . it was always a question of uncovering what had been hidden, of unmasking the disguises, of exposing duplicity and mendacity" (*OR*, 99–100). But once the hypocrisies were uncovered, French citizens also found themselves without a public legal *persona* by which to appear in public and which could protect them from the Terror.

We see the same search for true motives and hypocrisy in a variety of our own worst moments. Conspiracy theories have long thrived on the notion that fellow citizens have sinister hidden motives; witness recurring versions of the "international Jewish conspiracy" and the obsession with "homosexual agendas" in the public schools and on television.[25] Relatedly, governments sometimes assume to be able to discern a person's inner moti-

25 For example, the "International Jew" series in the *Dearborn Independent* in the 1920s, funded by Henry Ford or, more currently, the American Family Association website's discussion of the "Homosexual Agenda" at http://www.afa.net/homosexual_agenda/ (accessed December 12, 2006).

vation, hidden by their professions of loyalty and citizenship; witness the Japanese-American internment camps of World War II, the Red Scares, and the current threats to Middle Eastern immigrants. Yet the dangers do not need to be so acute to still have a negative effect on deliberative democracy and its focus of mutual democratic accountability. As Sennett argues, this sort of emphasis on the individual undermines "our rational understanding of society":

> A political leader running for office is spoken of as "credible" or "legitimate" in terms of what kind of man he is, rather than in terms of the actions or programs he espouses. The obsession with persons at the expense of more impersonal social relations is like a filter which discolors our rational understanding of society; it obscures the continuing importance of class in advanced industrial society; it leads us to believe community is an act of mutual self-disclosure and to undervalue the community relations of strangers, particularly those which occur in cities.[26]

Moreover, the unavoidable problem about someone's sincerity is that it is truly unknowable.[27] As Augustine describes the mystery of other human beings in City of God: "All human relationships are fraught with . . . misunderstandings. . . . Even if we could read [the hearts of friends] today, anything might happen tomorrow . . . no human judge can read the conscience of the man before him."[28] Arendt continues this line of thought, tying the futility of this quest to uncover the true person behind the mask to the character of human souls. She posits that our inner lives are obscure places that cannot be fully known by another human. Judging the true motives of another person, let alone finding out what they are, is impossible:

> Whatever the passions and the emotions may be, and whatever their connection with thought and reason, they certainly are located in the human heart. And not only is the human heart a

---

26. Sennett, Fall of Public Man, 4.

27. While they do not go so far as to think it is impossible to know, Steenbergen et al. acknowledge that sincerity poses unique measurement problems; it is therefore omitted from their measure of discourse quality. See Steenbergen et al., "Measuring Political Deliberation," 26.

28. Augustine, City of God (New York: Image/Doubleday, 1958), 443–44.

place of darkness which, with certainty, no human eye can pene-
trate. . . . To be sure, every deed has its motives as it has its goal
and principle; but the act itself, though it proclaims its goal and
makes manifest its principle, does not reveal the innermost motivation of the agent. His motives remain dark, they do not shine
but are hidden not only from others but, most of the time, from
himself, from his self-inspection, as well. (*OR*, 96, 98)

That is, motives are certainly causes of action, ones that may become apparent through a performed action. But one's innermost motivation is *not*
something another human can discern. As we saw in Chapter 3, Socratic
irony can highlight this fundamental problem for politics—the human psyche is a strange and mysterious place. "In politics, more than anywhere
else, we have no possibility of distinguishing between being and appearance" (*OR*, 98). We can *only* know a person through their appearance to
us.

Of course, Socrates did not limit his questioning to apparent or public
matters; instead, he links the health of one's soul to the health of the polis.
Yet his efforts draw attention to the point that the boundary between what
counts as public and what counts as private is fluid and contested. We cannot establish pre-politically what is going to be matter for public concern
and what is not. What one can do, however, is argue in support of particular
positions regarding particular aspects of our lives. An examination of the
dangers posed by a politics of sincerity in the contemporary United States
and historical traumas like the French Terror, as well as the probable impossibility of ever *truly* recognizing another person's sincerity, calls on us to
deemphasize the political importance of this personal virtue. However, the
exclusion of the interior life from politics is itself political, contingent on
context, and open to contestation. This does not mean that we must agree
with Arendt's division of the two spheres or that those matters currently
labeled "private" or "public" should necessarily remain labeled as such.
This is also not to say that virtue does not matter for politics—it does, since
it forms the foundation for the appearance we project into the public, as
both Aristotle and Arendt knew. It is the demand for *public transparency*
of one's inner motives that is my concern here. As Arendt highlights, the
interior life may motivate political action, but the interior life is unknowable and must be protected from the harsh light of the public arena. Democratic life depends on the presence of certain virtues among citizens, but

that fact alone gives us no resources to judge someone's character beyond its public manifestation in action. Must we critique the presumed interior life of fellow citizens? Or, in a more Arendtian fashion, could we perhaps limit our focus to one's public persona, judging another's political actions based on how well they comport with facts and our values, rather than trying to judge inner character and intentions? Admittedly, people will likely develop a reputation for often making factually or allegorically true and ethically appealing claims and we may mark them as people worthy of our political trust, but that does not necessarily mean we judge their hearts.

It is important to note that Arendt does not justify hypocrisy. Hypocrites take advantage of the fact that we have both public and interior lives by denying this duality and then hiding behind masks they pretend not to be wearing. According to Norma Moruzzi, they threaten the "disintegration of performative truth."[29] They thus encourage us to measure them by their intentions, not their conduct. Arendt calls on us not to play their game: "As witnesses not of our intentions but of our conduct, we can be true or false, and the hypocrite's crime is that he bears false witness against himself" (OR, 103).

The closing of the distance between our public and private selves poses a problem not only for political life but also for the private lives of citizens. Whenever such "qualities of the heart" as sincerity are proclaimed publicly, they lose their "innermost" quality and serve a strategic function. I argued in Chapter 1 that the strategic dimension of politics is unjustly derided, but here the claim of sincerity fails its own test; by invoking it, or having another person comment on it, one has made a claim with strategic effect (even if unintentional). Once the interior life is used strategically in a public setting, it begins to lose some of its ability to protect and comfort us from the glare of public life. While Arendt's strict split between the public and private is problematic and although she has been accused of prioritizing the public above all else, she was rightly concerned with protecting the private from the encroachment of public eyes. She warns against the search for innermost motives because it renders an inner life meaningless:

> The qualities of the heart need darkness and protection against the light of the public to grow and to remain what they are meant to

29. Norma Claire Moruzzi, *Speaking Through the Mask: Hannah Arendt and the Politics of Social Identity* (Ithaca: Cornell University Press, 2000), 34.

be, innermost motives which are not for public display. However deeply heartfelt a motive may be, once it is brought out and exposed for public inspection it becomes an object of suspicion rather than insight . . . when they appear they become "mere appearances" behind which again other, ulterior motives may lurk, such as hypocrisy and deceit. (OR, 96)

Sennett argues in a similar vein: "The world of intimate feelings loses any boundaries; it is no longer restrained by a public world in which people make alternative and countervailing investment in themselves. The erosion of a strong public life therefore deforms the intimate relations which seize people's wholehearted interest."[30] Thus, the existence of two spheres is critical to the protection of the one sphere (the private) we have unfortunately allowed to cannibalize the other (the public). We rely on persona and performance to protect our private lives from public intrusion. The impulse to look behind the mask, to uncover someone's true intentions is a strong one, made all the stronger by the large and small treasons of those who deliberately mislead. But instead of trying to strip people to some authentic being, we should move in the other direction, where we can acknowledge the performative aspect of all public interaction. To demand that someone reveal her true self, to remove all hypocrisy and hidden thoughts, recalls the Reign of Terror or the Taliban's Ministry for Promotion of Virtue and Prevention of Vice; it becomes a "tyranny of intimacy," to use Sennett's words. Our inner lives, as complicated and ambiguous as they are, are, at least, our own.

Removing questions of sincerity from politics does not mean we remove emotions—often considered part of the interior life—from politics. Instead, it requires, among other things, that we stop splitting the political world into inner and outer realms—which is required when we want to shore up our political arguments by referring to our inner lives as a foundation for our political claims. By focusing politics only on the public realm and assuming it is all there is for politics, we can avoid this split, accepting emotions as an important part of deliberation. The emotions (invariably mixed in with any statement or action) that are expressed publicly are important components of politics; they both inform and express political judgments. But emotions generally should not be the *substance* of politics;

30. Sennett, *Fall of Public Man*, 7.

the existence of a passion or emotion is not, alone, enough to sustain healthy deliberation (even when we take Hall's critique that deliberation depends on taking the passions into account). *Reasons,* inspired and informed by passions (which are in turn inspired and informed by reasons), offer us the opportunity for deliberation—the weighing of various sides of an issue, resulting in a judgment. Otherwise, politics becomes a discussion of the credibility of one's emotional responses to the world, rather than a discussion of those policies, goals, and histories that inform those responses.[31] The critical thing is to avoid assertions of the genuineness of one's emotions as evidence of their importance for politics.

To move out of this politics of forced intimacy, we put on the mask of a public *persona*. However, "masks" might still have reason to make us a bit wary; "masks" are not always constructed by the wearer, and they limit rights as well as grant them. As Susan Bickford puts it: "Feminist writers have used the metaphor of the mask not to solve but to describe the way 'what' we are can obscure our public appearance . . . so the stereotypic perception imposes a mask whose effect is to blur and muffle individuality rather than let it sound through."[32] Instead of being public *personas* that grant us each equality before the law regardless of our gender or sexuality or ethnic identity or economic position, masks often create a screen that makes it difficult for us to appear before our fellows. Arendt stops at legal equality, with little analysis of how social and economic inequality affects the prospects of our being heard without the mask of "what" we are (female, Catholic, poor, African-American, Jewish, physically handicapped, and so on) obscuring "who" we are. Bickford calls on us to be more skeptical of the possibility of equalizing masks and instead argues that we take these identities into account, disrupting Arendt's clear split between the

31. One might respond that the utility of emotions in politics depends on their sincerity: *one must really feel* a certain way for it to be valid; otherwise, we might succumb to cheap emotional ploys and pandering. But how do we judge this? One possibility would be to question whether someone *could* possibly feel that way, given the circumstances, obviating the need to really probe the individual's sincerity. Yet those judging often don't understand how a someone *could possibly* feel some particular way; conflict and misunderstanding remain. This is precisely why we shouldn't, once again, get into a discussion of their intentions and sincerity. If, for example, a wealthy white man from a privileged family background feels angry about an affirmative action at his local university, do we gain anything by saying he doesn't *really* feel that way? Instead, we try to work with those emotions, sorting out why the political arrangements have inspired such feelings. This requires an enormous amount of political trust, but I also think it is capable of generating such trust in return.

32. Bickford, *Dissonance of Democracy,* 101.

"political" and the "social." She argues that group identities not only ste-
reotype speakers but also exist as a "constitutive part of our public identity
because they provide the contexts in which we learned to speak and think
the languages that both shape us and enable us to give voice to our unique
selves."[33] That is, the masks that are imposed on us by virtue of being born
into a particular social context are not just disabling, but also empowering;
social identity is at least partially constitutive of our political identities.
Thus, even if it were possible to negate them through the mask of legal
equality, we would not want to, for we would become less than ourselves.
Moreover, there may arise situations in which wearing an otherwise hated
mask may be politically useful. Yet we do not necessarily want to affirm
the essentialism and stereotyping often imposed by social identities. We
want some in-between realm, where we can deny the naturalness of these
identities, but also appreciate the ways that they have shaped our lives for
both better and worse. Judith Butler speaks to this problem in her discussion of performativity in *Gender Trouble*.[34]

Butler shows that while feminist theory has largely discredited the idea
that gender is a natural and necessary foundation for identity, it has left
untouched the assumption that physical sex is inviolable.[35] In Arendt's language, Butler draws attention to the continued existence of a seemingly
necessary "what" that should be transformed into a "who," a thing that is
not a product of nature, but a human creation. Butler proposes a radical
interpretation of postmodernist identity construction, in which nothing is
left in a prediscursive state, but in which social change is possible. The
substance of this change is left open to continuous contestation, rather than
referring to an unassailable foundation (such as female or male sex organs).

33. Ibid., 103–4.

34. While Butler's work has long been criticized for what many see as its problematic
emphasis on subversion and instability, and its "cryptonormativity," I will generally pass by
these debates, since they have been ably discussed elsewhere and since I tend to agree with
Nancy Fraser's position that "the key is to avoid metaphysical entanglements. We should
adopt the pragmatic view that there are a plurality of different angles from which sociocultural
phenomena can be understood." Fraser, "Pragmatism, Feminism, and the Linguistic Turn,"
in *Feminist Contentions: A Philosophical Exchange*, ed. Linda Nicholson (New York:
Routledge, 1995), 166. While identity may be ultimately unstable, I do not think this makes
it meaningless to speak of identity or of character/*ethos*, as I do below. See also Eloise Buker,
Talking Feminist Politics: Conversations on Law, Science, and the Postmodern (Lanham, Md.:
Rowman and Littlefield, 1999), chaps. 8 and 10. For another perspective on the debate, see
Anderson, *The Way We Argue Now*, chap. 1.

35. Judith Butler, *Gender Trouble: Feminism and the Subversion of Identity* (New York:
Routledge, 1999), 10; henceforth cited in the text as *GT*.

There are no foundations, and the assumption of their existence amounts to a "normative injunction" that serves to mask both its origins and its regulatory goals (*GT*, 44). Butler's task is to remove the power that normative ideals have by permanently opening them to contestation. Otherwise, they are accepted as truths that essentialize and, by virtue of what they exclude, dehumanize.

In response to the critique that inevitably arises from this antifoundationalist viewpoint, Butler questions the assumed split between construction and agency. In standard epistemological frameworks, the "doer" must be prior to the "deed." That is, there is some stable, preexisting actor that engages in action; otherwise, social change cannot occur. Butler rejects the inevitability of the choice between construction and agency (*GT*, 181–82). In her view, the individual is constituted by discourse, but this does not remove her capacity for action. In fact, discourse is exactly what provides agency through the actor's ability to insert her own (possibly new and unpredictable) expressions into its flow. The "doer" *becomes* only through the "deed." According to Butler, "'Agency,' then, is to be located within the possibility of a variation of that repetition [of norms]. If the rules governing signification not only restrict, but enable the assertion of alternative domains of cultural intelligibility . . . then it is only *within* the practices of repetitive signifying that a subversion of identity becomes possible" (*GT*, 185). This process is never complete; it is repeated over time and subject to change. One's identity is therefore a changeable thing, subject to iterations that can vary over time. Although Arendt largely rejected feminism as a problematic intrusion of "what" we are into a realm where we should be disclosing "who" we are, this model of identity is reminiscent of Arendt's emphasis on appearance and the revelatory qualities of action. We can take on the masks that we are offered, using them to (possibly) subvert relations of domination, as well as to highlight the absence of an inviolable and natural inner core.

Instead of a natural "what," Butler conceptualizes sex and gender as performative (*GT*, 173–79). They are constituted through the repetition of certain acts, not decided once and for all. By altering these performances from the expected, the actor is able to subvert meaning and open new possibilities. Butler uses "drag" as her primary example. She argues that this performance serves to show how the "original" version of the feminine is not natural, but constructed. The drag performance opens both gender and sex up to subversion and change. "The performance suggests a dissonance not only between sex and performance, but sex and gender, and gender and performance. . . . *In imitating gender, drag implicitly reveals the imitative structure of gender itself—as well as its contingency"* (*GT*, 175). Drag is a mask in an obvious way: a covering that allows the speaker to be seen and heard. Instead of a mask of equality, this sort of mask differs from Arendt's *persona* in that it can call attention to the social inequalities that prevent true political equality. At the same time, we are not merely reduced to the "what" of our identity—there is room for the active (and interactive) creation of a "who," a political construction. However, prior to the performative action, we cannot delineate with much success the circumstances under which the performance will achieve a particular goal, recalling the argument of Chapter 3. The performance, like Socrates' irony and mythmaking, is dependent upon the context: "Parody by itself is not subversive, and there must be a way to understand what makes certain kinds of parodic repetitions effectively disruptive, truly troubling, and which repetitions become domesticated and recirculated as instruments of culture hegemony. A typology of actions would clearly not suffice, for parodic displacement, indeed parodic laughter, depends on a context and reception in which subversive confusions can be fostered" (*GT*, 176–77).

Butler's analysis opens a space for us to think of all action as a performance of sorts, reliant upon a certain type of mask we either choose to wear or must wear because society has invoked it. Sex is perhaps the last bastion of "natural" difference and of the irreducibly "social," but Butler's reading draws attention to not only the way sex exists and affects our political prospects (so as not to align herself with "postfeminists") but also to the danger of assuming that each person reveals some stable inner core (as opposed to engaging in a contingent performance): "The displacement of a political and discursive origin of gender identity onto a psychological 'core' precludes an analysis of the political constitution of the gendered subject" (*GT*, 174).

By reading Arendt through Butler, we can avoid the political/social split that marks Arendt's work, without also being handcuffed to particular identities as static formations that either deny or overly laud our agency to reconstruct the masks they impose. We also, again, are pushed to acknowledge the impossibility of a stable inner core that would make talk of sincerity truly meaningful.[36] "What" we are constructs the "who," and this

36. While critics argue that Butler's conception leaves no room for the active creation of an even momentarily stabilized identity that could then engage in intersubjective political deliberation, I do not see the need for such extremes (again, see Fraser and Buker). We can

analysis helps take into account the social differences that help to construct our identities. Appreciating these differences is actually quite Arendtian; social identity is no longer a realm of necessity, but one in which unique action is possible. As both Butler and Arendt argue, these masks enable political action. But this latter account allows more of the "personal" back into politics (for example, in debates over child care and education policy), while still rejecting the demand to expose one's interior life for all to see.

Not only do masks make possible a healthy democratic politics, they can also form an important component of the courage needed to engage in action. In *The Attack of the Blob: Hannah Arendt's Concept of the Social*, Hanna Pitkin describes ways to overcome the apathy and disconnection from politics that people feel. Her final recommendation is the adoption of a "just do it" mentality: "Though Arendt calls action a miracle, if you wait for your own action to befall you, it will not; you have to just do it. Others may or may not join you. Your action and the others may or may not succeed in extending freedom rather than furthering the social. There are no guarantees. But who will do it if we do not? . . . We are depressingly the problem; we are encouragingly the solution."[37] Political life requires action, and action requires a sort of mundane courage. In Chapter 2, I discussed how, in light of the analysis of *parrhesia*, contemporary discourse ethics would be better served by greater emphasis on problems of courage and duty. The courage and duty I mean here is not the heroism of Achilles, but rather a willingness to insert oneself in the world, to leave the comfort of home and hearth and begin a public story. In a politics of sincerity, in which one's good intentions are the most important quality one can have, this is an especially frightening prospect—so frightening that we often forget our commitment to democratic accountability, preferring to refrain from dealing with the issues that inevitably arise from living together. There is the danger of ridicule, of humiliation, of a righteous search for the *true you* behind the spun public facade. By refocusing our attention on the realm of appearance and the importance of a public *persona*, we can, as Bickford argues, "bolster our courage by reminding ourselves that criticisms are not of our most intimate selves, but of how we have performed, how we are acting in public."[38] Bolstering our courage should, in turn, strengthen our

---

still build our publicly projected character over time; what we do not do, however, is assume that this character is somehow authentic, inviolable, or natural.

37. Hanna Fenichel Pitkin, *The Attack of the Blob: Hannah Arendt's Concept of the Social* (Chicago: University of Chicago Press, 1998), 284.

38. Bickford, *Dissonance of Democracy*, 150.

commitment to democratic accountability, since the accounts offered and demanded should be less focused on one's moral worth. The person we disclose when we act publicly is certainly connected to the private self, but we should be comforted if we can accept that sometimes we may appear in a way that we did not intend or that our performance was not up to the standard we would have preferred. This failure does not necessarily indicate a great failure of either our innermost integrity or of our deeply held beliefs and values. Instead, we did not express them well. Moreover, because we have the opportunity to act again that failure need not be the whole of our story.

In other cases, the problem may be on the receiving end of the action. Given the unpredictability of public life and the plurality of individuals that compose it, we may be misunderstood by those before whom we appear. In such a case, we might look back to how our public mask might have obscured what we meant to say and shift our attention to the "social," renewing a commitment to changing the structural and cultural conditions that serve to maintain inequalities. The problem is also yet another argument in favor of paying attention to rhetoric, not as some way to hide our true motives and thoughts, but as the only way to express them. Others may have misheard what we meant to express; rhetoric can help bridge this gap by paying attention to those others and constructing one's appearance in public in a manner that will help them to understand. At the same time, our criticisms of other speakers should focus on what they said and what they did, not who we think they might be deep down inside (although this may very well inform what they said or did, it is not useful to judge this politically). For example, when asked if the request from a Fox network executive to include more white characters on a television show he wrote was racist, Dave Chappelle (a popular comedian) said, "It was racist. Look, I don't think these people sit around their house and call black people 'niggers' and all this kind of thing. But the idea that, unless I have white people around me on my show, that it's unwatchable or doesn't have a universal appeal, is racist."[39] Chappelle's reaction addresses the statement without making a presumption to know the "real" person who made the racist statement. Actions and statements pose the problem; they may be sexist, racist, or xenophobic. But to move from criticism of a statement or deed to indict-

39. Dave Chappelle, interview on *60 Minutes*, CBS News, December 29, 2004, http://www.cbsnews.com/stories/2004/10/19/60II/main650149.shtml/ (accessed January 6, 2005).

ing someone's inner life makes assumptions about our own powers of discernment and about the role of authenticity in politics that are not worthwhile risks in a democracy. Moreover, the political value of exposing whatever may in fact lurk in the human heart is not clear. As Judith Shklar has shown, hypocrisy may be an important element of a smoothly functioning democracy:

> We assume that our public roles carry greater moral responsibilities than our private ones. We expect to behave better as citizens and public officials than as actors in the private sphere. . . . It is, far more significantly, no longer acceptable in the United States to make racist and anti-Semitic remarks in public; yet in private conversation racism and anti-Semitism are expressed freely and frequently. . . . Would any egalitarian prefer more public frankness? Should our public conduct really mirror our private, inner selves? . . . Indeed one might well argue that liberal democracy cannot afford public sincerity. Honesties that humiliate and a stiff-necked refusal to compromise would ruin democratic civility in a political society in which people have many serious differences of belief and interest.[40]

Judging in a Plural World

Arendt's focus on the fact that we live among other unique actors who wear public masks makes her political ethic an appealing alternative to a politics of sincerity. Because of the human condition of plurality, we cannot make sense of our reality without paying attention to other people, thus opening the way for democratic accountability. The person who exists only privately—concerned with their job, their family, their abilities to consume—lives in a lesser reality, one that refuses to notice the existence of this human plurality and cannot understand even their own (albeit rare) actions. Arendt calls on us to take pleasure in the diversity of humanity, rather than giving in to the temptation of tyrannical control over others that appeals to Thrasymachus and Callicles. Arendt's conception of politics requires us to

---

40. Judith N. Shklar, *Ordinary Vices* (Cambridge: The Belknap Press of Harvard University Press, 1984), 78. See also Grant, *Hypocrisy and Integrity*, for more on the "ethical purist" and the role of hypocrisy, and Booth, *Rhetoric of Rhetoric*, 119–22.

listen to one another, a basic component of the democratic accountability based on universal moral respect central to Habermas's theory of deliberative democracy. Unlike the sincerity claims that motivate hyper-sincere pundits or Thucydides' Cleon, an Arendtian communicative ethic acknowledges that we cannot see reality without taking other people into account. "The reality of the public realm relies on the simultaneous presence of innumerable perspectives and aspects . . . only where things can be seen by many in a variety of aspects without changing their identity, can worldly reality truly and reliably appear" (*HC*, 57). That is, the multiple perspectives of individuals constitute the shared reality in which politics takes place. This immediately draws attention to the need for others, the impossibility of a single Archimedean point from which a *parrhesiastes* could speak intelligibly. This practice requires listening and listeners, not just courageous, critical, and truthful speaking. We thus set into motion some of the basic elements of democratic accountability, enabling and pushing people to offer accounts to one another. Arendt's conception involves both an acknowledgment of the other humans around us and a commitment to talk and listen.

This does not mean that we abandon ourselves or just go along with the crowd, however. We must remain committed to what Arendt calls *selbstdenken*, or thinking for oneself. Arendt makes clear that thinking for oneself is the only insurance we have against political disasters like the Third Reich. She asks, "Might the problem of good and evil, our faculty for telling right from wrong, be connected with our faculty of thought? . . . Could the activity of thinking as such, the habit of examining whatever happens to come to pass . . . could this activity be among the conditions that make men abstain from evil-doing or even actually conditions them against it?" (*LOM*, 5). But the act of thinking for oneself does not necessarily give a person special access to political authority. Once one joins in the community of others, the privileged position of "truthteller" has been vacated: "To look upon politics from the perspective of truth . . . means to take one's stand outside the political realm. This standpoint is the standpoint of the truthteller, who forfeits his position—and, with it, the validity of what he has to say—if he tries to interfere directly in human affairs and to speak the language of persuasion or violence" (*BPF*, 259).

In politics, our ability to understand ourselves and the world we live in requires the presence of at least some part of the plurality of humans, not just access to truth. The balance can be quite difficult, as we saw with Socrates, who ultimately sides with his own conscience (a sometimes necessary move). Kimberly Curtis discusses how plurality plays out practically with an example from contemporary community planning; writing about private gated communities, she argues that "such behavior creates a hermetic world . . . the reality of others who are different is difficult to comprehend in any politically and ethically significant (positive) manner."[41] This example draws attention to an important element of reality—the perspectives contributing to its formation must be diverse. We must seek out those unlike ourselves. When we are simply "multiplying and prolonging" our own perspective, we "become entirely private . . . deprived of seeing and hearing others, of being seen and being heard by them" (HC, 57). No matter how sincerely we feel an emotion or believe something, we leave the realm of politics when we refuse to live within a plurality of perspectives. We cannot form our opinions without listening to the perspectives of others; this does not necessarily mean adopting them, however—that would mean reducing the plurality to a multiplicity unmarked by distinctiveness. We must remain at the table, discussing; but we also must reject the temptation of believing that we can see it all from our seat (or that other guests might).

Let us assume that we have managed to extricate ourselves from our isolation and found a political community of truly different fellows. The promise of a plurality of perspectives is there, but how are we to move from just standing in their presence to the type of interaction that "assure[s] us of the reality of the world and ourselves" (HC, 50)? It happens in part with "representative thinking" or "visiting":

> Political thought is representative. I form an opinion by consider-
> ing a given issue from different viewpoints, by making present to
> my mind the standpoints of those who are absent. . . . This process
> of representation does not blindly adopt the actual views of those
> who stand somewhere else . . . this is a question neither of empathy
> . . . nor of counting noses and joining a majority but of being and
> thinking in my own identity where actually I am not. The more
> people's standpoints I have present in my mind while I am ponder-
> ing a given issue, and the better I can imagine how I would feel
> and think if I were in their place, the stronger will be my capacity

41. Kimberly Curtis, *Our Sense of the Real: Aesthetic Experience and Arendtian Politics* (Ithaca: Cornell University Press, 1999), 4.

for representative thinking and the more valid my final conclusions, my opinion. (*BPF*, 241)

In representative thinking, one is required to imagine one's own life in
another situation (and so the other person who lives in that situation does
not necessarily need to be present). According to Lisa Disch, visiting
"involves retelling the story of an event from a plurality of unfamiliar
standpoints, thereby making a shift from thinking from a private perspective to thinking from a public vantage point."[42] Furthermore, the effort of
representative thinking requires that "I think my own thought but from
the place of somebody else, permitting myself to experience the disorientation necessary for understanding how the world looks different to that person."[43] While Arendt calls on us to make "present to my mind the
standpoints of those who are absent," it seems doubtful that an upper-
class homeowner in Beverly Hills could understand what it is like to live in
Chicago's Cabrini Green without speaking to someone who has actually
lived there (even though she is trying to imagine what it would be like to
live there *herself* and although the other person may be absent during the
actual reimagining). As Bickford points out, this type of thinking is fraught
with difficulty:

> Representing to myself other opinions is tricky, for I cannot attri-
> bute opinions to specific others without knowing—without *hear-
> ing*—that they in fact hold that opinion. That is, we cannot confuse
> a possible judgment from a particular perspective with a specific
> person's actual judgment. By ourselves, we can never really know
> the innumerable perspectives in the world. The unpredictability of
> action and speech, the ability of humans to begin and give voice to
> something new, means that the opinions we hear may be—or per-
> haps even tend to be—surprising.[44]

It is thus not enough to *imagine* another's perspective. Given Arendt's
emphasis on being in the world with others, it seems that this practice

---

42. Lisa Disch, "Please Sit Down, but Don't Make Yourself At Home: 'Visiting' and the
Prefigurative Politics of Consciousness-Raising," in *Hannah Arendt and the Meaning of Politics*, ed. Craig Calhoun and John McGowan (Minneapolis: Minnesota University Press, 1997),
136.

43. Ibid.

44. Susan Bickford, *Dissonance of Democracy*, 86.

would actually require the presence of others, not just my imagining what their perspective would be like. Adopting a modified Arendtian ethic in this case, we can begin to see that to "tell it like it is" in the realm of politics requires other people, not just a single *parrhesiastes*. It requires that we stop talking for a bit and listen, shifting from a private point of view to a public one. I need to actually listen to others, incorporating (but not absorbing) that standpoint alongside my own. Arendt's vision requires that we engage one another, setting the stage for democratic accountability. We must energetically solicit the presence of others, which involves renewing our commitment to living with those unlike us. Thus, we should be weary of the isolation of the suburbs or predominantly upper-class liberal university towns or the appeal of private schools or the electronic enclaves of web logs and newsgroups that allow us to be with other people so like us that we may simply multiply similar perspectives. "But I see other people every day at the university!" "Politician X is a straight-shooter, so why bother listening to all that other noise?" "I talked about that issue with my entire listserv!" We must keep in mind that our efforts to solicit others with whom to speak and listen is never complete and that we can always do better.

Of course, there may be times when not-listening can be a response, albeit a drastic one, to political conditions. Yet this strategy tends to favor the powerful, who are more likely to be able to ignore those without as much as power. For example, it is easier for heads of state and finance ministers to ignore antiglobalization protestors than it is for antiglobalization protestors to ignore the police sent in to break up their demonstration. James Bohman has persuasively argued that while we may not be able to offer satisfactory reasons to one another in the end, the commitment to making the attempt defines democratic communication. "Not to offer a justification even to the unreasonable is to excuse them from the community of judgment and thus to violate the democratic commitments to political egalitarianism and nondomination."[45] Once we reject the reflexive challenge posed by the commitment to accountability, we have stepped outside democratic politics. There may be situations in which such a move may be warranted, but it is a perilous one that must be carefully considered.

When a person listens to the perspectives of others, he also must avoid the temptation to think he really "gets" where another person is coming

45. Bohman, "Deliberative Toleration," 768.

from. One more likely cannot fully understand what another person is talking about; Arendt's emphasis on plurality warns us away from the fantasy of full understanding or consensus. This preference for believing in our closeness, rather than our distance, has most often worked in favor of the already powerful. "Getting it" can be a way of trying to control another person's anger or sadness, by proclaiming that one already understands and therefore doesn't really need to continue listening. From the other direction, we need to also balance this listening with our own judgment, not least because there are certainly times when the majority is horribly wrong. "Free citizenship, then, is facilitated by the capacity to relate to others in this balanced way . . . attentive to their perspective without surrendering one's own judgment."[46] The point is to live somewhere in between the two poles of taking in the unique contributions of others and *selbstdenken*.

Arendt's discussion of common sense (or taste) in Kant's *Third Critique* also helps get to what might be involved in these democratic practices, trying to balance critical thoughtfulness with accountability. The key practice here is judgment, enabled by *sensus communis*, through which one is able to offer an account—an explanation of why one thinks the way one does. As Arendt explains, judgment itself is composed of two mental operations: imagination and reflection. Imagination makes present something which is no longer immediately there (allowing us to judge it), while reflection is the "actual activity of judging something."[47] The standard for reflection, and hence judgment, is communicability. That is, in order to judge, we must be able to submit that judgment to public scrutiny and stand by it. Thus, discursive accountability is critical to the very act of judging. These judgments are deeply intersubjective: "This *sensus communis* is what judgment appeals to in everyone, and it is this possible appeal that gives judgments their special validity. The it-pleases-or-displeases me, which as a feeling seems so utterly private and noncommunicative, is actually rooted in this community sense and is therefore open to communication once it has been transformed by reflection, which takes all others and their feelings into account" (*LKPP*, 72).

According to Beiner, "Judgment is contrasted with philosophical argument oriented towards truth. The latter, insisting upon demonstrable truth, seeks to *compel* agreement by a process of compelling proof. Judgment by

46. Pitkin, *Attack of the Blob*, 266.

47 Hannah Arendt, *Lectures on Kant's Political Philosophy*, ed. Ronald Beiner (Chicago: University of Chicago Press, 1992), 68; henceforth cited as *LKPP* in the text.

196 ★ THE POLITICS OF SINCERITY

taste, by contrast, is persuasive (like political opinions)—persuading in the hope of *coming* to an agreement with everyone else eventually."[48] It is not a matter of "harmonizing" views, as in the consensus theory of truth, but of taking others into account, trying to "woo" them to one's point of view through rhetorical appeals to this *sensus communis;* these appeals may be ironic, mythic, plainly styled—it is not their form that matters. Impartiality is thus redefined, not as an Archimedean point for conflict-free adjudication, but as an intersubjective activity:

> You see that *impartiality* is obtained by taking the viewpoints of others into account; impartiality is not the result of some higher standpoint that would then actually settle the dispute by being altogether above the melee . . . we find the notion that one can "enlarge" one's own thought so as to take into account the thoughts of others. . . . Hence, critical thinking, while still a solitary business, does not cut itself off from "all others." To be sure, it still goes on in isolation, but by the force of imagination it makes the others present and thus moves in a space that is potentially public, open to all sides. . . . To think with an enlarged mentality means that one train's one's imagination to go visiting. (*LKPP,* 42–43)

According to Bickford, this type of judgment "allows me not merely to see from another's location but to evaluate my own judgments through considering the judgments of others, and then to make a decision that I can live with," as well as provide (though not necessarily prove) intelligible reasons to others for my decision.[49] Citizens remain accountable to one another through an emphasis on the importance of individual—yet not solitary—judgment, allowing us an alternative for grounding political deliberations.

For instance, *The Daily Show* is ironic, insincere in what often might be considered cruel ways. Does that make it problematic for democratic deliberation (the process of weighing options and coming to a decision)? One person might believe the show offers a clever way to critique the U.S.-led war in Iraq and that the show helped her to come to a thoughtful deci-

48 Beiner, *Political Judgment*, 17.
49. Bickford, *Dissonance of Democracy,* 88.

sion about her position on the war. At the same time, that person should be able to explain that belief to others unlike herself, including someone who thinks Stewart makes light of U.S. soldiers' sacrifices or the threat of terrorism.[50] Imagining—based on actual listening in the world—and reflecting on the variety of perspectives on the program and then placing one's belief within that range offers a promise of democratic accountability by giving people the tools to continue a dialogue grounded by a commitment to reciprocity: "Communicability obviously depends on the enlarged mentality; one can communicate only if one is able to think from the other person's standpoint; otherwise one will never meet him, never speak in such a way that he understands. By communicating one's feelings, one's pleasures and disinterested delights, one tells one's *choices* and one chooses one's company" (*LKPP*, 74).

In this Arendtian account of democratic deliberation, we only have the possibility of taking others' viewpoints into account and then placing our own view within this collection, interpreting our own position in it and offering accounts to others. We are forced to live with the difficult but human prospect of forming a deep commitment to live with one another, visit with one another, and employ judgment all the while. This level of democratic accountability is precluded by our current emphasis on sincerity—a deeply sincere expression of my judgment, with its claim to truth and authority, does not require placement within the panoply of citizen views.

We can also see this Arendtian approach in the earlier analysis of Plato's dialogues. Chapter 3 examined the various ways of seeing Socrates, trying on different interpretations and seeing how the philosopher looks from a variety of different perspectives, giving us a better understanding of his meaning for democracy and relationship to *parrhesia*. Chapter 4 attempted a similar path with the *Republic*. Rather than trying to secure a final meaning for the dialogue, we can read it as a "summoner," something that is

---

50. Bickford's argument that one must strike a careful balance between "propriety" and "provocation" is useful here: "Because we might also think of the Little Rock controversy as illuminating the tension *between* propriety and judgment—that is, between following norms of appropriateness that would make our opinions communicable, or judging in a different mode and risking incommunicability. Most political action involves being between these two options somehow, or figuring out how not to get trapped in that either/or. And that 'figuring out' has to do in part with how we think about those others to whom we are communicating." Bickford, "Propriety and Provocation in Arendt's Political Aesthetic," in Calhoun and McGowan, *Hannah Arendt*, 88.

several things at once and that calls one to judgment. These are Arendtian readings of Plato, ones that neglect the sincerity question and instead focus on multiplicity and judgment. Accordingly, there is no universal rule by which to judge, but only a difficult process of trying to place one belief in relation to others and then communicate it. This is not intended to dull the conflict that often marks politics or to argue for more civility in politics; it is, however, a call to appreciate the balance between thinking for oneself and using an "enlarged mentality" to appreciate the rhetorical complexity of deliberative democracy.

Storytelling figures prominently in Arendt's thought as a way to acknowledge conflict and then to "go visiting" in the hopes of living with that conflict. Instead of a detached objectivity or earnest authority, stories invite discussion because of the way they proliferate meanings. Stories offers exemplars—concrete models that can, according to Disch, "spark visiting, a kind of cubist imagining by which one rewrites the story of an events from the plurality of perspectives it would engender in a particular context."[51] The *Republic* does exactly this; Socrates offers a variety of stories about justice, using myth and philosophy to destabilize the authority of hegemonic discourses and opening the field for discussion about justice and political ideals both for the Athenians and for us. Likewise, Socratic irony offers a proliferation of meanings, an invitation to understand something from a variety of perspectives. All of us have stories; the creation of a unique life story is the way we reveal ourselves to the world. These are not stories made by authors but stories which develop because of individuals who have decided to leave their "private hiding place[s]" and show through their actions who they are (*HC*, 186). Each of us takes part in these stories, and sharing them involves sharing our perspective with the public world, acknowledging our story's partiality at the same time. The emphasis on story also highlights the mediated nature of relating our experiences to one another. We do not simply let the facts shine through, unchosen and natural. We engage in a political practice of constructing narratives through rhetoric, choosing storylines that seem most important to us and choosing the facts and experiences that we believe best illustrate our points.

The goal of this type of communication is not just to arrive at a mutually agreed upon policy and allow administrators to take action from there. The point is to open and sustain deliberation in a contested space, while periodi-

51. Disch, "Please Sit Down," 145.

cally making judgments that momentarily close the discursive space (in contrast to Socrates' endless discussion, democratic deliberation often requires us to make decisions). Because of the emphasis on plurality and the importance to Arendtian political practice of thinking alongside other people, this understanding of politics is able to appreciate both the importance of *selbstdenken* and the presence of others. The political sphere is marked by contingency, and is constituted through our attention to it; deliberation is the working through of this problem of plurality and unpredictability, which is the very basis of politics. It also means not shying away from or denigrating conflict in political life; communication exists because conflicts exist in the political world. Conflict is not something to ignore or eliminate, but instead the very reason we have politics. We build political community *in order to account for* our inability to clearly judge one another's intentions and because our community is marked by disagreement and misunderstanding. Politics is meant to be a way to deal with these facts of life as fairly as possible, spreading both the risks and rewards across the community.[52] By being open to the act of listening to others, we acknowledge the potential for conflict and take responsibility for dealing with it.

Judgment, Truth, and Politics

Critics might be concerned that this vision of politics gives a pass to liars; an ethic of listening and offering accounts to others does not in itself tell us enough about the place of truth in politics. However, it is critical to this ethic of political action that we share Arendt's staunch commitment to the most basic factual truths. While she believed that politics is by definition concerned with things that lend themselves to disagreement and discussion, she did not believe that everything is up for discussion or should be viewed as an "opinion": "Facts inform opinions, and opinions, inspired by different interests and passions, can differ widely and still be legitimate as long as they respect factual truth. Freedom of opinion is a farce unless factual information is guaranteed and the facts themselves are not in dispute" (*BPF*, 238). Facts form the "texture" of politics (*BPF*, 231). The problem arises in that facts are fragile; once they are forgotten by history, they cannot be retrieved in the same manner in which geometry or calculus might reappear

52. See Allen, *Talking to Strangers*, chap. 8.

if forgotten. Furthermore, facts can be reframed as simply one of many opinions: "Factual truth is no more self-evident than opinion, and this may be among the reasons that opinion-holders find it relatively easy to discredit factual truth as just another opinion" (*BPF*, 243). Yet factual truth's fragility does not discount its importance; what it does do is help us think about how hyper-sincerity can obscure the facts. The more sincere-sounding person is considered to be the one with the correct facts; the other speakers, with their fancy locutions and ironic evasions, are trying to distort the truth, offering their partial opinions in the place of truth. According to Villa, "Audiences became passive spectators, convinced that what the truth of what any public speaker had to say reduced, finally, to the kind of person he was. The more adept at performing 'genuine' emotion—at displaying the private self in public—the politician is, the more believable he becomes."[53]

As usual, there is another side to Arendt's thinking on this subject. Arendt remains a committed political theorist, concerned with the realm of appearance and possibility. While "I know for certain that they will not say Belgium invaded Germany," there is a sense of uncertainty to much of the world, and Arendt is unwilling to make final decrees about any sort of truth other than "brutal elementary data" (*BPF*, 239). We must be committed to the facts, but we must also be willing to interrogate them (for eyewitness testimony can be false and documents forged [*BPF*, 243]). As Chapters 3 and 4 demonstrated, we should also remain skeptical of those who claim unfettered access to the truth *and* open to the possibility of deeper layers of understanding, as with myth; we can do this by encouraging the development of the individual judgment necessary to negotiate this difficult terrain. We live in an uncertain and fragile world, in which we must maintain faith in the possibilities of communication in order to stave off cynicism. Socratic irony and mythmaking can offer ways to temper this problem by drawing our attention to the complexity of both individuals and worldly truths while critiquing perversions of *parrhesia*. We may very well fail, as Socrates seems to have in Athens. But to stop talking or to invoke good intentions in place of argument is to dampen the spirit of democratic accountability that gives radically different people a way to live together without violence. We cannot be afraid to expose falsehood, or to connect issues to social structures and positions of privilege and to the values we hold dear. We will fight with one another about facts and the meanings of

53. Villa, *Politics, Philosophy, Terror,* 150.

those facts. But that is different from imputing hidden motives to others. Politics should not be a realm in which we shun conflict and "uncooperative" interlocutors are left out of the discussion; yet it is important to mitigate some of the negative effects of such conflict by ensuring that discussion focuses on politics, not the moral worth of individuals. When we start talking about the "real" motives lying behind appearances, we enable the hyper-sincere speakers who can make a farce of the truth, rendering citizens cynical and apathetic instead of skeptical and involved. In the highly meditated politics of the twenty-first century, we also deny citizens a real possibility of political judgment, for as Mark Warren points out, all they *can* rely on is appearance.[54] We can still hold one another accountable to the truth, not because it shows the type of person one really is in private, but because of the violence that lies do to the possibility of a shared reality.[55] This understanding of healthy democratic politics does not banish myth or allegory in favor of a separate rationality, but does require a commitment to accountability and an acceptance of the most basic facts as "the ground on which we stand and the sky that stretches above us" (*BPF*, 264). While the facts provide this ground, politics is generally concerned more with questions of *judgment* than "truth"; only one's ability to judge between competing visions of the world and between contrasting political ethics can provide a (somewhat) reliable foundation for politics.

This vision of politics is one that acknowledges the struggle and unpredictability of politics, consciously trying to forestall attempts to predetermine valid speech. Instead, our political life is one marked by contingency and difference; we cannot know beforehand what sorts of speech will meet our democratic obligations. If we silence unconventional voices—even inadvertently—by reifying ideas about rationality and valid deliberation, we both lose the plurality that defines politics and seriously undermine citizens' capacity for judgment. At the same time, this view of democracy depends on the fact that we remain connected to one another by the construction of political community in spite of difference, sharing a commitment to democratic accountability, as well as a language to articulate those differences (and in other acts of reflexivity, periodically challenging that shared language). We retain our own perspective, acknowledging that we attach different meanings and values to the world and resisting the authori-

54. Warren, "Democracy and Deceit," 161–67.
55. Thanks to Susan Bickford for this language.

tarian urge to erase all these differences. We must engage with others, for to live apart from one's fellows means to not really live at all, as Socrates understood when Crito offered him safe passage from Athens. At the same time, one must think for oneself (although the very expression "think for oneself" is unsatisfactory, for the process is incomplete without other people). Our need for other people exists alongside our own abilities to judge.

Of course, it is not enough to ask citizens in contemporary mass democracies to never rely on leaders or information sources. There are intense pressures that have led to the current obsession with straight talk and reliance on sincerity in politics. For example, media scholar and sociologist John Thompson has connected this politics of faux intimacy with the rise of communication media—"The more political leaders sought to present themselves through the media as ordinary individuals with ordinary lives, the more likely it was that the audiences whom they addressed would be inclined to assess them in terms of their character as individuals—their sincerity, their honesty, their integrity."[56] We live in a "society of self-disclosure," in which politicians feel the need to reveal their interior lives for all to see (or, rather, they try to project the image that they are revealing who they really are). This overarching concern for sincerity is not limited to the political realm. Paddy Scannell analyzes how, with the rise of radio and television, sincerity has come to replace other criteria of aesthetic judgment; instead of praising a singer who hit her notes perfectly, we laud her for putting her heart into the performance.[57] Meanwhile, Bernard Manin argues that, in addition to mass media's influence, the decline of party platforms as arenas for governance become wider and more complex has led to increased reliance on personalities in politics. "When standing for office, politicians know they will have to face the unforeseen; so they are not inclined to tie their hands by committing themselves to a detailed platform . . . the personal *trust* that the candidate inspires is a more adequate basis of selection."[58] These conditions must be taken into account in order to find relief from the politics of sincerity. We need political leaders we are willing to trust because few, if any, citizens are going to follow each issue and take their own policy position. We want a heuristic that can help ensure we elect or listen democratically beneficial leaders and civil society actors; as Chambers counsels, we need a deliberative rhetoric. In what fol-

---

56. Thompson, "New Visibility," 44.
57. Scannell, *Radio, Television and Modern Life*, chap. 3.
58. Manin, *Principles of Representative Government*, 220–21.

lows, I will offer a series of suggestions for strengthening democratic accountability in light of these considerations.

If Not Sincerity, What?

Both Foucault and Habermas suggest that *parrhesia* and sincerity be evaluated according to an individual consistency between word and deed over time. In these views, one can ascertain an actor's motivations by examining how well the words he speaks accord with the actions he undertakes. If a politician, for example, makes a speech in support of a universal healthcare system at a union rally, then returns to Washington, D.C., and votes to establish private healthcare savings accounts instead, suspicion is cast on the sincerity of the speech given at the rally. Because the words did not accord with the actions, the actor would be seen as an insincere speaker. The consistency of words and deeds are believed to point to an inner quality, that of sincerity or *parrhesia.* However, as has been shown, there are good reasons to eschew the language of sincerity. Nonetheless, given the facts of representation and mediation in contemporary democracies, we cannot simply expect citizens to be so participatory that they would never need a political proxy to act on their behalf or need a shorthand guide for political judgment. Thus, we need an alternative to sincerity, but one that avoids the emphasis on the interior motivations and qualities of the human heart, as well as allows a more nuanced understanding of truth. I propose that we judge our representatives not on the basis of their apparent or professed sincerity but on the basis of their trustworthy *ethos.*

We could look to consistency of action and words without looking to it for evidence of sincerity. Given the problems with sincerity, this seems advantageous. The politician in my example who advocated universal health care is inconsistent; the facts of his action did not correspond to the facts of his words. There may be reasons behind his decision—the political climate changed, making such a policy impossible, or convincing new information has come to light disputing the efficiency of such systems. That politician may also be an opportunistic manipulator, but we could never be certain about such a claim. One may be inconsistent, but that does not necessarily mean that he intends to deceive or that it is politically useful for his opponents to believe that of him. It is not one's heart and intentions that should be the issue, but that one has failed to act consistently according to one's own statements or according to the known facts about the world.

As tempting as relying on consistency without sincerity seems, Arendt warns against it, for several reasons. First, consistency is not always desirable. The ability to change is one of the most appealing aspects of humanity for Arendt, deeply tied to the fact of our natality and our ability to create new beginnings (*HC*, 178). The fact that we can act—that is, speak and do things in new and surprising ways, ways that could not be predicted—means that a strict application of a consistency rule would punish precisely what is most free about us. Cherishing consistency above all else holds the danger that we will be more concerned with avoiding the appearance of "waffling" than with responding to changing political realities and the other unique human beings that form our political community. While Patchen Markell has rightly drawn attention to the overstatements of Arendt's emphasis here, the possibility of a break must remain—otherwise, the choice that precedes action loses its meaning.[59] Action is unpredictable, in part, because of the kinds of beings humans are; this quality can be suffocated or neglected in different social constructions, but it remains a fundamental characteristic of individual humans. This accounts for Arendt's hostility toward "the social," a public realm in which she believed all people acted the same, obscuring the place of politics in favor of administration and denying the centrality of human plurality for public life.[60] (Arendt, however, neglected the fact that people may disagree and therefore deliberate about social needs, such as housing and health care—the needs and identities invoked are not identical all the way down.)[61]

The second reason we should be careful in our application of a consistency norm relates to the fact that action is unpredictable because we do not exist alone in the world. Not only are we ourselves unpredictable, but there are many such beings, leading to human plurality: "Human plurality is the paradoxical plurality of unique beings" (*HC*, 176). Much to our own chagrin, we cannot control the results of our actions, or how others interpret them:

59. Patchen Markell, "The Rule of the People: Arendt, *Arche*, and Democracy," *American Political Science Review* 100, no. 1 (February 2006), 7.

60. Commentators have interpreted "the social" several ways, referring to material needs, as well as to what we would now think of as Foucauldian normalization. I draw here on Pitkin's definition. See Pitkin, *Attack of the Blob*, 17, 252.

61. See Bickford, *Dissonance of Democracy*, 72–75, for a full discussion of this problem.

> The disclosure of "who" [one is] through speech, and the setting of a new beginning through action, always fall into an already existing web where their immediate consequences can be felt. Together they start a new process which eventually emerges as the unique life story of the newcomer, affecting uniquely the life stories of all those with whom he comes into contact. It is because of this already existing web of human relationships, with its innumerable, conflicting wills and intentions, that action almost never achieves its purpose. . . . Although everybody started his life by inserting himself into the human world through action and speech, nobody is the author or producer of his own life story. In other words, the stories, the results of action or speech, reveal an agent, but this agent is not an author or producer. Somebody began it and is its subject in the twofold sense of the word, namely, its actor and sufferer, but nobody is its author. (*HC*, 184)

When we act, we determine only part of the meaning of our actions. This does not mean that we bear no responsibility for them; Arendt was certainly not about to absolve people of the ramifications of their choices. But Arendt highlights for us the difficulty of trying to establish either the true intentions that preceded a particular action or its full meaning. Our ability to act, and the boundlessness of that action, is intimately tied to the fact that we are born unique individuals into a world composed of other unique individuals: "Action, the only activity that goes on directly between men without the intermediary of things or matter, corresponds to the human condition of plurality, to the fact that men, not Man, live on the earth and inhabit the world. While all aspects of the human condition are somehow related to politics, this plurality is specifically *the* condition—not only the *conditio sine qua non*, but the *conditio per quam*—of all political life" (*HC*, 7).

For Arendt, the essence of politics is this plurality, the fact we are not just copies of the same being, but each uniquely individual. It is into a web created by this plurality that we insert ourselves with actions, either through word or deed. Our actions are received by distinct others who bring their own perspectives to the table. They may understand our words and deeds to mean something quite different from what we intended them to mean and they may disagree among themselves about the meanings. For that reason, we cannot fully control the reception of our actions.

There is a final reason we cannot comprehensively predict the effects of our actions and should therefore avoid reliance on a consistency norm. Besides the fact that actions fall into this "existing web of human relations," the time period is simply too short. We cannot see the total effect of any action without distance from the event (*HC*, 192). While we may know some effects of the action during or soon after an event, it takes time for the full ramifications to reveal themselves. In politics, we are always living in circumstances shaped by previous history—and often those circumstances bring about unintended consequences for which we must still take political responsibility. A similar situation exists regarding the persons who act: "The essence of who somebody is . . . can come into being only when life departs, leaving behind nothing but a story" (*HC*, 193). Only once we are dead and incapable of a new beginning and changing the course of our story, can the full story of our actions be told. Again, we do not tell the story (although we set it into motion); we must rely on the plurality of other people to interpret our actions. In these ways, action seems unfree— that is, we do not control our own stories—but Arendt rejects the impulse to withdraw into oneself and away from politics because to do so would be to "exchange the real world for an imaginary one" (*HC*, 234). Thus, we see that consistency may be too blunt an instrument for evaluating speakers and their actions. Moreover, to make consistency more useful and to account for surface inconsistencies, it is tempting to go back to an investigation of true intentions—something that looks like a "flip-flop" might be explained by reference to what the speaker *really* meant to accomplish.

Given the difficulties of consistency and its long association with sincerity in the literature, let me propose that we look to some other aspect of character. According to Aristotle, the character projected by a particular speaker is his *ethos*:[62] "There is persuasion through character [*ethos*] whenever the speech is spoken in such a way as to make the speaker worthy of credence."[63] Thus, to project *ethos* is project a certain type of authority. Of course, this authority could be rooted in one's sincerity or Christian virtues or expertise in a particular craft. The relevant basis for authority and the type of character one should project differs according to context.[64] So we

---

62. For more on the variety of uses of the term, see Anderson, *The Way We Argue Now*, 136–37.

63. Aristotle, *On Rhetoric: A Theory of Civic Discourse*, trans. George Kennedy (Oxford: Oxford University Press, 1991), 38.

64. Ibid., 168.

must determine what sort of *ethos* is appropriate to speakers in a healthy deliberative democracy.

Current usages of *ethos* are often unsatisfying, linking *ethos* to the speaker's interior life and not making clear the distinction I advocate. For example, according to Eugene Garver's authoritative work on Aristotle's *Rhetoric*, "We assume that if someone can give good advice, he or she must be a good person."[65] Although Garver's work is persuasive on many counts and although the interior often leads to the appearance of a particular *ethos*, the emphasis on whether or not a political speaker is a good person (using appearance to determine the interior) is, as I have shown, deeply problematic for contemporary democratic political life. Likewise, Simone Chambers's notion of "virtuous character" noted in Chapter 1 is problematic, not necessarily because of her particular usage, but because of what "virtue" and "character" have come to mean in contemporary politics. As Amanda Anderson notes, "For many . . . 'character' is fatally shadowed by its long ideological history in the service of mystified notions of distinction, nobility, and worthiness."[66] Likewise, when citizens today think of the character of a politician or virtue, they tend to think of it in terms of such personal and intimate qualities. Even if we were to overcome this problem, we still need to know more about "virtuous character." That is, what is the content of the *ethos* appropriate to a mass-mediated representative democracy? If we were to work from Aristotle's description, which of the many virtues he describes do we mean? As Bernard Yack notes, "Character plays an especially weighty role in helping people decide when they are uncertain . . . it plays a crucial secondary role in public argument, since so many of the reputable opinions that provide its premises are more notable for the good or bad reputation of the person endorsing it than for the premise itself."[67] Citizens rely on character; the claim here pertains to what sort of character they should rely on. Given the critique here, a sincere *ethos* is not a suitable option; instead, I propose that the idea of a "trustworthy *ethos*" can get us where we want to go.

"Trustworthiness" offers an intersubjectively conscious foundation for critique as an alternative to the interiority of the sincerity ethic. While

65. Eugene Garver, *Aristotle's Rhetoric: An Art of Character* (Chicago: University of Chicago Press, 1994), 148.
66. Anderson, *The Way We Argue Now*, 137.
67. Bernard Yack, "Rhetoric and Public Reasoning: An Aristotelian Understanding of Political Deliberation," *Political Theory* 34, no. 4 (August 2006): 430.

"sincerity" pertains to an inner moral quality of purity and a lack of duplicity, to be "trustworthy" is, according to the *Oxford English Dictionary*, to
be "worthy of trust." It also means "taking responsibility for one's conduct
and actions," according to the WordNet database (at the Cognitive Science
Lab of Princeton University). While one may object that we should simply
redefine "sincerity," that term has a long history of referring to an inner
state; moreover, it differs from trustworthiness in that sincerity refers to
an individual quality, which one could have or not have regardless of other
people, while "trustworthiness" makes sense only in a context of intersub-
jectivity. Trustworthiness also does not pertain to a particular speech act,
the way "sincerity" is often used; instead, one must rely on the entire
context, making room for the ironist or mythmaker, in addition to promoting the rhetorical trust that is critical in a mass democracy.

A trustworthy *ethos* also moves us away from other glosses on *ethos*
that slide too easily back to a concern with the interior life of the speaker.
In keeping with the Athenian emphasis on appearances and public space,
Aristotle's *ethos* is the publicly displayed character, not a direct reference
to an internal quality of that person or to an established reputation. In his
discussion of *ethos*, Aristotle makes clear that we should concentrate on
character that results "from the speech, not from a previous opinion that
the speaker is a certain kind of person."[68] Although the revealed character
can in fact spring from that internal source (or could be a false representation), the interior is not where others may identify it. Thus, Aristotle's
work has an appreciation of the importance of appearances and continuous
audience attention to the speaker that is deeply appealing and which
inspired Arendt. An emphasis on a trustworthy *ethos* focuses on the public
aspects of a speaker's character and remains conscious of the difference
between that appearance and whatever private moral characteristics that
same speaker might have. We must reinvigorate the meaning of *ethos* as a
public projection that, while related to the interior, cannot be identified for
political life there. "In modern times we seem to have lost our sense of the
distinction between the private and the public spheres," and thus the audience is concerned with moral cores and has an "*ethos* that slights questions
of public life by setting personality above character, an *ethos* that denies
the importance of *ethos*."[69] Here we find an extremely useful sense of

68. Ibid. See also Garver, *Aristotle's Rhetoric*, 14.
69. S. Michael Halloran, "Aristotle's Concept of Ethos, or If Not His Somebody Else's,"
Rhetoric Review 1, no. 1 (September 1982): 62–63.

ethos, that of the *public* projection of character, defined not as personality or actions in the intimate, private sphere, but character as revealed in the realm of appearances. We are still using character as an aide in judgment, and we may refer to a variety of the speaker's attributes—such as former business dealings, publicly disclosed investments, previous statements and writings, and voting records. But we remain modest in our claims about what we can know about a person, in addition to remaining focused on which particular qualities matter in the political arena.

How can we identify a trustworthy *ethos?* This book has argued that for too long we have been attentive to those who project an aura of sincerity as the foundation for their authority. It went on to argue that sincerity is too chimerical a foundation, too seductive and too manipulable, leading to a dangerous obsession with the intimate in the public arena. Therefore, we should look for a trustworthy *ethos,* but not necessarily a sincere one. This emphasis on "trustworthy" actors allows citizens to rely on fellow citizens—a necessity in contemporary representative democracy—but it also allows for citizen judgment because this quality refers to the relationship of trust between a speaker and another person—is *this* particular person worthy of *my* trust at this point in time? Trustworthiness is a temporary quality; one can gain or lose it, depending on recent events. Speakers who get facts wrong or say things deeply at odds with our core values may not be worthy of our trust. This gain or loss occurs, not because of some objective standard of trustworthiness, but according to individual citizen judgment—I should not trust that speaker to make political decisions on my behalf. (Thus, this does not mean that the speaker is not "worthy" in other senses—such as worthy of life, friendship, other people's political trust, and interpersonal trust.) He or she is not worthy of *my political* trust, according to the judgment I have made in light of the context. This notion of trust is deeply intersubjective and discursive, taking seriously the deliberative imperatives of mutual respect and democratic accountability through speech. This notion of trust is *not* dependent on some loving friendship with others; instead I follow Allen in relying on an Aristotelian notion of civic friendship, highlighting trust (she calls it friendship in this passage) as a "set of hard-won, complicated habits."[70] This is a public foundation for community, one that eschews concern with fellow citizens' interior life and

70. Allen, *Talking to Strangers,* xxi. See also Jill Frank, *A Democracy of Distinction: Aristotle and the Work of Politics* (Chicago: University of Chicago Press, 2005), chap. 5.

instead focuses on the shared stage of appearances. Assessing the political character of speakers is a critical way for individual citizens to exercise their own political judgment; it requires continuous effort—reminiscent of the Athenian attention to accountability mechanisms—while also acknowledging that we do not live in a direct democracy and instead rely on leadership and mass media.[71]

Because of the importance of context to this judgment, it can be difficult to spell out the circumstances under which one gains or loses a reputation for trustworthiness. Still, there are certain citizen practices we can encourage to promote this heuristic and to temper the desire for sincere politicians. Trustworthy individuals provide good arguments rooted in factual truth (although myth and allegory may come into play), with appropriate normative commitments (that is, appropriate for the listener). Thus, this notion allows for a robust link between *ethos* and *logos,* as judgments of a speaker's trustworthiness would depend on the speaker's arguments. Trustworthy speakers focus on their actions and speeches, rather than the true—but unseen—intentions behind their actions; one does not earn trust by consistently failing to fulfill one's one good intentions, nor does one achieve it by fulfilling one's lousy intentions. Attention should be on performance, rather than inwardly focused. It is through one's public actions that one's trustworthiness is revealed. Rhetoric becomes especially important in this context; since the presentation of self on the public stage is a choice, it is precisely the speaker's choice to invoke the intimate that should indicate poor judgment on her part. In short, trustworthy politicians spend little time talking about how trustworthy they are. Meanwhile, when one does face uncontrolled or unintended events, the trustworthy citizen takes political (not personal) responsibility for them, regardless of one's intentions, highlighting the second meaning of "trustworthy." For example, when discussing Eichmann's trial, Arendt maintains that "every government assumes political responsibility for the deeds and misdeeds of the past."[72] We inherit political legacies, in addition to creating them for others; we cannot refuse political responsibility simply because we do not feel we have personal responsibility. A politically trustworthy individual takes responsibility for the situation (not just control of) and refrains from invoking good intentions in spite of failures. The trustworthy individual also responds

71. Much thanks for Gerry Mara for this point.

72 Hannah Arendt, *Eichmann in Jerusalem: A Report on the Banality of Evil* (New York: Penguin, 1994), 297–98.

fully to the institutional mechanisms of accountability and acknowledges the reciprocity necessary for democratic governance. As Danielle Allen has shown, without this reciprocity, it becomes very difficult, if not impossible, to generate political trust.[73]

Over time, actions will create a subtext against which current actions and statements can be read. But each new opportunity for action poses a chance to begin again—a new "irrevocable event . . . and point of departure."[74] Because humans are the types of beings they are, there is no guarantee that the actor of past history will choose yet again to act in a trustworthy way—there is a choice to be made. While these actions will not always break with the past, they should represent a practical engagement with the world, and so the possibility of choice and change must remain. It is therefore crucial that the public not rely solely on a reputation for trustworthiness—each new situation could be a signal that this person needs to lose or gain this designation; this is one reason for Aristotle's emphasis on character revealed through speech, not "previous opinion." If we were to take a reputation as a guarantor of that person's commitment to democratic politics and therefore a license to cease the activities that ensure accountability, we would lose our own commitment to democratic politics. There can be no guarantees and the effort to establish the precise nature of an actor's consistency or lack of it is a complex and long-term one. While one may establish a reputation as a person who is worthy of trust, because democratic politics is iterative and performative, reputation is not a sufficient substitute for the relentless questioning and answering required of democratic accountability. (Nor should it necessarily be taken to be a reflection of that person's moral core.) Thus, a reliance on a speaker's trustworthiness is a contingent thing that requires steady examination.

How can we encourage a reliance on speakers with a trustworthy *ethos*, rather than assertions of sincerity? First, we should pay more attention to institutional ways to ensure accountability. Institutional mechanisms are critically important, as discourse ethics of any sort remain an unstable and easily perverted foundation for democratic deliberation. Because of the freedoms embedded within it, democracy requires sure and regular ways to question and probe political actions, as the Athenians knew. Yet we do not have to make assumptions about one another's sincerity; we should

73 See Allen, *Talking to Strangers*.
74. Markell, "Rule of the People," 7.

acknowledge that assertions and claims about our own and others' inner core are unreliable. Instead, we must institute formal mechanisms of questioning and performance review. Too often we engage in a political discourse that seems to be centrally focused on the interior life and presumed commitments of various actors. Instead, we should take claims about hidden and true intentions out of politics, removing one source of vitriol and apathy. We need various institutions that serve as an actual check on whether actions serve democratic interests, depersonalizing deliberation and acknowledging that such testing is the only reliable way to protect our democracy from those who will, invariably, lie.[75] Since there is "no people of gods," we need to develop more institutional ways to hold actors accountable for their speeches; Athenian mechanisms of accountability can provide a source of inspiration for this task. As Socrates did in a reflection of Athenian practices, we must test the speech of others, conscious of the instability of democratic discourse, even as we try to create foundations that can provide avenues of accountability. As Arlene Saxonhouse writes, "The assemblies of ancient Greece do not make the moral demands on their citizens that contemporary deliberative democrats do; the challenge is to test the speeches of concrete individuals, with personalities and interests, against one another in the search for what the city must do in its own interest."[76] Note that Saxonhouse talks about testing the *speeches*, not the personalities of individuals, although she acknowledges that personalities play a role; the key difference is whether assertions of personal traits can take the place of such *testing* and whether the interior life, rather than actions and statements, is the proper focus of investigations.

Such a vision of politics would better account for both the difficulty and the promise of deliberation, as well as the unique qualities of political action and community noted by Arendt. Certain measures may necessitate rethinking what we demand of public officials; certainly, mandating regular open forums in which any interested constituent is able to ask any (that is, not prescreened) question of officials would require a great deal of political will. In other ways, our contemporary practices may just need some tweak-

75. Anderson argues in chapter 7 of *The Way We Argue Now* that Habermas's conception of proceduralism already "shifts the perspective to that of political institutions and collective practice, explicitly refusing the notion that individuals carry the burden of cultivating the virtue required for a well-ordered polis" (176). In the end, then, my position here is quite close to her reading of Habermas.

76. Saxonhouse, "Democratic Deliberation," 70.

ing. Current institutions in the United States seem to fall far short too often. For example, public officials are already required to account for expenditures and file public reports; however, these reports (such as campaign finance reports) are often filed late and erroneously filled out, and difficult for the average citizen to find. Strengthened and extended accountability practices—more reminiscent of the *euthunai* and *dokimasia* of ancient Greece—would help improve the quality of democratic discourse, as well as citizens' capacity for judgment. We should, for example, increase funding for venues that compile candidate records and statements. Several of these already exist—such as www.opensecrets.org—yet these are largely the province of political junkies and are inhibited by the continued "digital divide."[77] Likewise, the oft-maligned area of opposition research might also be seen as a useful public service (as long as it refrains from the sort of personal dirty-laundry airing that has led to its bad reputation).[78] Especially in contemporary democracy, with its representative institutions and mass media, it is unlikely that we would actually need to investigate the private person in order to make a political judgment of his or her character. For example, say a particular congressperson privately believes that his wife should submit to his authority based on religious belief, and that, at home, he lives such a life. Would a feminist want such a person making political decisions as her representative? Probably not. But this information isn't necessarily indicative of his political decisions, nor is it necessary to judge his political impact. He may cherish his religious beliefs and lifestyle, but he may also cherish his commitment to democratic toleration or liberal government enough to have a very different political agenda than others might assume is a necessary result of his private beliefs. Even if that politician would in fact pose a problem for a feminist political agenda, the candidate most likely has a public record of votes, proposals, public statements,

---

77. This may be changing as the Internet evolves. In 2006, the CEO of Google, Inc., warned politicians that the Internet could soon be used to hold politicians to account. "One of my messages to them (politicians) is to think about having every one of your voters online all the time, then inputting 'is this true or false.' We (at Google) are not in charge of truth but we might be able to give a probability." Reuters, "Google Boss Warns Politicians about Internet Power," October 3, 2006, http://reuters.myway.com/article/20061004/2006–10–04T005304Z_01_L03419567_RTRIDST_0_NEWS-GOOGLE-POLITICIANS-DC.html/ (accessed October 21, 2006).

78. For a more sinister view of this field, see Joshua Green, "Playing Dirty," *Atlantic Monthly* (June 2004). On the other hand, I once worked as an opposition researcher, compiling votes and statements of state legislators who were not owning up to less desirable aspects of their public records.

and campaign literature that one could rely on to make the decision, without digging into his family life or religious beliefs (although those things likely inform his public decisions).

Instead of lauding sincerity, contemporary democracy would benefit from greater emphasis on skeptical listening, based not on a speaker's personal traits, but on the relation of that speaker's actions and statements to truth and values—did the speech remain faithful to the facts? Did it promote democracy, mutual respect, and accountability (or whatever value the listener feels is important)? We should encourage citizens to be pesky questioners with a developed sense of rhetorical literacy, less swayed by professions of intent. Instead of looking for a sincere politician to rely on, citizens should be looking to establish contingent relationships of trust with leaders, relationships that are often tested through various institutions. As Chapters 3 and 4 showed, reading Plato's Socratic dialogues can be one way to help develop the judgment that could underpin such relationships. These dialogues are already part of the accepted "Western Canon"; of course, they are not always taught in such a way as to develop an individual's judgment. Yet that they can and ought to be. Such democratic ideology, coupled with serious attention to formal institutions of accountability, could help provide the foundation that a representative democratic polity based on speech needs and which deliberative democrats are seeking.

To this end, we should encourage the development of "rhetorical literacy" programs within political science departments and in secondary civics education akin some of the "media literacy" programs gaining popularity with educators[79] or the "Rhet-Ed" program suggested by Wayne Booth.[80] Media literacy programs, for example, are designed to equip young people with the analytical skills to recognize different messages in the media and to learn to evaluate the claims made based on their own values; they have been shown to increase students' critical thinking skills, as well as lower rates of substance abuse (depending on the program).[81] The Alliance for a Media Literate America explains its mission:

79. See http://www.amlainfo.org or www.medialit.org/ (accessed August 1, 2006).
80. Booth, *Rhetoric of Rhetoric*, chap. 5.
81. Renee Hobbs and Richard Frost, "Measuring the Acquisition of Media Skills," *Reading Research Quarterly* 38, no. 3 (July/August/September 2003): 330–55. Other programs focus directly on drug, alcohol, and tobacco abuse prevention. For information of the effectiveness of programs related specifically to alcohol, see E. W. Austin, B. E. Pinkleton, and S.J.T. Hust, "Evaluation of an American Legacy Foundation/Washington State Department of Health Media Literacy Pilot Study," *Health Communication*, 18, no. 1 (2005): 75–79, and P. L. Ellickson, R. L. Collins, K. Hambarsoomians, and D. F. McCaffrey, "Does Alcohol Advertising

Media literacy is seen to consist of a series of communication competencies, including the ability to ACCESS, ANALYZE, EVALUATE, and COMMUNICATE information in a variety of forms, including print and non-print messages. Interdisciplinary by nature, media literacy represents a necessary, inevitable, and realistic response to the complex, ever-changing electronic environment and communication cornucopia that surround us.[82]

These programs are funded in a variety of ways, although no single national effort to implement these programs currently exists (the Canadian school system, in contrast, has a program in every school district). At the same time, civic education efforts in the United States are on the decline, leaving young people with fewer and fewer resources to negotiate our increasingly complex and large democracy.[83] Instead, we must increase funding and support for civic education, with a curricular model based on these other literacy programs. While many English and Communications programs already strive to develop this literacy among students, my concern here is with the neglect of rhetorical literacy in political science and civics education. Until political scientists accept the central importance of rhetoric for political practices, we will be doing a disservice to both students and democracy. These programs might incorporate my understanding of the ethos of trustworthiness; I would also suggest using Danielle Allen's guidelines for listening (as an effort to promote trust among citizens),[84] as well as Wayne

Promote Adolescent Drinking? Results from a Longitudinal Assessment," *Addiction* 100, no. 2 (2005): 235–46.

82. http://www.amlainfo.org/home/media-literacy/ (accessed August 1, 2006).

83. See, for example, "Does a Downturn in Civic Education Signal a Disconnect to Democracy?" *Carnegie Reporter* 2, no. 3 (Fall 2003), and Nat Hentoff, "What You Don't Know Can Hurt You," *USA Today*, July 12, 2006.

84. According to Danielle Allen (*Talking to Strangers*, 158), these are "1. Separate a speaker's claims about facts from the principles on which her conclusions are based; assess both; 2. Ask whether a speaker has a history of making pragmatically correct decisions; 3. Ask who is sacrificing for whom, whether the sacrifices are voluntary, and honored; whether they can and will be reciprocated; 4. Ask whether the speaker has spoken as a friend [in the Aristotelian sense; meaning the person recognizes the shared life they have together and acts in accordance with "ethical reciprocity"]; 5. Insist on opportunities to judge political arguments; and 6. Judge." The first recommendation helps avoid collapsing the claim to factual truth alongside other claims, a problem noted in Chapter 1; numbers 5 and 6 get at the importance of judgment for politics and the importance of accountability. Meanwhile, numbers 2–5 involve components of trustworthiness—does this person merit political trust? Does this person acknowledge our shared context? Are they taking political responsibility for sacrifices made? Is there democratic accountability?

Booth's guidelines for teaching "listening rhetoric."[85] These sources provide a useful starting point for thinking about the kind of political literacy we should encourage in citizens. Using the Arendtian vision of politics outlined here—one that privileges the public-ness of politics and encourages judgment—is, of course, key. Students must learn to differentiate between appeals grounded in the claim to moral goodness and trustworthy appeals that refuse the temptations of a personalized, impoverished public stage. We need to change the *ethos* of the audiences through a rhetorically literate and Arendtian-inspired civics and political science education. Coupled with the judgment that develops from negotiating Plato's dialogues, we have the foundation for a new type of civic education.

Speech will always remain a frustrating tool in our political life. Paradoxically, the best way to ensure a genuine commitment to truth in politics is to relax our wholesale endorsement of sincerity in politics—a commitment that perversely enables Machiavellian realists, in addition to drawing our attention away from the original concern and away from possible institutional remedies. Democratic communication requires more complex and difficult efforts than the sincerity ethic recommends or the popular fascination with straight talk encourages. This does not mean we abandon other normative commitments in deliberative theory or that "anything goes" in democratic discourse. We must work toward a healthy democratic discourse on multiple fronts. We should embrace an Arendtian understanding of democratic discourse, one that emphasizes the importance of appearances, plurality, and judgment for a healthy polity. Coupling this vision of deliberative processes with an emphasis on listening to those speakers with an ethos of trustworthiness will better equip citizens to attend to the imperatives of reciprocity and mutual respect that invigorate democratic commitments. To support these efforts, we must revitalize institutional means of accountability, relying on actual examination instead of individual goodwill to ensure the quality of democratic governance. We must also renew our commitment of civic education, acknowledging that rhetorical literacy is a critical tool for citizenship practices. Of course, these challenges are extremely difficult ones. Yet as we have seen since the first attempts at self-governance in Athens, democracy requires a sustained effort to forestall the routinization of its radical impulses and the dulling of democratic judgment.

85. Booth, *Rhetoric of Rhetoric*.

BIBLIOGRAPHY

Abizadeh, Arash. "Historical Truth, National Myths and Liberal Democracy: On the Coherence of Liberal Nationalism." *Journal of Political Philosophy* 12, no. 3 (2004): 291–313.

Ahl, Frederick. "The Art of Safe Criticism." *American Journal of Philology* 105, no. 2 (Summer 1984): 174–208.

Alcoff, Linda. "The Problem of Speaking for Others." In *Theorizing Feminisms: A Reader*, ed. Elizabeth Hackett and Sally Haslanger, 78–92. Oxford: Oxford University Press, 2006. Originally published as "The Problem of Speaking for Others," *Cultural Critique*, no. 20 (Winter 1991–92): 5–32.

Allen, Danielle. *Talking to Strangers: Anxieties of Citizenship since Brown v. Board of Education.* Chicago: University of Chicago Press, 2004.

Alterman, Eric. "Bush Lies, Media Swallows." *Nation*, November 25, 2002.

Anderson, Amanda. *The Way We Argue Now: A Study in the Cultures of Theory.* Princeton: Princeton University Press, 2006.

Anzaldúa, Gloria. "En rapport, In Opposition: Cobrando cuentas a las neustras." In *Making Face, Making Soul, Haciendo Caras: Creative and Critical Perspectives by Feminists of Color*, ed. Gloria Anzaldúa, 142–48. San Francisco: Aunt Lute Books, 1990.

Arendt, Hannah. *Between Past and Future.* New York: Penguin Books, 1977.

———. *Eichmann in Jerusalem: A Report on the Banality of Evil.* New York: Penguin, 1994.

———. *The Human Condition.* Chicago: University of Chicago Press, 1998.

———. *Lectures on Kant's Political Philosophy.* Edited by Ronald Beiner. Chicago: University of Chicago Press, 1992.

———. *The Life of the Mind: Thinking, Willing.* Two vols. New York: Harcourt Brace Jovanovich, 1977.

———. *On Revolution.* New York: Penguin/Pelican Books, 1977.

———. *The Origins of Totalitarianism.* New York: Harcourt Brace Jovanovich, 1973.

Aristotle. *On Rhetoric: A Theory of Civic Discourse.* Edited by George Kennedy. Oxford: Oxford University Press, 1991.

Augustine. *City of God.* New York: Image/Doubleday, 1958.

Aune, James Arnt. *Selling the Free Market: The Rhetoric of Economic Correctness.* New York: Guilford Press, 2001.

Austin, E. W., B. E. Pinkleton, and S.J.T. Hust. "Evaluation of an American Legacy Foundation /Washington State Department of Health Media Literacy Pilot Study." *Health Communication* 18, no. 1 (2005): 75–79.

Bakhtin, M. M. *The Dialogic Imagination: Four Essays.* Austin: University of Texas Press, 1981.

Barber, Benjamin. "Misreading Democracy: Peter Euben and the *Gorgias.*" In *Demokratia: A Conversation on Democracies Ancient and Modern,* ed. Josiah Ober and Charles Hedrick, 361–76. Princeton: Princeton University Press, 1996.

Beiner, Ronald. *Political Judgment.* London: Methuen, 1983.

Benhabib, Seyla, ed. *Democracy and Difference: Contesting the Boundaries of the Political.* Princeton: Princeton University Press, 1996.

———. Introduction to *Democracy and Difference: Contesting the Boundaries of the Political,* ed. Benhabib, 3–18. Princeton: Princeton University Press, 1996.

———. *Situating the Self: Gender, Community, and Postmodernism in Contemporary Ethics.* New York: Routledge, 1992.

———. "Toward a Deliberative Model of Democratic Legitimacy." In *Democracy and Difference: Contesting the Boundaries of the Political,* ed. Benhabib, 67–94. Princeton: Princeton University Press, 1996.

Bennett, W. Lance, and Robert M. Entman. Introduction to *Mediated Politics: Communication in the Future of Democracy,* ed. Bennett and Entman, 1–29. Cambridge: Cambridge University Press, 2001.

———, eds. *Mediated Politics: Communication in the Future of Democracy.* Cambridge: Cambridge University Press, 2001.

Benardete, Seth. *Rhetoric of Morality and Philosophy.* Chicago: University of Chicago Press, 1991.

Beversluis, John. Cross-Examining Socrates: A Defense of the Interlocutors in Plato's Early Dialogues. Cambridge: Cambridge University Press, 2000.

Bickford, Susan. *The Dissonance of Democracy: Listening, Conflict, and Citizenship.* Ithaca: Cornell University Press, 1996.

———. "Propriety and Provocation in Arendt's Political Aesthetic." In *Hannah Arendt and the Meaning of Politics,* ed. Craig Calhoun and John McGowan, 85–95. Minneapolis: University of Minnesota Press, 1997.

Blair, Sara B. "Good Housekeeping: Virginia Woolf and the Politics of Irony." In *The Politics of Irony: Essays in Self-Betrayal,* ed. Daniel Conway and John Seery, 99–118. New York: St. Martin's Press, 1992.

Bloom, Allan. *The Republic of Plato.* New York: Basic Books, 1991.

Bohman, James. "The Coming of Age of Deliberative Democracy." *Journal of Political Philosophy* 6, no. 4 (1998): 400–425.

———. "Deliberative Toleration." *Political Theory* 31, no. 6 (December 2003): 757–79.

Bohman, James, and William Rehg, eds. *Deliberative Democracy: Essays on Reason and Politics.* Cambridge: MIT Press, 1997.

Booth, Wayne C. *The Company We Keep: An Ethics of Fiction.* Berkeley and Los Angeles: University of California Press, 1988.

———. *A Rhetoric of Irony.* Chicago: University of Chicago Press, 1974.

———. *The Rhetoric of Rhetoric: A Quest for Effective Communication.* Malden, Mass.: Blackwell, 2004.

Brisson, Luc. *Plato the Mythmaker.* Chicago: University of Chicago Press, 1998.

Buker, Eloise. *Talking Feminist Politics: Conversations on Law, Science, and the Postmodern.* Lanham, Md.: Rowman and Littlefield, 1999.

Butler, Judith. *Gender Trouble: Feminism and the Subversion of Identity.* New York: Routledge, 1999.

Button, Mark. "'A Monkish Kind of Virtue'? For and Against Humility." *Political Theory* 33, no. 6 (December 2005): 840–68.

Calhoun, Craig, ed. *Habermas and Public Sphere.* Cambridge: MIT Press, 1992.

Calhoun, Craig, and John McGowan, eds. *Hannah Arendt and the Meaning of Politics.* Minneapolis: Minnesota University Press, 1997.

Carey, Christopher. "Rhetorical Means of Persuasion." In *Persuasion: Greek Rhetoric in Action,* ed. Ian Worthington, 26–45. New York: Routledge, 1994.

Carmola, Kateri. "Noble Lying: Justice and Intergenerational Tension in Plato's *Republic.*" *Political Theory* 31, no. 1 (February 2003): 39–62.

Carter, April, and Geoffrey Stokes, eds. *Democratic Theory Today.* Cambridge: Polity Press, 2002.

Chambers, Simone. "Behind Closed Doors: Publicity, Secrecy, and the Quality of Deliberation." *Journal of Political Philosophy* 12, no. 4 (December 2004): 389–410.

———. *Reasonable Democracy.* Ithaca: Cornell University Press, 1996.

Cohen, Joshua. "Procedure and Substance in Deliberative Democracy." In *Deliberative Democracy: Essays on Reason and Politics,* ed. James Bohman and William Rehg, 407–37. Cambridge: MIT Press, 1997.

Cole, Susan Guettel. "Oath Ritual and the Male Community at Athens." In *Demokratia: A Conversation on Democracies Ancient and Modern,* ed. Josiah Ober and Charles Hedrick, 227–48. Princeton: Princeton University Press, 1996.

Conover, Pamela J., Donald D. Searing, and Ivor Crewe. "The Deliberative Potential of Political Discussion." *British Journal of Political Science* 32, no. 1 (2002): 21–62.

Conway, Daniel W., and John E. Seery. Introduction to *The Politics of Irony: Essays in Self-Betrayal,* ed. Conway and Seery, 1–4. New York: St. Martin's Press, 1992.

———, eds. *The Politics of Irony: Essays in Self-Betrayal.* New York: St. Martin's Press, 1992.

Consigny, Scott. *Gorgias: Sophist and Artist.* Columbia: University of South Carolina Press, 2001.

Curtis, Kimberly. *Our Sense of the Real: Aesthetic Experience and Arendtian Politics.* Ithaca: Cornell University Press, 1999.

Deacon, Terrence W. *The Symbolic Species.* New York: W. W. Norton, 1997.

Dickinson, Tim. "Have Clip Art, Will Dissent." *Mother Jones,* April 3, 2003.

Dietz, Mary G. "Trapping *The Prince:* Machiavelli and the Politics of Deception." *American Political Science Review* 80, no. 3 (September 1986): 777–99.

Disch, Lisa. "Impartiality, Storytelling, and the Seductions of Narrative: An Essay at an Impasse." *Alternatives* 28 (2003): 253–66.

———. "More Truth Than Fact: Storytelling as Critical Understanding in the Writings of Hannah Arendt." *Political Theory* 21, no. 4, (1993): 665–94.

———. "Please Sit Down, But Don't Make Yourself at Home: 'Visiting' and the Prefigurative Politics of Consciousness-Raising." In *Hannah Arendt and the*

Meaning of Politics, ed. Craig Calhoun and John McGowan, 132–65. Minneapolis: Minnesota University Press, 1997.

Dodds, E. R. Plato's Gorgias: *A Revised Text with Introduction and Commentary.* Oxford: Oxford University Press, 1959.

Dryzek, John. *Deliberative Democracy and Beyond: Liberals, Critics, Contestations.* Oxford: Oxford University Press, 2000.

Elias, Julius A. *Plato's Defense of Poetry.* London: MacMillan Press, 1984.

Ellickson, P. L., R. L. Collins, K. Hambarsoomians, and D. F. McCaffrey. "Does Alcohol Advertising Promote Adolescent Drinking? Results from a Longitudinal Assessment." *Addiction* 100, no. 2 (2005): 235–46.

Elster, Jon, ed. *Deliberative Democracy.* Cambridge: Cambridge University Press, 1998.

Euben, J. Peter. *Corrupting Youth: Political Education, Democratic Culture, and Political Theory.* Princeton: Princeton University Press, 1997.

———. *Platonic Noise.* Princeton: Princeton University Press, 2003.

———. *The Tragedy of Political Theory: The Road Not Taken.* Princeton: Princeton University Press, 1990.

Euben, J. Peter, John R. Wallach, and Josiah Ober. Introduction to *Athenian Political Thought and the Reconstruction of American Democracy,* ed. Euben, Wallach, and Ober, 1–26. Ithaca: Cornell University Press, 1994.

Fishkin, James, and Peter Laslett, eds. *Debating Deliberative Democracy.* Malden, Mass.: Blackwell Publishing, 2003.

Flood, Christopher G. *Political Myth: A Theoretical Introduction.* New York: Routledge, 2002.

Fontana, Benedetto, Cary J. Nederman, and Gary Remer, eds. *Talking Democracy: Historical Perspectives on Rhetoric and Democracy.* University Park: Pennsylvania State University Press, 2004.

Foucault, Michel. *Fearless Speech.* Los Angeles: Semiotext(e), 2001.

Frank, Jill. *A Democracy of Distinction: Aristotle and the Work of Politics.* Chicago: University of Chicago Press, 2005.

Frank, Thomas. *The Conquest of Cool.* Chicago: University of Chicago Press, 1998.

———. *What's the Matter with Kansas: How Conservatives Won the Heart of America.* New York: Metropolitan Books, 2004.

Frankfurt, Harry. *On Bullshit.* Princeton: Princeton University Press, 2005.

———. *On Truth.* New York: Knopf, 2006.

Fraser, Nancy. "Pragmatism, Feminism, and the Linguistic Turn." In *Feminist Contentions: A Philosophical Exchange,* ed. Linda Nicholson, 151–71. New York: Routledge, 1995.

———. "Rethinking the Public Sphere: A Contribution to the Critique of Actually Existing Democracy." In *Habermas and the Public Sphere,* ed. Craig Calhoun, 109–42. Cambridge: MIT Press, 1992.

Frazer, Michael L. "Esotericism Ancient and Modern: Strauss Contra Straussianism on the Art of Political-Philosophical Writing." *Political Theory* 34, no. 1 (February 2006): 33–61.

Freydberg, Bernard. *The Play of the Platonic Dialogues.* New York: Peter Lang, 1991.

Garsten, Bryan. *Saving Persuasion: A Defense of Rhetoric and Judgment.* Cambridge: Harvard University Press, 2006.

Garver, Eugene. "After *Virtù:* Rhetoric, Prudence, and Moral Pluralism in Machia-velli." In *Prudence: Classical Virtue, Postmodern Practice,* ed. Robert Hariman, 67–97. University Park: Pennsylvania State University Press, 2003.

———. Aristotle's Rhetoric: *An Art of Character.* Chicago: University of Chicago Press, 1994.

Gaus, Gerald F. "Reason, Justifications, and Consensus: Why Democracy Can't Have It All." In *Deliberative Democracy: Essays on Reason and Politics,* ed. James Bohman and William Rehg. Cambridge: MIT Press, 1997.

Gill, Christopher, Norman Postlethwaite, and Richard Seaford, eds. *Reciprocity in Ancient Greece.* Oxford: Oxford University Press, 1998.

Goffman, Erving. *The Presentation of Self in Everyday Life.* New York: Anchor Books, 1959.

Goodin, Robert E. "Sequencing Deliberative Moments." *Acta Politica* 40, no. 2 (July 2005): 182–96.

Gordon, Jill. "Against Vlastos on Complex Irony." *Classical Quarterly* 46, no. 1 (1996): 131–37.

Grant, Ruth. *Hypocrisy and Integrity: Machiavelli, Rousseau, and the Ethics of Politics.* Chicago: University of Chicago Press, 1997.

Green, Joshua. "Playing Dirty." *Atlantic Monthly* 293, no. 5 (June 2004).

Greene, Joshua D., R. Brian Sommerville, Leigh E. Nystrom, John M. Darley, and Jonathan D. Cohen. "An fMRI Investigation of Emotional Engagement in Moral Judgment." *Science* 293 (2001): 2105–8.

Grice, Paul. *Studies in the Way of Words.* Cambridge: Harvard University Press, 1989.

Griswold, Charles L., Jr., ed. *Platonic Readings / Platonic Writings.* University Park: Pennsylvania State University Press, 2002.

Gutmann, Amy, and Dennis Thompson. *Democracy and Disagreement.* Cambridge: Belknap Press of Harvard University Press, 1996.

Habermas, Jürgen. *Between Facts and Norms: Contributions to a Discourse Theory of Law and Democracy.* Cambridge: MIT Press, 1996.

———. On the Pragmatics of Social Interaction: *Preliminary Studies in the Theory of Communicative Action.* Cambridge: MIT Press, 2001.

———. Moral Consciousness and Communicative Action. Cambridge: MIT Press, 1990.

———. A Theory of Communicative Action. Vol. 1, *Reason and the Rationaliza-tion of Society.* Boston: Beacon Press, 1984.

———. A Theory of Communicative Action. Vol. 2, *Lifeworld and System: A Cri-tique of Functionalist Reason.* Boston: Beacon Press, 1987.

———. "Three Normative Models of Democracy." In *Democracy and Difference: Contesting the Boundaries of the Political,* ed. Seyla Benhabib, 21–30. Princeton: Princeton University Press, 1996.

———. The Transformation of the Public Sphere. Cambridge: MIT Press, 1989.

Hackett, Elizabeth, and Sally Haslanger, eds. *Theorizing Feminisms: A Reader.* Oxford: Oxford University Press, 2006.

Haiman, John. *Talk Is Cheap: Sarcasm, Alienation, and the Evolution of Language.* Oxford: Oxford University Press, 1998.

Hall, Cheryl. "Recognizing the Passion in Deliberation: Toward a More Democratic Theory of Deliberative Democracy." *Hypatia: A Journal of Feminist Philoso-phy* 22, no. 4 (forthcoming).

Halliwell, Stephen. "Comic Satire and Freedom of Speech in Classical Athens." *Journal of Hellenic Studies* 111 (1991): 48–70.

———. "Philosophy and Rhetoric." In *Persuasion: Greek Rhetoric in Action*, ed. Ian Worthington, 222–43. New York: Routledge, 1994.

———. "The Uses of Laughter in Greek Culture." *Classical Quarterly* 41, no. 2 (1991): 279–96.

Halloran, S. Michael. "Aristotle's Concept of Ethos, or If Not His Somebody Else's." *Rhetoric Review* 1, no. 1 (September 1982): 62–63.

Hansen, Mogens Herman. *The Athenian Democracy in the Age of Demosthenes: Structures, Principles, and Ideology.* Norman: University of Oklahoma Press, 1999.

Harding, Philip. "Comedy and Rhetoric." In *Persuasion: Greek Rhetoric in Action*, ed. Ian Worthington, 196–221. New York: Routledge, 1994.

Hariman, Robert. *Political Style: The Artistry of Power.* Chicago: University of Chicago Press, 1995.

———, ed. *Prudence: Classical Virtue, Postmodern Practice.* University Park: Pennsylvania State University Press, 2003.

———. "Prudence in the Twenty-First Century." In *Prudence: Classical Virtue, Postmodern Practice*, ed. Robert Hariman, 287–322. University Park: Pennsylvania State University Press, 2003.

Hatzistavrou, Antony. "Socrates' Deliberative Authoritarianism." *Oxford Studies in Ancient Philosophy* 29 (Winter 2005): 75–113.

Heilke, Thomas. "Realism, Narrative, and Happenstance: Thucydides' Tale of Brasidas." *American Political Science Review* 98, no. 1 (February 2004): 121–38.

Henderson, Jeffrey. "Attic Comedy, Frank Speech, and Democracy." In *Democracy, Empire, and the Arts in Fifth-Century Athens*, ed. Deborah Boedeker and Kurt A. Raaflaub, 266–73. Cambridge: Harvard University Press, 1998.

Hesiod. *Theogony* and *Works and Days.* Translated by M. L. West, Oxford: Oxford University Press, 1988.

Hesk, Jon. *Deception and Democracy in Classical Athens.* Cambridge: Cambridge University Press, 2000.

Hobbs, Renee, and Richard Frost. "Measuring the Acquisition of Media Skills." *Reading Research Quarterly* 38, no. 3 (July/August/September 2003): 330–55.

Honig, Bonnie. "Difference, Dilemmas, and the Politics of Home." In *Democracy and Difference: Contesting the Boundaries of the Political*, ed. Seyla Benhabib, 257–77. Princeton: Princeton University Press, 1996.

Hunter, Virginia. *Policing Athens: Social Control in the Attic Lawsuits.* Princeton: Princeton University Press, 1994.

Johnson, James. "Arguing for Deliberation." In *Deliberative Democracy*, ed. Jon Elster, 161–84. Cambridge: Cambridge University Press, 1998.

Kahn, Charles H. "Drama and Dialectic in Plato's *Gorgias*." *Oxford Studies in Ancient Philosophy* 1 (1983): 75–121.

Kahn, Victoria. "*Virtù* and the Example of Agathocles in Machiavelli's *Prince*." *Representations*, no. 13 (Winter 1986): 68–83.

Kang, John M. "The Irrelevance of Sincerity: Deliberative Democracy in the Supreme Court." *Saint Louis University Law Journal* 48, no. 305 (April 2004): 305–26.

Kennedy, George A. "Historical Survey of Rhetoric." In *Handbook of Classical Rhetoric in the Hellenistic Period, 330 B.C.–A.D. 400*, ed. Stanley E. Porter, 3–41. New York: E. J. Brill, 1997.

Kiss, Elizabeth. "Alchemy or Fool's Gold? Assessing Feminist Doubts About Rights." In *Reconstructing Political Theory: Feminist Perspectives*, ed. Uma Narayan and Mary Shanley, 1–24. University Park: Pennsylvania State University Press, 1997.

Kohanski, Alexander S. *The Greek Mode of Thought in Western Philosophy*. Rutherford: Fairleigh Dickinson University Press, 1984.

Koziak, Barbara. *Retrieving Political Emotion:* Thumos, *Aristotle, and Gender*. University Park: Pennsylvania State University Press, 2000.

Kuklinski, James H., Paul J. Quirk, Jennifer Jerit, David Schweider, and Robert F. Rich. "Misinformation and the Currency of Democratic Citizenship." *Journal of Politics* 62, no. 3 (August 2000): 790–816.

Laclau, Ernesto, and Chantal Mouffe. *Hegemony and Socialist Strategy: Towards a Radical Democratic Politics*. New York: Verso, 2001.

Lakoff, George. *Moral Politics: How Liberals and Conservatives Think*. Chicago: University of Chicago Press, 2002.

Lane, Melissa. *Plato's Progeny: How Socrates and Plato Still Captivate the Modern Mind*. London: Gerald Duckworth, 2001.

Lanni, Adriann M. "Spectator Sport or Serious Politics? οἱ περιεστηκότες and the Athenian lawcourts." *Journal of Hellenic Studies* 117 (1997): 183–89.

Lear, Jonathan. "Allegory and Myth in Plato's *Republic*." In *Blackwell's Companion to Plato's* Republic, ed. Gerasimos Santas, 25–43. London: Blackwell, 2005.

———. *Therapeutic Action: An Earnest Plea for Irony*. New York: Other Press, 2003.

Lee, Benjamin. "Textuality, Mediation, and Public Discourse." In *Habermas and the Public Sphere*, ed. Craig Calhoun, 402–18. Cambridge: MIT Press, 1992.

Lewis, J. D. "*Isegoria* at Athens: When Did It Begin?" *Historia* 20 (1971): 129–41.

Lieb, Ethan J. *Deliberative Democracy in America: A Proposal for a Popular Branch of Government*. University Park: Pennsylvania State University Press, 2004.

Loftus, Elizabeth. *Eyewitness Testimony*. Cambridge: Harvard University Press, 1996.

Loraux, Nicole. *Born of the Earth: Myth and Politics in Athens*. Ithaca: Cornell University Press, 2000.

Macedo, Stephen, ed. *Deliberative Politics: Essays on Democracy and Disagreement*. Oxford: Oxford University Press, 1999.

Machiavelli, Niccoló. *Selected Political Writings*. Edited and translated by David Wootton. Indianapolis: Hackett, 1994.

Mackie, Gerry. "All Men Are Liars: Is Democracy Meaningless?" In *Deliberative Democracy*, ed. Jon Elster, 69–96. Cambridge: Cambridge University Press, 1998.

Manin, Bernard. "On Legitimacy and Public Deliberation." *Political Theory* 15, no. 3 (August 1987): 338–68.

———. *The Principles of Representative Government*. Cambridge: Cambridge University Press, 1997.

Mansbridge, Jane S. *Beyond Adversary Democracy*. New York: Basic Books, 1980

Manville, Philip Brook. *The Origins of Citizenship in Ancient Athens.* Princeton: Princeton University Press, 1990.

Mara, Gerald M. "Politics and Action in Plato's *Republic*." *Western Political Quarterly* 36, no. 4 (December 1983): 596–618.

———. *Socrates' Discursive Democracy:* Logos *and* Ergon *in Platonic Political Philosophy.* Albany: SUNY Press, 1997.

Markell, Patchen. "The Rule of the People: Arendt, *Arche*, and Democracy." *American Political Science Review* 100, no. 1 (February 2006): 1–14.

Markovits, Elizabeth. "Economizing Debate: Rhetoric, Citizenship, and the World Bank." *Poroi: An Interdisciplinary Journal of Rhetorical Analysis and Invention* 3, no. 1 (June 2004).

———. "The Trouble with Being Earnest: Deliberative Democracy and the Sincerity Norm." *Journal of Political Philosophy* 14, no. 3 (September 2006): 249–69.

Matthews, Chris. *Now, Let Me Tell You What I Really Think.* New York: Touchstone Books, 2001.

McCloskey, D. N. *The Vices of Economists, The Virtues of the Bourgeoisie.* Amsterdam: Amsterdam University Press, 1996.

McCloskey, D. N., and Robert M. Solow, eds. *The Consequences of Economic Rhetoric.* Cambridge: Cambridge University Press, 1988.

McKim, Richard. "Shame and Truth in Plato's *Gorgias*." In *Platonic Readings / Platonic Writings,* ed. Charles L. Griswold, Jr., 34–48. University Park: Pennsylvania State University Press, 2002.

McWhorter, John H. *The Power of Babel: A Natural History of Language.* New York: Times Books, 2001.

Michelini, Ann N. "ΠΟΛΛΗ ΑΓΡΟΙΚΙΑ: Rudeness and Irony in Plato's *Gorgias*." *Classical Philology* 93, no. 1 (January 1998): 50–59.

Miller, David. *On Nationality.* Oxford: Oxford University Press, 1995.

Momigliano, Arnoldo. "Freedom of Speech in Antiquity." In *Dictionary of the History of Ideas: Studies of Selected Pivotal Ideas,* ed. Philip Weiner, 252–63. New York: Scribner's, 1973.

Monoson, S. Sara. *Plato's Democratic Entanglements: Athenian Politics and the Practice of Philosophy.* Princeton: Princeton University Press, 2000.

Morgan, Kathryn. *Myth and Philosophy from the Presocratics to Plato.* Cambridge: Cambridge University Press, 2000.

Moruzzi, Norma Claire. *Speaking Through the Mask: Hannah Arendt and the Politics of Social Identity.* Ithaca: Cornell University Press, 2000.

Mouffe, Chantal. "Democratic Citizenship and the Political Community." In *Dimensions of Radical Democracy,* ed. Chantal Mouffe, 225–39. New York: Verso, 1992.

Nails, Debra. *The People of Plato: A Prosopography of Plato and Other Socratics.* Indianapolis: Hackett, 2002.

Narayan, Uma, and Mary Lyndon Shanley, eds. *Reconstructing Political Theory: Feminist Perspectives.* University Park: Pennsylvania State University Press, 1997.

Nehamas, Alexander. *The Art of Living: Socratic Reflections from Plato to Foucault.* Berkeley and Los Angeles: University of California Press, 1998.

———. *Virtues of Authenticity: Essays on Plato and Socrates.* Princeton: Princeton University Press, 1999.

Nehamas, Alexander, and Paul Woodruff. Introduction to *Plato's Phaedrus*, ed. Alexander Nehamas and Paul Woodruff, ix–xlviii. Indianapolis: Hackett, 1995.

Nichols, Mary P. "The *Republic*'s Two Alternatives: Philosopher-Kings and Socrates." *Political Theory* 12, no. 2 (May 1984): 252–74.

———. *Socrates and the Political Community: An Ancient Debate.* Albany: SUNY Press, 1987.

Nightingale, Andrea Wilson. *Genres in Dialogue: Plato and the Construct of Philosophy.* Cambridge: Cambridge University Press, 1995.

Nunberg, Geoffrey. *Going Nucular: Language, Politics, and Culture in Confrontational Times.* New York: PublicAffairs, 2004.

Nussbaum, Martha. *The Fragility of Goodness: Luck and Ethics in Greek Tragedy and Philosophy.* Cambridge: Cambridge University Press, 1986.

———. *Plato's* Republic: *The Good Society and the Deformation of Desire.* Washington, D.C.: Library of Congress, 1998.

Ober, Josiah. *The Athenian Revolution: Essays on Ancient Greek Democracy and Political Theory.* Princeton: Princeton University Press, 1996.

———. *Mass and Elite in Democratic Athens: Rhetoric, Ideology, and the Power of the People.* Princeton: Princeton University Press, 1989.

———. *Political Dissent in Democratic Athens: Intellectual Critics of Popular Rule.* Princeton: Princeton University Press, 1998.

Ober, Josiah, and Charles Hedrick, eds. *Demokratia: A Conversation on Democracies Ancient and Modern.* Princeton: Princeton University Press, 1996.

Ong, Walter. *Orality and Literacy: The Technologizing of the World.* New York: Routledge, 1988.

O'Reilly, Bill. *The No Spin Zone.* New York: Broadway Books, 2001.

Ostwald, Martin. *From Popular Sovereignty to the Sovereignty of Law.* Berkeley and Los Angeles: University of California Press, 1986.

Panagia, Davide. "The Force of Political Argument." *Political Theory* 32, no. 6 (December 2004): 825–48.

Pew Research Center for the People and the Press. "Cable and Internet Loom Large in Fragmented Political News Universe." Released January 11, 2004. http://people-press.org/reports/display.php3?ReportID = 200/.

———. "The 2004 Political Landscape: Evenly Divided and Increasingly Polarized." Released November 5, 2003. http://peoplepress.org/reports/display.php3?ReportID = 196/.

Pinker, Steven. *The Language Instinct.* New York: Morrow, 1994.

Pitkin, Hanna Fenichel. *The Attack of the Blob: Hannah Arendt's Concept of the Social.* Chicago: University of Chicago Press, 1998.

Popper, Karl. *The Open Society and Its Enemies: Vols. 1 and 2.* Princeton: Princeton University Press, 1971.

Purdy, Jedediah. *For Common Things: Irony, Trust, and Commitment in America Today.* New York: Knopf, 1999.

Plato. *The Complete Works.* Edited by John Cooper. Indianapolis: Hackett, 1997.

Przeworski, Adam. "Deliberation and Ideological Domination." In *Deliberative Democracy*, ed. Jon Elster, 140–60. Cambridge: Cambridge University Press, 1998.

Raaflaub, Kurt. "Democracy, Oligarchy, and the Concept of the Free Citizen in Late Fifth-Century Athens." *Political Theory* 11, no. 4 (November 1983): 517–44.

Radin, Max. "Freedom of Speech in Ancient Athens." *American Journal of Philology* 48, no. 3 (1927): 215–30.

Rees, David. *Get Your War On.* Brooklyn: Soft Skull Press, 2002.

Reeve, C.D.C. *Philosopher-Kings: The Argument of Plato's Republic.* Indianapolis: Hackett, 2006.

Roberts, Jennifer Tolbert. *Accountability in Athenian Government.* Madison: University of Wisconsin Press, 1982.

Rocco, Christopher. *Tragedy and Enlightenment: Athenian Political Thought and the Dilemmas of Modernity.* Berkeley and Los Angeles: University of California Press, 1997.

Rorty, Richard. *Contingency, Irony, and Solidarity.* Cambridge: Cambridge University Press, 1989.

Rosenblatt, Roger. "The Age of Irony Comes to an End." *Time,* September 24, 2001.

Rowe, Christopher. "Democracy and Sokratic-Platonic Philosophy." In *Democracy, Empire, and the Arts in Fifth-Century Athens,* ed. Deborah Boedeker and Kurt Raaflaub, 241–53. Cambridge: Harvard University Press, 1998.

———. "The Portrait of Aeschines in the Oration on the Crown." *Transactions and Proceedings of the American Philological Association* 97 (1966): 397–406.

Runciman, David. *The Politics of Good Intentions: History, Fear, and Hypocrisy in the New World Order.* Princeton: Princeton University Press, 2006.

Salkever, Stephen. "Socrates' Aspasian Oration: The Play of Philosophy and Politics in Plato's Menexenus." *American Political Science Review* 87, no. 1 (March 1993): 133–43.

Sampson, Geoffrey. *Educating Eve.* London: Cassell, 1997.

Saxonhouse, Arlene. "Comedy in the Callipolis: Animal Imagery in the Republic." *American Political Science Review* 72, no. 3 (September 1978): 888–901.

———. "Democratic Deliberation and the Historian's Trade: The Case of Thucydides." In *Talking Democracy: Historical Perspectives on Rhetoric and Democracy,* ed. Benedetto Fontana, Cary Nederman, and Gary Remer, 57–85. University Park: Pennsylvania State University Press, 2004.

———. "Democracy, Equality, and *Eide:* A Radical View from Book 8 of Plato's *Republic.*" *American Political Science Review* 92, no. 2 (June 1998): 273–83.

———. *Free Speech and Democracy in Ancient Athens.* Cambridge: Cambridge University Press, 2006.

———. "The Philosophy of the Particular and the Universality of the City: Socrates' Education of Euthyphro." *Political Theory* 16, no. 2 (May 1988): 281–99.

———. "The Tyranny of Reason in the World of the Polis." *American Political Science Review* 82, no. 4 (December 1988): 1261–75.

Scannell, Paddy. *Radio, Television and Modern Life: A Phenomenological Approach.* Malden, Mass.: Blackwell Publishers, 1996.

Scott, Joan W. "Experience." In *Feminists Theorize the Political,* ed. Judith Butler and Joan W. Scott, 22–40. New York: Routledge, 1992.

Seaford, Richard. Introduction to *Reciprocity in Ancient Greece,* ed. Christopher Gill, Norman Postlethwaite, and Richard Seaford, 1–11. Oxford: Oxford University Press, 1998.

Seery, John E. "Politics as Ironic Community: On the Themes of Descent and Return in Plato's *Republic.*" *Political Theory* 16, no. 2 (May 1988): 229–56.

————. *Political Returns: Irony in Politics and Theory from Plato to the Antinuclear Movement*. Boulder, Colo.: Westview Press, 1990.

Sennett, Richard. *The Fall of Public Man*. New York: W. W. Norton, 1976.

Shiffman, Gary. "Deliberation versus Decision: Platonism in Contemporary Democratic Theory." In *Talking Democracy: Historical Perspectives on Rhetoric and Democracy*, ed. Benedetto Fontana, Cary Nederman, and Gary Remer, 87–114. University Park: Pennsylvania State University Press, 2004.

Shklar, Judith N. *Ordinary Vices*. Cambridge: The Belknap Press of Harvard University, 1984.

Sinclair, R. K. *Democracy and Participation in Athens*. Cambridge: Cambridge University Press, 1988.

Sparks, Holloway. "Dissident Citizenship: Democratic Theory, Political Courage, and Activist Women." *Hypatia* 12, no. 4 (Fall 1997): 74–111.

Spragens, Thomas. *Reason and Democracy*. Durham: Duke University Press, 1990.

Steenbergen, Marco R., Andre Bächtiger, Markus Spörndli, and Jürg Steiner. "Measuring Political Deliberation: A Discourse Quality Index." *Comparative European Politics* 1 (2003): 21–48.

Stokes, Susan. "Pathologies of Deliberation." In *Deliberative Democracy*, ed. Jon Elster, 123–39. Cambridge: Cambridge University Press, 1998.

Strauss, Barry. "The Cultural Significance of Bribery and Embezzlement." *Ancient World* 2 (1985): 67–74.

Strauss, Leo. *The City and Man*. Chicago: University of Chicago Press, 2004.

————. *Persecution and the Art of Writing*. Chicago: University of Chicago Press, 2004

Sullivan, Andrew. *The Conservative Soul: How We Lost It, How to Get It Back*. New York: HarperCollins, 2006.

Tarnopolski, Christina. "Prudes, Perverts, and Tyrants: Plato and the Contemporary Politics of Shame." *Political Theory* 32, no. 4 (August 2004): 468–94.

Tessitore, Aristide. "Courage and Comedy in Plato's *Laches*." *Journal of Politics* 56, no. 1 (February 1994): 115–33.

Thompson, John B. "The New Visibility." *Theory, Culture and Society* 22, no. 6 (2005): 31–51.

Thucydides. *The Peloponnesian War*. New York: Modern Library, 1982.

Traugott, John. "'Shall Jonathan Die?' Swift, Irony, and a Failed Revolution in Ireland." In *The Politics of Irony: Essays in Self-Betrayal*, ed. Daniel Conway and John Seery, 31–51. New York: St. Martin's Press: 1992.

Trilling, Lionel. *Sincerity and Authenticity*. Cambridge: Harvard University Press, 1972.

Vernant, Jean-Pierre. *The Origins of Greek Thought*. Ithaca: Cornell University Press, 1982.

Veyne, Paul. *Did the Greeks Believe Their Myths? An Essay on the Constitutive Imagination*. Chicago: University of Chicago Press, 1988.

Villa, Dana. *Politics, Philosophy, Terror: Essays on the Thought of Hannah Arendt*. Princeton: Princeton University Press, 1999.

————. *Socratic Citizenship*. Princeton: Princeton University Press, 2001.

Vlastos, Gregory. "The Paradox of Socrates." In *The Philosophy of Socrates: A Collection of Critical Essays*, ed. Gregory Vlastos, 1–21. Notre Dame: Notre Dame University Press, 1971.

————. *Socrates, Ironist and Moral Philosopher*. Ithaca: Cornell University Press, 1991.

Wallace, Robert W. "Law, Freedom, and the Concept of Citizens' Rights in Democratic Athens." In *Demokratia: A Conversation on Democracies Ancient and Modern*, ed. Josiah Ober and Charles Hedrick, 105–19. Princeton: Princeton University Press, 1996.

————. "The Sophists in Athens." In *Democracy, Empire, and the Arts in Fifth-Century Athens*, ed. Deborah Boedeker and Kurt Raaflaub, 203–22. Cambridge: Harvard University Press, 1998.

Wallach, John R. *The Platonic Political Art: A Study of Critical Reason and Democracy*. University Park: Pennsylvania State University Press, 2001.

Wallach, John R., J. Peter Euben, and Josiah Ober, eds. *Athenian Political Thought and the Reconstitution of American Democracy*. Ithaca: Cornell University Press, 1994.

Warren, Mark. "Deliberative Democracy." In *Democratic Theory Today*, ed. April Carter and Geoffrey Stokes, 173–202. Cambridge: Polity Press, 2002.

————. "Democracy and Deceit: Regulating Appearances of Corruption." *American Journal of Political Science* 50, no. 1 (January 2006): 160–74.

White, James Boyd. *When Words Lose Their Meaning: Constitutions and Reconstitutions of Language, Character, and Community*. Chicago: University of Chicago Press, 1984.

Wiser, James L. "Philosophy as Political Action: A Reading of the *Gorgias*." *American Journal of Political Science* 19, no. 2 (May 1975): 313–22.

Wolfe, Alan. *Does American Democracy Still Work?* New Haven: Yale University Press, 2006.

Wolin, Sheldon. *Politics and Vision: Continuity and Innovation in Western Political Thought*. Princeton: Princeton University Press, 2004.

Worthington, Ian, ed. *Persuasion: Greek Rhetoric in Action*. New York: Routledge, 1994.

Yack, Bernard. "Rhetoric and Public Reasoning: An Aristotelian Understanding of Political Deliberation." *Political Theory* 34, no. 4 (August 2006): 417–38.

Young, Iris Marion. "Communication and the Other: Beyond Deliberative Democracy." In *Democracy and Difference: Contesting the Boundaries of the Political*, ed. Seyla Benhabib, 120–35. Princeton: Princeton University Press, 1996.

————. *Inclusion and Democracy*. Oxford: Oxford University Press, 2001.

INDEX

reflective challenge. *See* accountability
representative thinking, 192–99
Republic
  and censorship, 133–37
  and emotion, 135, 145, 153
  and heterogeneity, 143–44, 167
  and *parrhesia*, 138, 162–64, 167
  and poetry, 133–37
  and philosopher–kings, 133
  as myth, 159–65
  as summoner, 132, 152, 159, 167, 197–98
  and violence, 141, 143–44
  critiques of democracy, 163–65
  historical context of, 160–61
  scholarly interpretations of, 132
reputation, 31, 41, 60–61, 182, 207–8, 211
Rhet-Ed, 214
rhetoric
  and flattery, 93, 110
  and *parrhesia*, 70–71, 75–77, 84, 106–10
  and Plato, 7, 10, 62, 92–93
  anxieties about, 63–64, 75–77, 86, 112
  definition of, 10–11
  deliberative, 108, 202
  development in Athens, 62
  rejection of, 10–11, 36–42
  See also listening rhetoric; Socrates as
    rhetorician
rhetoric of anti-rhetoric, 74–77
rhetorical literacy, 214–16
Roberts, Jennifer Tolbert, 56
Rocco, Christopher, 118
Rorty, Richard, 4 n. 5, 87, 91, 111
Rosenblatt, Roger, 82
Runciman, David, 171

Salkever, Stephen, 117
sarcasm. *See* irony
Saxonhouse, Arlene, 6, 52, 66, 115, 131, 212
Scannell Paddy, 202
Schwartzman, Micah, 34 n. 61
Scott, Joan, 32
Seery, John, 152
Sennett, Richard, 171, 180, 183
September 11th, 41, 81–83
Shiffman, Gary, 173
Shklar, Judith, 190
sincerity
  alternatives to, 207–13
  appearance of, 44, 171–72, 176, 200, 202
  and accountability, 180, 188–91, 197, 200
  and consistency, 21, 203, 204
  and courage, 68–70, 73

  and transparency, 32, 43, 70, 172, 181
  and truth claims, 71–72
  obsession with, 1, 14, 170, 180, 202
  redemption through third parties, 73
  usefulness of, 176
  links with *parrhesia*, 68–73
  See also discourse ethics; plain speech; *par-*
    rhesia; realist rhetorical style
Socrates
  ambiguity of, 96, 104, 121, 165, 198
  and comedy, 101, 112, 131
  and democracy, 91–92. *See also* Plato and
    democracy
  and *parrhesia*, 77–78, 86–87, 91–106,
    109–10
  and Plato, 5–7, 85–86, 119
  as gadfly, 116–17
  as *parrhesiastes*, 122
  as *politikos*, 112–17
  as rhetorician, 106–12
  death of, 6, 118–19
  failures of, 118–19, 137
  negative aspects of, 99–100, 102, 104, 113,
    117–19, 121
  See also Plato
Solon, 52–54
sophism, 10, 62–63, 75–76, 134, 161
Sophocles, 63
sophrosyne, 57, 76
Sparta, 51, 62, 139, 164
storytelling, 36, 38–39
  Arendtian, 154–57, 198–99
  dangers of, 156
  See also myth
straight talk, 1–2, 25–36, 176. *See also* plain
    speech; zero-degree trope; realist rhetor-
    ical style
Strauss, Barry, 65
Strauss, Leo, 132
Swift, Jonathan, 103

Talking Democracy, 9
Tarnopolsky, Christina, 85, 99
Thompson, John, 202
Thrasymachus, 47–48, 62, 148, 155–56, 161
Thucydides, 74–77, 129
transparency, 118, 121–22, 158, 179–80,
    188–90, 201–2, 209, 212
  and *parrhesia*, 70, 74, 130
  and sincerity, 32, 43, 70, 172, 181
Trilling, Lionel, 21 n. 23, 34 n. 60
trust
  and deliberative theory, 20, 31, 45
  experts, 33, 43, 71–72, 75–76, 158, 202